Divine Love and Wisdom

Emanuel Swedenborg

Translated by
George F. Dole

Swedenborg Foundation
West Chester, Pennsylvania

*Sapientia angelica de Divino Amore
et Divina Sapientia,* by Emanuel Swedenborg

Translated by George F. Dole
*Angelic Wisdom concerning the
Divine Love and Wisdom*

First published in Latin, 1763
First English translation published in
    the U.S.A., 1851
First Dole translation, 1985
First reprint, 1994

For information, contact:
    Swedenborg Foundation
    320 North Church Street
    West Chester, Pennsylvania 19380

Library of Congress Catalog Card Number 85-050918
ISBN 087785-129-8

Cover design by Nancy Crompton. Cover photo by Serendip,
© 1984: "Annular Solar Eclipse with Corona and Prominences."

Manufactured in the United States of America

CONTENTS

(chapter titles by W.R. Woofenden)

TRANSLATOR'S PREFACE

The paired volumes *Divine Love and Wisdom* and *Divine Providence* occupy a special place in Swedenborg's theological output. Immediately after his call, Swedenborg turned to the study of Scripture. He began writing a massive exposition of the spiritual meaning of Scripture (posthumously published as *The Word Explained*), abandoned it, and then wrote and published the equally massive *Arcana Coelestia*, dealing with inner levels of meaning in Genesis and Exodus.

Having seen this through the press, he drew on it to publish several topical works—*Earths in the Universe, Heaven and Hell, The Last Judgment, The New Jerusalem and its Heavenly Doctrine,* and *The White Horse*. He then turned back to Scripture, and carried a detailed but discursive treatment of the book of Revelation almost to completion (this has been published posthumously as *The Apocalypse Explained*). About seven years later, he published a more concise commentary, *The Apocalypse Revealed*.

In the seven years between his first and his final efforts to present an exegesis of the book of Revelation, he wrote and published *The Four Doctrines* (of the Lord, Sacred Scripture, Life, and Faith), a *Continuation on the Last Judgment,* and *Divine Love and*

Wisdom and *Divine Providence*. In *The Four Doctrines*, he seems particularly concerned to gather Scriptural evidence for basic doctrines, while the latter two works set the same doctrines in a philosophical and metaphysical context.

Examination of *The Apocalypse Explained* suggests a rationale for this sequence. As he progressed in writing it, he adapted a device he had used in writing *Arcana Coelestia*. There, he had appended material on various topics to the several exegetical chapters. Now he began to append material to each (numbered) paragraph, again carrying single themes for some time, with the repeated subheading *Continuatio*.

As the work progressed, these "continuations" grew larger and larger, and the exegesis of the text of Revelation grew more and more cursory. It looks very much as though his conscious intent to focus his mission on Scripture was being overridden by a sense of urgency about other things that needed to be said. So while the Bible is cited copiously in *The Four Doctrines*, it is systematic theology rather than Scripture that provides the framework; and the appeal of *Divine Love and Wisdom* and *Divine Providence* is more to the reader's sense of philosophical coherence than to the authority of Scripture. Scripture citations in *Divine Love and Wisdom*, in fact, are few and far between.

Divine Love and Wisdom is literally cosmic in its scope. The ground it covers is summarized in the Table of Contents, so it would be prolix to repeat it here. For the present translator, though, the work gives every evidence of intensity, of being a book that "had to be written." The single focus and concise style of *The Apocalypse Revealed* surely testify to an author who had no other agenda to distract him.

The present translation rests on quite specific criteria of fidelity. Historically, translators have debated the relative merits of "literal" and "free" translations, and while fashions have changed from time to time, no clear "winner" has emerged.

To me, most of this debate has overlooked the fact that different authors use language differently. Wilhelm Busch, for example, wrote *Max und Moritz* with tongue in cheek, and took full advantage of the potentials of the German language for phonetic humor. His translator is, I believe, obliged to respect this priority, and therefore to take full advantage of parallel resources in the "target language." This will normally preclude literalism; literalism would in fact be infidelity to Busch's own language.

In regard to Swedenborg, it is my conviction that he strove above all for clarity and directness. He uses a relatively limited vocabulary and very straightforward syntax, and copes with complex ideas by writing extensively rather than intricately. Above all, he wants the reader to understand; and I cannot regard myself as "free" to render his clarity into abstruse English in the name of literal fidelity.

Specifically, I have translated with a persistent suspicion of cognates. The extensive Latinate vocabulary of English is largely one of abstract ideas, in sharp contrast to the concreteness of our Anglo-Saxon vocabulary. There is no such dichotomy in Swedenborg's Latin, so the choice of the cognate is usually the choice of the abstract rather than the concrete, both of which are normally implicit in the original. This choice may often be warranted, but it should be conscious and considered, not merely a reflex action.

Syntax presents the translator with no less a challenge. English style has had its Latinate excursions, and as a result, most of Swedenborg's standard constructions have English counterparts that are grammatically admissible. To the contemporary ear, though, they are often stilted and difficult, and rarely occur in good serious prose.

Divine Love

My own effort has therefore been to find devices in good English style that preserve the relationships of Swedenborg's Latin—to build a kind of lexicon of syntax, in which a Latin construction has one or more English constructions that accomplish the same thing. This, together with the recognition that Swedenborg used colons and semicolons the way we use periods, allows the writing of reasonably good English without abandoning a consistent representation of the Latin text.

The first draft of the present translation was published serially in *Studia Swedenborgiana* between 1977 and 1984, with an ongoing request for critical comments. Those few individuals who responded will find, I trust, that their suggestions have been both appreciated and heeded. I would repeat the invitation. Translation is for the sake of communication, and it seems obvious that it is helpful to know both what has communicated and what has not.

This revision of the first draft has had the benefit of a careful reading by the Rev. Dr. William R. Woofenden, and is materially improved as a result. I am most grateful to him for his labor. I wish also to express my gratitude to Mary Bryant for her extraordinarily good-natured competence at the typewriter.

My greatest debt of gratitude is to the Swedenborg Foundation. Its moral and financial support have been invaluable, and the provision of word-processing equipment for the task of editing has vastly simplified a formerly burdensome chore.

Sharon, Massachusetts
October 1985.

CHAPTER 1

[The Creator]

LOVE IS HUMAN LIFE

1. People know that love exists, but they do not know what love is. They realize that love exists because of everyday language—for example, people say, "He loves me," "The subjects love their ruler," "The husband and wife love each other," "The mother and her children love each other," and "He loves his country, his fellow-citizen, his neighbor." People say the same sort of thing about inanimate objects—for example, "He loves this or that thing." But in spite of the fact that "love" is so pervasively present in speech, scarcely anyone knows what love is.

Since people cannot formulate any concept of it when they reflect on it, they say either that it isn't really anything, or that it is merely something that flows in from sight, hearing, touch, and conversation and therefore exerts an influence. People are utterly unaware that it is their very life—not just the general life of their whole body and the general life of all their thoughts, but the life of their every element.

This is something a wise person can perceive as in saying, "If you take away affection, which belongs to love, can you think anything? Can you do anything? As affection (which belongs to love) cools off, do not thought and speech and action cool off? As the one warms up do not the others warm up?" But this wise person is not perceiving these matters on the basis of a thought that love is a person's life, but on the basis of his or her experience that this is how things happen.

2. Without knowing what love is, no one knows what human life is. Without knowing this, one individual can believe that human life is feeling and acting, and another that it is thinking; when actually thinking is a first result of life, and acting is a second result.

We say that thinking is a first result of life; but there is more and more inward thinking and more and more outward thinking. The most inward thinking, the perception of goals, is really the first result of life. But more on this below, when we discuss levels of life.

3. We can gain some idea of love—of its being our life—on the basis of the sun's warmth in this world. We realize that this is, so to speak, the shared life of all earth's plants, since when it increases, as happens in springtime, all kinds of plants spring up from the soil. They deck themselves with leaves, then with blossoms, and finally with fruits; they are thus virtually alive. But when the warmth declines, as happens in autumn and winter time, they are stripped of the signs of their life, and droop.

It is the same with love in the case of human beings, since love and warmth correspond to each other. For this reason, love also has a warming effect.

GOD ALONE—HENCE THE LORD—IS LOVE ITSELF, SINCE HE IS LIFE ITSELF; ANGELS AND PEOPLE ARE RECEIVERS OF LIFE

4. This will be highlighted by many considerations in [my coming] treatments of *Divine Providence* and *Life*. Here we need state only that the Lord, who is God

of the universe, is uncreated and infinite, while people and angels are created and finite. And since the Lord is uncreated and infinite, He is the very reality [*Esse*] which is called Jehovah: He is life itself or intrinsic life. From that which is uncreated, infinite reality itself and life itself, no one can be created directly, because what is divine is a unity and is not divisible. This creation, rather, must occur using things created and limited, so formed that the divine can be in them. Since this is the nature of mortals and angels, they are recipients of life.

So if people allow themselves to be misled in thought to the point that they believe they are not recipients of life but are life, they cannot be led away from the thought that they are God. The feeling people have that they are life, and the resultant belief that this is the case, stem from an illusion. The fundamental cause is perceived in the working cause only as an integal part of it.

The Lord teaches in *John* that He is intrinsic life—

> Just as . . . the Father has life in Himself, He has granted the Son to have life in Himself (John 5:26).

and that He is life itself (John 11:25; 19:6).

Now, since life and love are one and the same (as we can see from the statements in nn. 1 and 2 above), it follows that the Lord, being life itself, is love itself.

5. If this is to fit into our understanding, though, we need to realize that the Lord, being love in its very essence or divine love, looks like the sun to angels in heaven. We need to realize that warmth and light emanate from that sun, that the emanating warmth is essentially love and the emanating light essentially wisdom. We need to realize that angels are recipient of that spiritual warmth and that spiritual light to the extent that they are "loves" or "wisdoms"—not loves and wisdoms on their own, but from the Lord.

That spiritual warmth and that spiritual light do not flow into and influence angels alone; they flow into and influence people on earth as well, precisely to the extent that they become recipients. And they become recipients in the measure of their love to the Lord and their love toward their neighbor.

That very sun (or divine love) cannot use its own warmth and its own light to create anyone directly from itself—the result of this would be love in its essence, which is the Lord Himself. But it can create by using substances and materials so formed that they can receive actual warmth and actual light. In much the same way, the world's sun cannot use its warmth and light to produce sprouting things in the earth directly. It uses rather materials from the soil which it can be in by means of its warmth and light, thus making things sprout.

The reader may see in the book *Heaven and Hell* (nn. 116-140) that the Lord's divine love looks like a sun in the spiritual world, and that a spiritual warmth and a spiritual light emanate from it which are the sources of angels' love and wisdom.

6. So since people are not life but are rather recipients of life, it follows that a person's being conceived by his father is not the conception of life. It is the conception rather of the first and purest forms that can receive life—forms to which, as to a [weaver's] warp or an outline, there are added in the womb, step by step, substances and materials in forms fitted to receive life in their own pattern and on their own level.

THE DIVINE IS NOT IN SPACE
7. The fact that the divine, or God, is not in space (even though He is present everywhere, with every person on earth, every angel in heaven, and every spirit under heaven) cannot be grasped by means of

a merely natural concept, but it can be grasped by means of a spiritual concept.

The reason it cannot be grasped with a natural concept is that space is involved in such a concept. Natural concepts are actually formed out of the sorts of thing that exist in the world, and in each and every item the eyes see, space is involved. Whenever we say "large" or "small," it is a matter of space; whenever we say "long," "wide," or "high," it is a matter of space. This is why we stated that it is impossible to grasp in a merely natural concept the divine's not being in space, when it is stated that He is everywhere.

Yet people can grasp this with natural thinking if only they let some spiritual light into it. So let us first say something about a "spiritual concept" and the spiritual thinking that follows from it.

A spiritual concept does not draw on space for anything; it draws rather on state for everything. State is predicated of love, life, wisdom, affections, and the delights they bring—broadly speaking, of the good and the true.

A really spiritual concept of these elements has nothing to do with space. It is higher, and looks at concepts of space the way heaven looks at earth. However, since angels and spirits see with their eyes just as much as people on earth do, and since objects cannot be seen unless they are in space, "spaces" like spaces on earth do appear in the spiritual world where spirits and angels are. They are not spaces, though, but appearances. Actually, they are not fixed and prescribed as on earth. They can be stretched out or contracted, altered and varied. And since they cannot be delineated by measurement, they cannot there be encompassed by any natural concept, only by a spiritual one. This means that [spiritual] spatial distances reflect simply distances of what is good or distances of what is true, which are affinities and likenesses depending on their state.

8. We can conclude from these considerations that humans, on the basis of a merely natural concept, cannot grasp either the fact that the divine is everywhere and yet not "in space," or the fact that angels and spirits grasp this clearly. We can conclude that in consequence, we too could grasp this if only we let some spiritual light into our thought.

The reason we are able to understand is that our bodies do not think, but rather our spirits. This means that our natural aspect does not think, but rather our spiritual aspect.

9. The reason most people do not grasp this is that they love what is natural and therefore do not want to lift the thoughts of their discernment above it into spiritual light. And people who are unwilling are unable to think in any way but spatially, even about God. Thinking spatially about God is thinking about the expanse of nature.

We need to present this material in preface, because without the information—and some perception—that the divine is not in space, we cannot understand anything about divine life, which is love and wisdom, which are our present topics. As a result there could be little understanding of divine providence, omnipresence, omniscience, infinity, and eternity, which we will need to deal with in sequence.

10. We stated that in the spiritual world, spaces—and therefore distances, are apparent just as much as they are in the natural world, but that they are "appearances" dependent on spiritual affinities which are matters of love and wisdom, or of the good and the true.

This is why the Lord, even though He is in the heavens with the angels everywhere, still appears high above them as a sun. And since acceptance of love and wisdom constitutes affinity with Him, the heavens containing angels in closer affinity with Him (because of their acceptance) look closer to Him than those in less close affinity. This is also why the heavens (three in number) are distinguished from each other, as are the communities of each heaven. Too, it is why the hells are far from Him in keeping with their rejection of love and wisdom.

It is the same with people on earth, in whom and with whom the Lord is present throughout the whole globe. The only reason for this is that the Lord is not in space.

GOD IS THE ESSENTIAL PERSON

11.   The only concept of God throughout all the heavens is the concept of a Person. This is because heaven, overall and in its parts, is like a person in form, and the divine which is among angels constitutes heaven. Thought progresses acccording to heaven's form; so angels are incapable of thinking about God in any other way. This is why all the people in the world who are united to heaven think of God in a similar way when they think more deeply, or in the spirit.

Because God is Person, all angels and all spirits are people in perfect form. Heaven's form accomplishes this, resembling itself in its greatest and its smallest instances (on heaven's being like a person in form, overall and in its parts, see the book *Heaven and Hell*, nn 59-87; and on thoughts progressing according to heaven's form, *ibid.* nn. 203-4).

It is recognized that people were created in the image and likeness of God, from Genesis 1:26-7; also that God appeared to Abraham and others as a Person.

People of early times, both wise and simple ones, thought about God only as a Person. Even when they began to worship many gods, as they did at Athens and Rome, they worshipped them all in human form.

Divine Love

We can illustrate these observations with the following material treated in a previous booklet:

Gentiles—especially Africans—who recognize and worship a single God as Creator of the universe, have a concept of God as a Person. They say that no one can have any other concept of God.

When they hear that most people cling to a concept of God as something like a small cloud at the center of everything, they ask where these people are. And when they hear that these people are among Christians, they deny that this can be.

They are told in reply, though, that they have this kind of concept because God is called "a spirit" in the Word, and the only way they think about a spirit is as a small bit of cloud. They do not know that every spirit and every angel is a person. However, an inquiry was made as to whether their spiritual concept was the same as their natural one, and it was discovered that it was not the same for people who on a deeper level recognized the Lord as God of heaven and earth.

I heard a particular Christian elder stating that no one could have a concept of the Divine-Human. I saw him transferred to various heathen peoples, more and more inward, from them to their heavens, and eventually to the Christian heaven. Everywhere, he was allowed to share in people's more inward perception of God; and he observed that they had no concept of God except as a Person—which is the same thing as a concept of the Divine-Human (see *Continuation on the Last Judgment*, n. 74).

12. In Christendom, the ordinary concept of God is one of Person, because God is called *"Persona"* in the Athanasian doctrine of the Trinity. But people who are "wiser" than ordinary folk present God as invisi-

ble. This happens because they cannot grasp how God as Person could have created heaven and earth and then have filled the universe with His presence—along with many other matters that cannot fit into understanding as long as people do not realize that the divine is not in space. But people who approach the Lord alone reflect on the Divine-human, and so reflect on God as Person.

13. We can determine how important it is to have a fair concept of God from the fact that one's concept of God constitutes the very core of thinking in all people who have a religion. In fact, all elements of religion and all elements of worship focus on God. And since God is involved—overall and in detail—in all elements of religion and worship, there can be no communication with the heavens unless there is a fair concept of God.

This is why each nation is given its portion in the spiritual world in keeping with its concept of God as Person. Their concept of the Lord is actually contained within this concept and nowhere else. The dependence of the life-state after death on the concept of God avowed by the individual is observable in the opposite phenomenon, that denial of God constitutes hell—in Christianity, denial of the Lord's divinity.

REALITY [Esse] AND PRESENCE [Existere] ARE DISTINGUISHABLY ONE IN THE GOD-MAN

14. Where there is reality [Esse], there is presence [Existere]; neither occurs without the other. Reality in fact exists by means of presence and not apart from it. The rational faculty can grasp this by weighing whether there can occur any reality that does not become present and whether there can be any presence except from reality. And since each does occur with the other and not apart from the other, it follows that they are one, but "distinguishably one."

They are distinguishably one like love and wisdom. Nay, love is reality and wisdom is presence; love actually does not occur except within wisdom, nor wisdom except from love. So when love is within wisdom, then it *becomes present*.

These two constitute a unity of such nature that they can indeed be distinguished in thought, but not in performance. And since they can be distinguished in thought and not in performance, we use the phrase, "distinguishably one."

In God-Man, reality and presence are distinguishably one like soul and body. A soul does not occur apart from its body, nor a body apart from its soul. The divine soul of the God-Man is what we mean by "the divine reality;" and the divine body is what we mean by "the divine presence."

The notion that a soul can become present apart from a body, can think and be wise, is an error that flows from misconceptions. Actually, every person's soul is in a spiritual body after it has shed the material trappings it carried around in the world.

15. The reason reality is not reality unless it *becomes present*, is that it is not in a form until it does. And if it is not in a form, it has no quality; and that which has no quality is not anything.

What *becomes present* from reality makes one with reality by virtue of its derivation from reality. This is the source of their union into one; and this is why each belongs to the other reciprocally, why each is intrinsically, so to speak, the all-in-all of the other.

16. We can conclude from these considerations that God is Person, and by this means is God becoming present—not becoming present away from Himself, but becoming present in Himself. The one who becomes present in himself is God, the source of everything.

IN THE GOD-MAN, INFINITE ELEMENTS ARE DISTINGUISHABLY ONE

17. God's infinity is recognized—He is in fact called "the infinite one." But He is called "the infinite one" because He is infinite. He is not the infinite one simply because He is intrinsically reality and presence itself, but because there are infinite elements within Him. An infinite entity without infinite elements is an infinite entity in name only.

The infinite elements within Him cannot be called either "infinitely many" or "infinitely all" because of the natural concept of "many" and "all." For the natural concept of "infinitely many" is limited; and while there is something unlimited about "infinitely all," it does depend on limited elements within the universe.

Humans therefore, possessing a natural concept, cannot attain perception of the infinite elements in God by raising their concept or by analogy. But angels, being involved in a spiritual concept, can get higher than the human level by being raised up and by analogy, though they cannot completely attain perception.

18. Everyone who believes that God is Person can maintain inwardly that there are infinite elements within God. Since He is Person, He has a body and everything a body entails. So He has a face, a chest, an abdomen, loins, feet—without these He would not in fact be a person. And because He has these features, He also has eyes, ears, nose, mouth, and tongue. Then He also has the organs that are within a person, such as heart and lungs and the organs that depend on them, all of which, taken collectively, make a person a person.

In created people, these elements are many: seen in their interconnections, they are countless. But in God-Man they are infinite. Nothing is missing. As a result, He has an infinite completeness.

The reason for the comparison of the uncreated Person, who is God, with created man, is that God is Person. He is the reason it is stated that earthly man was created after His image and in His likeness (Genesis 1:27-27).

19. Angels can see very plainly that there are infinite elements within God, on the basis of the heavens they live in. The entire heaven, made up of myriads of angels, is like a person in its overall form. The same holds true of every community, larger or smaller. Further, this is why an angel is a person, an angel actually being a heaven in its smallest form. The truth of this may be seen in the book *Heaven and Hell*, nn. 51-86.

Heaven is in this form overall, regionally, and in individuals, as a result of the divine which angels accept. For the amount of the divine that angels do accept determines the extent to which they are in a perfect human form. This is why angels are said to be in God, and God in them, why God is said to be "their all."

There is no possibility of describing how many things exist in heaven. And since the divine constitutes heaven—which means that there indescribably many things are from the divine—it is easy to see that there are infinite elements in that very Person who is God.

20. We can arrive at the same conclusion on the basis of the created universe, when we look at this in regard to uses and the things which correspond to them. But before this can be understood, we may preface some material that will be illustrative.

21. Since there are infinite elements within God-Man, which are visible in heaven, in angels, and in people as in a mirror, and since God-Man is not within space (as presented above, nn. 7-10), we can to some extent see and grasp how God can be all-present, all-knowing, and all-providing, and how as a Person

He could create everything, even how as a Person He can forever sustain what He has created in his design.

22. As to the proposition that infinite elements are distinguishably one in God-Man, this too we can determine by using the human being as a kind of mirror. There are many elements—countless elements—within a person, as already stated, yet the person still feels them as one. On the basis of their senses, people know nothing of their brains, their heart, their lungs, their liver, spleen, and pancreas. They know nothing of the countless elements within their eyes, tongue, belly, reproductive organs, and so on. And since they do not know them on a sensory basis, they are like single entities to themselves.

The reason is that all these things exist within a kind of form which does not permit a single element to be lacking. It is in fact the form which receives life from God-Man (as shown in nn. 4-6 above). From the patterning and linking of all these elements in this kind of form, there is presented a feeling and a consequent concept of their not seeming many or countless, but virtually one.

We can conclude from these considerations that the many and countless elements that constitute a kind of "one" in the human being, are distinguishably one in the essential person who is God—are even most clearly distinguishably "one."

THERE IS ONE GOD WHO IS THE SOURCE OF EVERYTHING

23. All the elements of human reason come together and virtually center in this fact—that one God is the creator of the universe. So the individual possessed of reason neither does nor can think anything else, on the basis of general understanding. Tell someone of sound reason that there are two creators of the universe, and you will discover the resistance to you

which results, perhaps simply from the tone of the person's voice in your ear. We can see from this that all the elements of human reason do come together and center in the fact that there is one God.

There are two reasons why this is so. *First*, the very ability to think rationally does not, in its own right, belong to the person, but belongs to God within the person. Human reason depends on this in general, and this general dependence so operates that reason sees with apparent independence. *Second*, it is by means of this ability that a person either participates in heaven's light or derives the common thread of his or her thinking from it. And the universal principle of heaven's light is that God is one.

It is different if individuals have used this ability to corrupt the lower elements of their understanding. They may indeed use this ability effectively, but by virtue of having disarranged the lower elements, they turn it astray. In this manner, their reason becomes unsound.

24. Every individual, whether he or she realizes it or not, thinks about an aggregate of people as an individual person. So people understand immediately when someone says that the ruler is the head and the subjects are the body, or when it is said that one or another person has this role in "the body politic"—meaning the nation. It is the same with a spiritual body as it is with a civic one. A spiritual body is a church: its head is God-Man.

We can see from this what kind of person the church would look like in this view, if the thought were not of one God as creator and sustainer of the universe, but rather of several. In this view, the church would look like a single body with several heads on it—not like a human being, then, but like a monster.

If someone were to claim that these heads had a single essence, and thereby taken together constituted a single head, the only concept this could produce would be either of one head with several faces, or of several heads with a single face. In this view, then, the church would be presented deformed. The fact is, though, that one God is the head, and the church is the body which acts at the bidding of the head and not on its own, which is also what happens in a person.

This is also why there is only one king to a kingdom. Several kings would fragment it, but one can hold it together.

25. It would be the same with the church scattered throughout the world (called "the Communion") because it is, so to speak, a single body governed by a single Head.

We know that a head rules its subject body at will. In fact, discernment and intentionality dwell in the head, and the body is activated out of discernment and intentionality, even to the point that the body is simply obedience. The body cannot do anything except out of discernment and intentionality in the head. In the same way, the church person cannot do anything except from God.

It does look as though the body acted on its own. It looks, for example, as though hands and feet acted on their own while they act, as though the mouth and tongue made their quick little movements on their own during speech. Yet not a shred of this is on their own; it is rather out of intentionality's affection and discernment's consequent thought in the head.

Reflect then: if a single body had several heads, each head self-governing as a result of its own discernment and its own intentionality, could the body continue to exist? The kind of single-mindedness that one head has is impossible for those several heads.

It is the same in the heavens, made up of myriads of myriads of angels, as it is in the church. If each and every one did not focus on the one God, they would fall out with each other, and heaven would come apart. So if an angel of heaven simply thinks about several gods, he or she vanishes instantly, is hurled to the very edge of heaven, and falls away.

26. Since the entire heaven and all its elements go back to a single God, angelic speech is of such nature that it settles in a unity through a harmony derived from heaven's own harmony. This is evidenced by their inability to think except in terms of one God, since speech is a result of thought.

27. What person with healthy reason does not perceive that the divine is not divided? That consequently several infinite, uncreated, omnipotent beings, several gods, do not occur? If some other, irrational person were to maintain that there could be several infinite, uncreated, omnipotent beings, several gods, provided they had a single defined essence, and that this would result in a single infinite, uncreated, omnipotent being, a single God, is not a single defined essence a single defined entity? And a single defined entity does not occur in a plurality. If it were maintained that one of these derived from another, then the derivative one would not be God in itself; yet God in Himself *is* God, the source of everything (see above, n. 16).

THE ACTUAL DIVINE ESSENCE IS LOVE AND WISDOM

28. If you gather together everything that is known, and subject it to your mind's close attention, if you search out what is common to everything with your spirit lifted up somewhat, you cannot help concluding that this common element is love and wisdom. These are in fact the two essential elements of all aspects of human life—everything civic, moral, and spiritual that pertains to human beings depends on these two and is nothing without them.

It is the same with a collective person, who as already stated is a larger or smaller community, a nation, an empire, a church, and also the angelic heaven. Abstract love and wisdom from them, and reflect—are they then anything? You will discover that apart from love and wisdom as their source, they are nothing.

29. No one is capable of denying that in God there is love, and at the same time wisdom in its very essence. For He loves everyone out of a love within Himself, and guides everyone out of a wisdom within Himself.

Further, when the created universe is looked at from the point of view of design, it is so full of wisdom from love that you would say the whole thing, grasped together, is wisdom itself. There are actually boundless elements in such patterns of sequence and coexistence that taken together they constitute a unity. This is the only reason they can be held together and maintained forever.

30. It is because the very divine essence is love and wisdom that we have two abilities of life, one giving us discernment, and the other giving us intentionality. The ability that results in discernment derives everything it has from an inflow of wisdom from God. The ability that results in intentionality derives everything it has from an inflow of love from God.

An individual's failure to be properly wise and properly loving does not abolish these abilities: it simply closes them in. As long as one does close them in, while the names discernment and intentionality are indeed used, still they do not really exist. So if the abilities were taken away, everything human would perish—that is thinking, speaking as a result of thinking, intending, and acting as a result of intending.

We can see from this that in the human being, the divine dwells in these two abilities—the ability to be

17

wise and the ability to love—the fact that the person can do these things.

An abundance of experience (which you will find amply presented elsewhere) has shown me that the ability to be wise and to love is within people even though they are not wise and do not love as they can.

31. It is because the very divine essence is love and wisdom that everything in the universe goes back to what is good and what is true. Everything in fact that comes forth from love is called good; and everything that comes forth from wisdom is called true. But more on this below.

32. It is because the very divine essence is love and wisdom that the universe and everything in it, living and inert, remains in existence as a result of warmth and light. Warmth in fact corresponds to love, and light corresponds to wisdom. So spiritual warmth is love, and spiritual light is wisdom. But more on this too below.

33. Out of divine love and out of divine wisdom, which constitute the very essence that is God, arise all affections and thoughts within human beings. Our affections arise from divine love and our thoughts from divine wisdom. Each and every part of a person is nothing but affection and thought—these are the wellsprings of all elements of human life. All the delights and graces of our life derive from them—the delights from the affection of our love, and the graces from our consequent thought.

Now then, since the human beings were created to be recipients, and are recipients to the extent that they love God and are wise because of that love for God (that is, to the extent that they are affected by things that come from God and think because of that affection), it follows that the divine essence, the Creatress, is divine love and wisdom.

DIVINE LOVE BELONGS TO DIVINE WISDOM, AND DIVINE WISDOM TO DIVINE LOVE

34. On the fact that divine reality and divine presence in the God-Man are distinguishably one, see above (nn. 14-16); and since divine reality is divine love and divine presence is divine wisdom, these latter are therefore distinguishably one in the same way.

We call them distinguishably one because love and wisdom are two distinct things; but they are united in such a way that love belongs to wisdom and wisdom to love. In fact, love exists [est] in wisdom, and wisdom becomes present [existit] in love. And since wisdom does derive its presence from love (as stated in n. 15 above), divine wisdom too is reality. It follows from this that love and wisdom taken together are the divine reality, while taken separately, love is called the divine reality and wisdom the divine presence. This is what the angelic concept of divine love and divine wisdom is like.

35. Since there is this kind of oneness of love and wisdom and wisdom and love in the God-Man, the divine reality is one. Actually, the divine reality is divine love because that belongs to divine wisdom, and is divine wisdom because that belongs to divine love. Then, too, since they have this kind of oneness, the divine life is one as well—life is the divine essence.

The reason divine love and divine wisdom are one is that the uniting is mutual, and mutual uniting makes a one. But we will have more to say elsewhere about mutual uniting.

36. The uniting of love and wisdom exists also in every divine work. This is the source of its constancy, its eternity. If there were more divine wisdom than divine love in any created work, or more divine wisdom than divine love, it would not last except to the extent that there were equal proportions within it—any excess passes off.

37. In its activities of re-forming, re-generating, and saving people, divine providence partakes equally of divine love and divine wisdom. An individual cannot be re-formed, re-generated, or saved out of an excess of divine love over divine wisdom, or out of an excess of divine wisdom over divine love. Divine love intends to save everyone, but is able to save only through divine wisdom. All the laws through which salvation is accomplished belong to divine wisdom, and love cannot transcend these laws because divine love and divine wisdom are one and act in unity.

38.   In the Word, divine love and divine wisdom are meant by "justice" [*justitia*] and "judgment" [*judicium*]—divine love by "justice" and divine wisdom by "judgment." For this reason, justice and judgment are predicated of God in the Word. In Psalms, for example,

> Justice and judgment are the foundation of your throne (Psalm 89:14).

Again,

> [Jehovah] will bring forth justice as light . . . and judgment as noonday (Psalm 37:6).

In Hosea,

> I will betroth Myself to you forever . . . in justice and judgment (Hosea 2:19).

In Jeremiah,

> I will raise up for David a righteous branch, who will reign as King . . . and he will work judgment and justice in the land (Jeremiah 23:5).

In Isaiah,

> [He will sit] on the throne of David and over his kingdom, to make it firm . . . in judgment and in justice (Isaiah 9:7).

Again,

> Jehovah will be exalted,...because He has filled [the earth] with judgment and justice (Isaiah 33:5).

In Psalms,

> Once I have learned the judgments of your justice:...seven times a day will I praise You because of the judgments of your justice (Psalm 119:7, 164).

Much the same is meant by "life" and "light" in John:

> In Him was life, and the life was the light of men (John 1:4).

In this verse, "life" means the Lord's divine love, and "light" means his divine wisdom. Much the same is also meant by "life" and "spirit" in John:

> Jesus said, "The words which I say to you are spirit and life" (John 6:63).

39. In a human being, love and wisdom seem to be two separate entities; yet intrinsically they are distinguishably one, since in a human being the quality of love determines the quality of wisdom and the quality of wisdom determines that of love.

Wisdom that does not make one with its love seems to be wisdom; however, it is not. And love that does not make one with its wisdom seems to be wisdom's love; however, it is not. Each one derives its essence and its life from the other.

The reason for the appearance in humans that love and wisdom are two separate entities is that the ability to discern in humans can be raised into heaven's light, but not the ability to love, except to the extent that people act in accord with what they discern.

In consequence, the portion of seeming wisdom that does not make one with wisdom's love slips back into the love that does make one with it, which may be not wisdom's but madness's love. People can actually know, from wisdom, that they ought to do something or other, and yet not do it because they do not love it. But to the extent that they do, from love, what belongs to wisdom, they are images of God.

DIVINE LOVE AND DIVINE WISDOM IS [sic] SUBSTANCE AND IS [sic] FORM

40. In the concept ordinary folk have of love and wisdom, they are like something volatile, something that flows in a tenuous gas or "ether," or like an emanation from some such thing. Hardly anyone thinks that they are really and effectively substance and form.

Even people who do see that they are substance and form still perceive love and wisdom as outside their subject and emanating from it. And what they perceive as outside a subject and emanating from it they call substance and form even though it is volatile and fluid. They are unaware that love and wisdom are the actual "subject," and that what they perceive outside the subject, as volatile and fluid, is nothing more than the appearance of the intrinsic subject's state.

There are many reasons why the actual situation has not yet been seen. Among others, there is the fact that "appearances" are the raw material out of which the human mind shapes its understanding, and that these appearances cannot be dispelled except by careful inquiry into causes. If a cause is deeply hidden, it cannot be investigated unless the mind is held for some considerable time in spiritual light; and the mind cannot be held there very long because of the natural light which persistently pulls it back.

But the truth is that love and wisdom are real and effective substance and form, which constitute the actual subject.

41. However, since this goes against the way things seem, it can seem unworthy of belief unless it is described; and the only way to describe it is with the aid of the kinds of thing a person can perceive with his physical senses. So we will use these for our description.

People have five outward senses, called touch, taste, smell, hearing, and sight.

The "subject" of touch is the skin that envelops us. The very substance and form of skin make it feel things that come in contact with it. The sense of touch is not in those things that come in contact; it is in the skin's substance and form, which are the subject. The sense is simply the way it is affected by the impinging objects.

It is the same with taste. This sense is simply the change of state [*affectio*] of the tongue's substance and form; the tongue is the subject.

It is the same with smell. It is recognized that an odor affects the nostrils and their components, that there is a change of state [*affectio*] in them occasioned by impinging odors.

It is the same with hearing. It does seem as though hearing were in the place where a sound originates; but hearing is within the ear, and is a change of state [*affectio*] of its substance and form. It is an appearance only that hearing is outside the ear.

It is the same with sight. When a person is seeing objects at a distance, it seems as though sight were over there. However, sight is in the eye, which is the subject, and, as in the other cases, is its change of state [*affectio*]. The element of distance derives from a judgment made about space on the basis of intervening objects, or from the object's reduction in size and consequent loss of clarity, the object's image being formed within the eye as determined by the angle of incidence.

We can see from this that sight does not go out from the eye to the object, but that an image of the object enters the eye and affects the eye's substance and form. It is the same with sight as with hearing; hearing does not go out from the ear to seize on a sound, rather the sound enters the ear and affects it.

We can conclude from these observations that the change of state [*affectio*] of substance and form which constitutes the senses is not some entity separate from its subject, but simply effects a change in that subject, with the subject continuing to be the subject at that point, as it was before and will be afterwards.

It follows from this that sight, hearing, smell, taste, and touch are not some volatile effluent from their organs, but are the organs regarded as to their substance and form; when these are affected, sensation occurs.

42. It is much the same with love and wisdom. The one difference is that the substances and forms which are love and wisdom are not visible to the eye like the organs of the outer senses. Nevertheless, no one can deny that those matters of wisdom and love called thoughts, perceptions, and affections are substances and forms, that they are not fluid entities that flow from nothing, or removed from the real and effective substance and form which are their subjects. Actually, the brain contains countless substances and forms in which dwells every deeper sense that goes back to discernment and intentionality.

We can conclude from the preceding statements about the outward senses that all affections, perceptions, and thoughts in the brain are not emanations from its substances and forms, but are effectively and really subjects, which do not emit anything from themselves but simply undergo changes in response to impingements that affect them. We will have more to say below about the impingements that affect them.

43. We can now see on this basis that divine love and divine wisdom are intrinsically substance and form—are in fact actual reality and presence. And if reality and presence did not have the nature of substance and form, they would be nothing but a rational construct which intrinsically is nothing.

DIVINE LOVE AND DIVINE WISDOM ARE INTRINSIC SUBSTANCE AND FORM; THEY ARE THEREFORE AUTHENTIC [*Ipsum*] AND UNIQUE

44. We have just established the premise that divine love and divine wisdom is [*sic*] substance and form, and have also stated that divine reality and presence is intrinsic [*in se*] reality-and-emergence. We cannot say that it is reality-and-emergence from itself, because this implies a beginning, and implies further that it comes from something in that beginning which would be intrinsic reality-and-emergence.

Authentic, intrinsic reality-and-emergence is uncreated, and everything created can exist only from the uncreated. Further, what is created is also finite, and the finite can emerge only from the infinite.

45. Anyone who can, with some thought, catch and grasp intrinsic reality-and-emergence, will inevitably catch and grasp the fact that it is authentic and unique. "Authentic" means that which alone *exists*, and "unique" means that which is the source of everything else.

Since then the authentic and unique is substance and form, it follows that it is the authentic and unique substance and form. And since that authentic substance and form is divine love and divine wisdom, it follows that it is the authentic and unique love and the authentic and unique wisdom. We may therefore conclude that it is the authentic and unique essence, and the authentic and unique life, since love-and-wisdom is life.

46. We can determine from this how sensory, how dependent on the physical senses and their shadows in spiritual matters, is the thinking of people who claim that nature exists from itself. They are thinking from the eye, and are incapable of thinking from discernment. Thinking from the eye closes off discernment, while thinking from discernment opens the eye.

These people are incapable of thinking anything about intrinsic reality-and-emergence, of thinking that it is eternal, uncreate, and infinite. They cannot think anything about life except as something volatile that trails off into nothing. This is the only way they can think about love and wisdom—they are utterly incapable of thinking that love and wisdom are the source of all elements of nature.

It is impossible to see that they are the source of all elements of nature unless nature is looked at from the point of view of uses, in its sequence and its design. This does not happen when the focus is on some of its forms, which are objects of sight only.

In fact, uses exist only from life, with their sequence and design from wisdom and love; while the forms are the things which contain the uses. So if the focus is on forms alone, no element of life can be seen in nature, let alone any element of love and wisdom; so nothing of God can be seen there.

DIVINE LOVE AND DIVINE WISDOM CANNOT HELP EXISTING AND BECOMING PRESENT IN OTHERS CREATED BY ITSELF

47. The identity [*ipsum*] of love is not loving self, but loving others and being united to others through love. The essence of love is also being loved by others; this is in fact how the uniting occurs.

The essence [*essentia*] of every love consists of uniting. This applies to its life, which we call pleasure, charm, delight, sweetness, blessedness, prosperity, and happiness. Love consists of having what belongs to oneself belong to someone else; feeling another person's joy as joy in oneself—that is loving. But feeling one's own joy in someone else is not loving. This latter is loving oneself; the former is loving the neighbor.

These two kinds of love are exact opposites. Both do form a bond, and it does not look as though loving what is one's own (that is, oneself in someone else) divides. However, this does divide, so much so that to the extent someone else has been loved in this fashion, he is later hated. In fact, this bond gradually dissolves of its own accord, and then the love becomes hatred on a comparable level.

48. If anyone can explore love's essence, can he or she fail to see this? What does it in fact mean to love oneself alone, loving no one beyond oneself by whom he may be loved in return? This is breaking apart rather than bonding together.

Love's uniting stems from a mutual element, and a mutual element does not occur in oneself alone. If anyone thinks it does so occur, it stems from some imagined mutual element in others.

We can see from this that divine love cannot help existing and becoming present in others whom it loves and by whom it is loved. For given the presence of this characteristic in every love, it is at its zenith—infinitely so, that is—in Love itself.

49. Specifically concerning God, this loving and being loved in return cannot occur with others who have in themselves something of the infinite, or something of the essence and life of intrinsic love, or something of the divine. If there actually were something of the infinite in them, something of the essence and life of intrinsic love, or something of the divine, that is, then He would not be loved by others, He would be loving Himself. For the infinite, or the divine, is unique. If this were in others, it would be itself, and that would be

actual love of self; and there cannot be a shred of that in God. It is in fact wholly opposite to the divine essence. For this reason, [mutual love] occurs with others in which there is nothing of the intrinsic divine. We shall see below that this happens with beings created by the divine.

But for this to happen there must be an infinite wisdom that must make one with an infinite love. That is, divine love must belong to divine wisdom and divine wisdom to divine love (see above, nn. 34-39).

50. On a grasp of and reflection on this *arcanum* depends the grasp and recognition of the emergence or creation of everything, and of everything's enduring or maintenance by God—that is, of all God's works in the created universe. We need to deal with these matters below.

51. I beg you, though, not to muddle your concepts with time and with space. The more of time and space you have in your concepts as you read what follows, the less you will understand. For the divine is not within time and space, as will be seen clearly as the present work progresses, especially in the treatment of eternity, infinity, and omnipresence.

EVERYTHING IN THE UNIVERSE WAS CREATED OUT OF THE DIVINE LOVE AND DIVINE WISDOM OF GOD-MAN

52. The universe in its greatest and its smallest, its first and its last elements, is so full of divine love and divine wisdom that we might say it is divine love and divine wisdom in reflection.

The truth of this is clearly established on the basis of the correspondence of all components of the universe with all components of humans. Absolutely all the things that take form in the created universe have such a correspondence with all the components of humans, so that you could say that a person is a kind of universe.

The correspondence of our affections and resultant thoughts is with all members of the animal kingdom; the correspondence of our intentionality and consequent discernment is with all members of the vegetable kingdom; and the correspondence of our outmost life is with all members of the mineral kingdom.

The existence of this correspondence is not apparent to anyone in the natural world, though it is apparent to any observant person in the spiritual world. All the things that take form in the natural world, in its three kingdoms, exist in the spiritual world, being correspondences of the affections and thoughts, the affections from intentionality and thoughts from discernment, and the outmost aspects of life, of the people who are there. All of these things are visible in the environment of these people, with the same kind of appearance the created universe has, except that they are in smaller likeness.

The angels can clearly see from this that the created universe is an image depicting God-Man, and that it is his love and wisdom which are presented in image in the universe.

Not that the created universe is God-Man—it is rather from Him. For nothing whatever in the created universe is intrinsic substance and form or intrinsic life or intrinsic love and wisdom. Even the human being is not intrinsically human. No, everything is from God, who is Person, Wisdom and Love, Form and Substance, intrinsically.

Whatever is intrinsic is uncreate and infinite. Whatever is from Him, since it involves nothing intrinsic, is created and finite. This portrays an image of Him from whom it exists and emerges.

53. We can predicate of created and finite things reality and presence, substance and form, life, and even love and wisdom, but these predicates are all

created and finite. The reason we can make this predication is not that anything divine belongs to them, but that they are in the divine and the divine is in them. Actually, every created thing is intrinsically lifeless and dead, but is quickened and brought to life by the presence of the divine in it, and by its presence in the divine.

54. The divine does not have one kind of presence in one subject and another kind in another. Rather, one created subject is different from another. No two identical things occur, which is why they contain something different. This is why the divine takes on different appearances in its image. We will discuss later the presence of the divine in its opposites.

ALL THE THINGS IN THE CREATED UNIVERSE ARE RECIPIENTS OF GOD-MAN'S DIVINE LOVE AND DIVINE WISDOM

55. It is recognized that each and every component of the universe was created by God. This is why the universe, including each and every component, is called "the work of Jehovah's hands" in the Word.

Some people claim that the whole world was created out of nothing, and they cherish a concept of nothing as really nothing at all. But out of "really nothing at all" nothing is made: nothing can be made. This is an abiding truth.

For this reason, the universe—being an image of God and therefore full of God—must have been created in God, from God. God is in fact essential reality, and whatever does exist must come from reality. To create what does exist out of a "nothing" that does not exist is absolutely self-contradictory.

However, something created by God from God is not a continuation of God. For God is intrinsic reality, and there is no intrinsic reality in created things. If there were some intrinsic reality in created things, it would be a continuation of God, and any continuation of God is God.

The angelic concept of the situation is like this. What is created by God from God is like something which individuals have brought forth out of their life, but from which their life has then been withdrawn. It is the sort of thing that is appropriate to their life but is not actually his life. Angels support this concept with many things which happen in their heaven, where they say that they are in God and God in them, while still they possess nothing of God which actually is God in his reality.

We will cite more resources for support of this later; for the present, the above may serve for information.

56. Because of this origin, every created thing is in its own nature fit to be a recipient of God—not by being a continuation but by being in contact. This is the only means to the possibility of uniting. Because everything is created in this way, everything is an analogue, and by being united is a virtual mirror-image of God.

57. This is why angels are not angels on their own, but as a result of this bond with God-Man. This bond depends on their acceptance of the Divine-Good and the Divine-True which are God, which seem to emanate from Him even though they are actually within Him. Their acceptance, further, depends on their applying to themselves the laws of order, which are divine truths, freely thinking and intending according to reason, which freedom and reason are given them by the Lord as though they belonged to the angels themselves.

This is the source of their apparently independent acceptance of the Divine-Good and the Divine-True, and this is the source of the mutual aspect of love. For as already stated, love does not exist unless it is mutual. It is the same with people on earth.

We can now see, on the basis of these statements, that everything in the universe was created a recipient of the divine love and divine wisdom of God-Man.

58. At this point, there is no way to explain to the discerning mind that those other components of the universe which are not like angels and people are also recipients of God-Man's divine love and divine wisdom—things, for example, like those below humanity in the animal kingdom, below these in the vegetable kingdom, and below these again in the mineral kingdom. There are many things that need to be said first about levels of life and levels of recipients of life.

The union with these things depends on their functions [usus]. All good functions do actually find their origin in a union with God similar in kind but unlike as to level. The nature of this union changes as it descends, becoming such that in involves no element of freedom because it involves no element of reason. As a result, it contains no appearance of life; yet these are still recipients. Because they are recipients, they are also reactive entities; for by being reactive entities, they are containants.

We will discuss functions that are not good after we have described the origin of evil.

59. We can determine on this basis that the divine is in each and every created thing and that the created universe is therefore the work of Jehovah's hands, as it says in the Word. That is, it is a work of divine love and divine wisdom, for this is what "Jehovah's hands" means.

Further, even though the divine is in each and every component of the created universe, nothing of the intrinsic divine is in these components' reality. The created universe is not in fact God, but is from God. And being from God, there is an image of Him within it, like the image of a person in a mirror: the person does indeed appear there, and yet there is nothing of the person in the image.

60. I heard a number of people in the spiritual world talking near me, saying that they did want to acknowledge the presence of the divine in each and every component of the universe because they saw God's wonders there, and the deeper they looked, the more wonderful things they saw. Yet when they heard that the divine was actually within each and every component of the created universe, they were distressed. This was a sign that while they did say this, they did not believe it.

They were therefore asked whether they could not see this simply from the marvelous ability, inherent in every seed, of producing in proper sequence its own plant all the way to new seed. Within each seed there is a concept of what is infinite and eternal, an actual effort within seeds to multiply and bear fruit to infinity and to eternity.

Or they might see this from any animal, even the smallest. Each has within it sense organs, brains, heart, lungs, and such other things as arteries, veins, fibers, muscles, and their consequent activities. Beyond this, there are incredible aspects of their instinctual nature, about which we can find whole books written.

All these marvelous things are from God. However, the forms in which they are clothed are made from elements of this earth. Plants are made from these elements, and so in its own design is the human being. This is why it is said of [the first] person

> that he was created from the ground, and that he is the dust of the earth, and that the breath of lives was breathed in (Genesis 2:7).

We can see from this that the divine does not belong to us, but is added to us.

EVERY CREATED THING REFLECTS THE HUMAN IN A PARTICULAR IMAGE

61. We can support this proposition with each and every member of the animal kingdom, each and every member of the vegetable kingdom, and each and every member of the mineral kingdom.

We can see *a relationship of the human to each and every member of the animal kingdom* on the basis of the following observations. Animals of all kinds have limbs for moving themselves, organs for sensing, and internal organs which serve to energize them, which they hold in common with us. They also have appetites and affections like the natural ones we have. They have inborn data corresponding to their affections—in some of these data we can see an apparently spiritual element, which in earth's larger animals, heavens's birds, bees, in worms, ants, etc., is more or less evident to sight. This is why merely natural people make living members of this kingdom like themselves, with the exception of speech.

We can see *a relationship to the human in each and every member of the vegetable kingdom* from the following observations. They emerge from seed, and step by step advance from this point into their own stages of life. They have something like marriage, followed by reproduction. Their "plant-soul" is a function of which they are forms. Then there are many other things which are relationships to the human, which other writers have also described.

We can see *a relationship to the human in each and every member of the mineral kingdom* only in their effort to produce forms which do have relationship—these, as mentioned, are all the members of the vegetable kingdom—and in this way fulfilling a use. The moment a seed is dropped into the bosom of the earth, earth does cherish it, and from all about supplies it for sprouting and presenting itself in a form that is representative of the human. We can see the presence of this tendency within earth's fluids from corals in the ocean depths, from flowers in mines that are formed from minerals and metals.

The tendency to grow into plants and thus to fulfill a use is the final product of the divine in created things.

62. Just as there is in earth's mineral substances an effort to grow into plants, there is in plants an effort to become alive. This is the reason for the different kinds of insects, which are responsive to the fragrant vapors of plants. We will see below that this does not happen *as a result of* the warmth of earth's sun, but *by means of* that warmth, as a result of life, in keeping with the recipient entities.

63. One may know from the material just cited that there is a relationship of all things in the created universe to the human, and yet see it only dimly. In the spiritual world, though, this is clearly seen.

All the members of the three kingdoms exist there, with each angel in their midst. Angels see them around themselves, and further know that they are "representations" of themselves. In fact, when the deepest level of their discernment is opened, they recognize themselves and see their image in them, almost as though they were seeing it in a mirror.

64. Given these facts and many others which agree with them, which we have not time to cite here, we can know with certainty that God is Person, and that the created universe is an image of Him. There is actually an overall relationship of everything with Him, just as there is a specific relationship with the individual person.

THE FUNCTIONS (*USUS*) OF ALL CREATED THINGS RISE BY STEPS FROM LOWEST THINGS TO MAN, AND THROUGH MAN TO GOD THE CREATOR, THEIR SOURCE

35

65. The *lowest things* [*ultima*], as we have stated, are all the members of the mineral kingdom—various kinds of matter, some composed of stony substance, of saline or oily or mineral or metallic substance, or deposited on the soil by the vegetable and animal matter that is constantly disintegrating into very fine dust. Within these, there lie hidden both the end ["purpose"] and the beginning of all the functions derived from life. The purpose of all functions is the effort to produce them, while the beginning is the active force derived from that effort. These have to do with the mineral kingdom.

The *intermediate things* [*media*] are all the members of the vegetable kingdom—grasses and herbs of every kind, all kinds of plants and shrubs, and all kinds of trees.

Their functions are devoted to all the members of the animal kingdom, whether imperfect or perfect. They nourish and please and quicken them. They nourish their bodies with their substances, they delight their senses with their taste, smell, and beauty, and they quicken their affections. The effort toward these functions is inherent in them as a result of their life.

The *primary* [*prima*] things are all the members of the animal kingdom. We call the lowest of these worms and insects, the intermediate ones birds and beasts, and the highest, people. For there are in every kingdom lowest, intermediate, and highest members, the lowest to serve the intermediate, and the intermediate to serve the highest.

In this way, the functions of all created things rise in sequence from the lowest elements to man, who is first in the sequence.

66. Vertically, there are three levels in the natural world and three levels in the spiritual world. All living things are recipients of life. The more perfect living

things are recipients of the life of the three levels of the natural world; the less perfect ones are recipients of life of two levels of that world; and the imperfect ones are recipients [of the life] of one of its levels. But human beings alone are recipients of the life of the three levels of the spiritual world in addition to that of the three levels of the natural world.

This is why people can be raised above nature, unlike any other living thing. They can think analytically and rationally about civic and moral issues that are within nature, and even about spiritual and heavenly matters that are above nature. They can even be raised into wisdom, so that they see God.

We will discuss the six levels—the levels through which the uses of all created things rise in their sequence to God the creator—in their own proper place.

We can see from this brief treatment that there is an ascent of all created things to a First, who alone is life, and we can see that the functions of all these things are the actual recipients of life, that the things are therefore forms of function.

67. Let us now describe how people climb from the last [ultimo] level to the first—that is, how they are lifted up.

People are born into the lowest [ultimum] level of the natural world. They are later raised to the second level by means of information, and as their discernment is perfected with information, they are raised to the third level, and at that point become rational.

68. There is something else we should be aware of about the raising up of the more inward parts of people, which belong to their minds.

Reaction is inherent in everything created by God. Action is proper to life alone; and reaction is occasioned by life's action. This reaction seems to belong to the created being, since it takes form when an "action" is performed. In the case of human beings, it seems to belong to them because they feel entirely as though life belonged to them; yet in fact people are only recipients of life.

This is why people react against God out of their inherited will. But to the extent that individuals believe that their whole life is from God, that all life's good stems from God's action and all life's evil from their reaction, the "reaction" becomes "action"—they are acting with God, in apparent independence.

The balance of all things results from action and reaction at the same moment, and everything must be in a balance.

We have mentioned these matters so that people would not believe that they climb up to God on their own—it is the Lord's doing.

THE DIVINE FILLS EVERY SPACE OF THE UNIVERSE, BUT IS NON-SPATIAL

69. Nature has two characteristics, *space* and *time*. It is from these that people in the natural world form their thought-concepts and consequently their discernment. If they persist in these concepts, not raising their minds higher, there is no way for them to grasp anything spiritual and divine. For they combine these latter with concepts dependent on space and time; and to the extent that they do, the light [*lumen*] of their discernment becomes merely natural.

Thinking on this basis in calculating about spiritual and divine matters is like thinking on the basis of the gloom of night about things visible only in daylight. This is where materialism comes from.

But if people know how to raise their minds above thought-concepts that depend on space and time, they pass from gloom into light [*lux*]. They savor spiritual and divine matters, eventually seeing things which are in them and things which are derived from them. Then, because of that light, they dispel the gloom of natural light, and banish its deceptions from the center to the fringes.

Everyone who possesses discernment is able to think on a higher level than that of things characteristic of nature, and does indeed so think. At such times, people assert and see that the divine, being omnipresent, is not within space. They are able also to assert and see what we have mentioned above. But if they deny divine omnipresence and give nature credit for everything, then they do not want to be lifted up, even though it is possible.

70. These two characteristics of nature (which are space and time, as stated) are left behind by everyone who dies and becomes an angel. In fact, people enter spiritual light at that point, the light in which the subjects of sight are similar to ones in the natural world but are in correspondence with the angels' thoughts.

The subjects of their thought (which as stated are things which are true) are wholly independent of space and time. And while the subjects of their sight seem to be in space and time, they do not think on the basis of these subjects.

This is because "spaces" and "times" are not fixed there the way they are in a natural world. They are, rather, changeable, depending on the state of angels' lives. As a result, state of life is substituted for space and time in their thought-concepts, with matters pertinent to the state of love being substituted for spaces, and matters pertinent to the state of wisdom being substituted for times.

This is why there is such a great difference between spiritual thought with its consequent spiritual speech, and natural thought with its consequent natural speech—such a difference that they have nothing in common except in the deeper levels of subjects, which levels are all spiritual. We will discuss these differences further elsewhere.

Now since angels' thoughts do not derive anything from space and time, but depend on states of life, we can see that angels do not understand when someone says that the divine "fills spaces"—they actually do not know what spaces are. But they do understand clearly when someone says, without any concept of space, that the divine fills everything.

71. Perhaps the following illustration will show that a merely natural person thinks about spiritual and divine matters on the basis of space, while a spiritual person does so apart from space.

Merely natural people do their thinking on the basis of concepts they have acquired from objects of their sight, all of which involve a shape dependent on length, width, and height, and a form, angular or curved, bounded by these dimensions. These aspects are obviously present in their thought-concepts about the things they see on earth, and they are present as well in their thought-concepts about invisible things, such as civic and moral issues. They do not actually see these aspects, but they are still present as constants.

It is different for spiritual people, and especially for heaven's angels. Their thought has nothing in common with shape and form in any way dependent on spatial length, width, and height, but [depends] on the state of the matter depending on the state of life. So in place of spatial length, they think about the good of the matter from the good of life. In place of spatial width they think about the truth of the matter from the truth of life; and in place of height, they think about their levels. So they think from correspondence, which is an interrelationship between spiritual and natural things. This correspondence determines that length in the Word means the good of a matter, width the truth of a matter, and height, their level.

We can see from this that an angel of heaven can

think of divine omnipresence only as the Divine filling everything without [being bounded by] space. Whatever angels think is true, because the light that enlightens their discernment is divine wisdom.

72. This is the fundamental thought about God. For without it, while some of the statements about the God-Man's creation of the universe, His Providence, omnipotence, omnipresence, and omniscience can be understood, they cannot be retained. This is because when people who are merely nature-centered understand them, they still lapse back into their life's love, which is their intentionality. This scatters these thoughts and submerges thinking in space, where they find that light which they call rational—not realizing that to the extent that they deny these matters, they are irrational.

The truth of this can be supported using the concept of this true proposition—"God is person." Try reading carefully nn. 11-13 above, and what follows them. You will then understand that this proposition is true. But then drop your thinking back into the natural light that depends on space—do not these ideas seem like paradoxes? And if you drop your thinking much lower, you will reject them.

This is why we have said that the divine fills all spaces in the universe and have not said that God-Man fills them. If we made this latter statement, the merely natural light would not sustain it. But that light does sustain the proposition that the divine fills everything, since this agrees with the theologians' stock statement that God is omnipresent and hears and knows everything (more on this above, nn. 7-10).

THE DIVINE IS IN ALL TIME, AND IS TIMELESS

73. Just as the divine is in all space, and is non-spatial, it is in all time, and is timeless. Actually, we cannot predicate of the divine any characteristic of

nature, and nature's characteristics are space and time.

Space in nature can be measured, and so can time. Time is measured in days, weeks, months, years, and centuries. Days are measured in hours, weeks and months in days, years in the four seasons, and centuries in years. The nature of this measurement comes from the earth's rotation and from its circling the sun.

But it is different in the spiritual world. Stages of life do seem similarly to occur in time there. People do live together the way people on earth do, which does not happen without some appearance of time. But time there is not marked off into "times" the way it is in this world, since their sun is constantly in its East and does not move in any direction. In fact, it is the Lord's divine love that is visible to angels as the sun.

So they do not have days, weeks, months, years, or centuries; but in their stead they have states of life which result in some segmenting. This segmenting cannot be termed a segmenting of time, only of state.

This is why angels do not know what time is, and why they perceive state when time is mentioned. Further, when state determines time, time is only an appearance. For a pleasant state makes the time seem short, while an unpleasant state makes the time seem long.

We can see from all this that time in the spiritual world is nothing but a quality of state. This is why "hours," "days," "weeks," "months," and "years" in the Word indicate states and their stages, in sequence and *in toto*. This is also why, when times are predicated of the church, its morning means its first state, noon its full state, evening its decline, and night its end. There is similar significance to the four seasons of the year: spring, summer, fall, and winter.

74. These considerations enable us to conclude that time makes one with thought derived from affection.

This thought is in fact the source of the quality of an individual's state.

There are many ways to illustrate the proposition that the distances involved in motion through space in the spiritual world make one with advancing stages of time. Paths are actually shortened there in proportion to eagerness—which amounts to thoughts from affection—or, conversely, lengthened. This is why space is even described as belonging to time. However, in the kinds of state when thought is not united with an individual's characteristic [*propria*] affection, as in sleep, time does not seem to exist.

75. Granted, then, that the "times" which are characteristic of nature in its own world are nothing but states in the spiritual world, states which are apparently progressive there owing to angels' and spirits' finitude, we can conclude that they are not progressive in God because He is infinite, with infinite things being one in Him (according to the matters set forth above, nn. 17-22). It follows from all this that the Divine within all time is itself timeless.

76. If people do not know this, and cannot with some measure of perception think about God as timeless, they are utterly incapable of thinking about eternity except as an eternity of time. Then they cannot help thinking like lunatics about God from eternity. They are then in fact thinking on the assumption of a beginning, and a beginning is strictly a temporal concept. Then their lunacy reaches the conclusion that God emerged from Himself, and from here they slip down to nature's originating from itself. To extricate them from this concept it takes a spiritual or angelic concept of eternity. This is a concept devoid of time, and given the absence of time, the eternal and the divine are the same thing, the divine being the divine in itself, not from itself.

Angels say that it is possible for a person to perceive "God from eternity" but in no way "nature from eternity," and that it is even less possible to perceive nature being "in itself." For anything that exists "in itself" is reality itself, the source of everything. Reality itself is life itself which is divine wisdom's divine love and divine love's divine wisdom.

To angels, this is the eternal, quite apart from time, just as the uncreate is apart from the created or the infinite from the finite, with no ratio occurring between them.

THE DIVINE IS THE SAME IN THE GREATEST AND THE SMALLEST THINGS

77. This follows from the two sections immediately preceding on the divine being non-spatially in all space and timelessly in all time. There are greater and greater spaces and smaller and smaller ones; and since space and time make a single unit, the same holds true of times.

The reason the divine is the same in them is that the divine cannot vary and change as can everything characterized by time and space, or everything that belongs to nature. The divine is unvarying and unchangeable—this is why it is everywhere and forever the same.

78. It does seem as though the divine were not the same in one person as in another—for example, as though it were different in a wise person than in a simple one, different in an elderly person than in an infant.

But this stems from outward appearance, and is therefore deceptive. The person is different, but the divine is not different within. The person is a recipient, and a recipient or receiver is a changeable thing.

A wise person is a recipient of divine love and divine wisdom more adequately and therefore more fully than a simple person is, and an elderly person who is also wise, more than an infant or child, Yet the divine is the same in each one.

In the same way, outward appearance occasions the deceptive notion that the divine is different in heaven's angels than in people on this earth, since heaven's angels are involved in indescribable wisdom, while we are not. But the apparent difference is in particular subjects depending on the quality of their acceptance of the divine; it is not in the Lord.

79. We can illustrate the fact that the divine is the same in greatest and smallest things, by heaven and by an individual angel there. The divine in the whole heaven is the same as the divine within one angel; for this reason, the whole heaven can look like a single angel. It is the same with the church and the individual church person.

The largest entity in which the divine is, is the whole heaven and the whole church together; the smallest is a angel of heaven or a church person.

Several times, a complete community of heaven has appeared to me as a single angel-person, and I have been told that it can appear as a person large as a giant or small as a baby. This is because the divine is the same in greatest and smallest things.

80. The divine is also the same in the greatest and smallest parts of all created things which are not alive. It is in fact within the good aspect of their function [usus]. The reason they are not alive is that they are forms of functions rather than forms of life, and the form is varied depending on the goodness of the functions.

But we shall discuss how the divine is in them later, when we deal with creation.

81. Take space away, and utterly exclude any vacuum, and then think about divine love and divine wisdom as being essence itself once space is taken

away and vacuum excluded. Then, think on the basis of space, and you will realize that the divine is in the greatest and the smallest divisions of space alike. Neither "great" nor "small" occurs in an essence removed from space—it remains the same.

82. Let us now talk about "vacuum." I once heard some angels talking with Newton about vacuum, saying that they would not tolerate a concept of a vacuum as nothing. This was because in their world (which is a spiritual one, within or above the natural world's spaces and times) they too felt, thought, were moved, loved, intended, breathed—even spoke and acted. There is no way these things could happen in a vacuum which was nothing, since nothing is nothing, and no attribute can be predicated of nothing.

Newton stated that he knew that the divine which Is, fills everything. He said he himself abhorred the "nothing-concept" of a vacuum, since it tended to destroy everything. He urged the angels who were discussing vacuum with him to guard themselves against the concept of nothing, calling it an offense because no reality of mind occurs in "nothing."

CHAPTER 2

[THE MEANS OF CREATION]

DIVINE LOVE AND DIVINE WISDOM APPEAR IN THE SPIRITUAL WORLD AS A SUN

83. There are two worlds, a spiritual one and a natural one. The spiritual world does not derive anything from the natural world, nor the natural world from the spiritual world. Their only avenue of communication is correspondences, whose nature has been amply discussed elsewhere.

The following may serve as an illustrative example. Warmth in the natural world corresponds to the good content of charity in the spiritual world, and light in the natural world corresponds to the true content of faith in the spiritual world. Does anyone fail to see that warmth and the good content of charity are two distinct things, or that light and the true content of faith are?

At first glance they seem so distinct as to be wholly different entities. They seem so even if one ponders what the good content of charity has in common with warmth, or the true content of faith with light. Yet spiritual warmth is that good content, and spiritual light is that true content.

47

In spite of the fact that these entities are intrinsically distinct, they make one by means of correspondence. They make one in such a way that when a person reads "warmth" and "light" in the Word, the spirits and angels who are with him perceive charity in place of warmth and faith in place of light.

We have cited this example to let the reader know that the two worlds, spiritual and natural, are so distinct that they have nothing in common with each other. Yet they have been so created that they do communicate—they are even bonded together—by means of correspondences.

84. Since those two worlds are so distinct, a perceptive person can see that the spiritual world is under a different sun than the natural world. There is in fact just as much warmth and light in the spiritual world as in the natural world, but the warmth there is spiritual, and so is the light. Spiritual warmth is the good content of charity, and spiritual light is the true content of faith.

Now, since warmth and light can have no other source than a sun, we may conclude that there is a different sun in the spiritual world than in the natural; and we may further conclude that the spiritual world's sun is essentially of such nature that spiritual warmth and light can emerge from it, and that the natural world's sun is essentially of such nature that natural warmth [and light] can emerge from it.

The only possible source of every spiritual reality (which goes back to what is good and what is true) is divine love and divine wisdom. Everything good is in fact a matter of love, and everything true is a matter of wisdom. Any wise person can see that there is no other source.

85. Hitherto, people have not known of the existence of a sun other than the sun of the natural world. This is because our spiritual part has so assimilated itself

to [*transiit in*] his natural part that we do not know what "the spiritual" is. People therefore do not know that there is a spiritual world where spirits and angels live, different and distinct from the natural world.

Since the spiritual world has become so thoroughly obscured to people who are in the natural world, the Lord has graciously opened my spirit's sight, so that I could see things that exist in that world just as I see things in the natural world, and so that I could then describe that world, as has been done in the book *Heaven and Hell*. There is a chapter there describing the sun of that world. I have in fact seen it, and it looked to be the same size as the natural world's sun and to have the same kind of fiery look, though more reddish. I have been informed that the whole angelic heaven lies beneath that sun, that angels of the third heaven see it constantly, angels of the second heaven very often, and angels of the first or outmost [*ultimi*] heaven occasionally.

The reader will see below that this sun is the source of all their warmth and light and of everything visible in that world.

86. That sun is not the Lord Himself; it is rather derived from the Lord. It is the emanating divine love and divine wisdom which appear as a sun in that world. And since in the Lord love and wisdom are one (as shown in Chapter I), it is said that that sun is divine love. Divine wisdom actually belongs to divine love, so it too is love.

87. The reason that sun looks fiery to angels' eyes is that love and fire correspond to each other. They cannot actually see love with their eyes, but they see what corresponds to it instead.

Angels do have an "inner" and an "outer" like people. Their inner is what thinks and is wise, what intends and loves as well; and their outer is what feels, sees, speaks, and acts. Further, all their outer at

49

tributes are correspondences of inner ones—but they are spiritual and not natural correspondences.

Divine love is also felt as fire by spiritual beings. This is why, when fire is mentioned in the Word, it indicates love. The sacred fire in the Israelite church used to indicate love. This is the source of the custom of asking in prayers to God that heavenly fire may kindle the heart—that is, divine love.

88. There being such a difference between what is spiritual and what is natural (as shown in n. 83 above), no least particle derived from the natural world's sun can cross over into the spiritual world—that is, no trace of its light and warmth, or of any object on earth. The natural world's light is gloom in the spiritual world, and its warmth is death there.

However, this world's warmth can be brought to life by an inflow of heaven's warmth, and this world's light can be brightened by an inflow of heaven's light. The inflow occurs by means of correspondences, and cannot occur by means of a continuum.

FROM THE SUN WHICH EMERGES FROM DIVINE LOVE AND DIVINE WISDOM, WARMTH AND LIGHT EMANATE

89. In the spiritual world where angels and spirits live there is just as much warmth and light as in the natural world where people live. Then too, the warmth is felt as warmth and the light is seen as light in the same way.

Nevertheless, the warmth and light of the spiritual world are so different from those of the natural world that, as we have already stated, they have nothing in common. They are as different as something alive and something dead.

The spiritual world's warmth is intrinsically alive, and so is its light; the natural world's warmth is however intrinsically dead, and so is its light. Actually, the spiritual world's warmth and light emanate from a sun that is pure love, while the natural world's warmth and light emanate from a sun that is pure fire. And love is alive, and divine love is life itself; while fire is dead and solar fire is death itself. We can call it that because there is absolutely no trace of life within it.

90. Angels, being spiritual, cannot live in any warmth or light that is not spiritual. People cannot live in any warmth or light that is not natural. For the spiritual suits a spiritual being, and the natural suits a natural being. If an angel were to take in the tiniest trace of natural warmth and light, he would die—this is utterly unsuited to his life.

Every individual is a spirit, as far as the more inward elements of mind are concerned. When people die, they leave the natural world completely behind and let go of everything that pertains to it, and they enter a world where there is nothing that belongs to nature. In that world, they live so separated from nature that there is no communication along a continuum like something purer to something coarser, but like something prior to something posterior. Correspondence is the only avenue of communication for them.

We can determine from this that spiritual warmth is not a purer natural warmth, nor spiritual light a purer natural light. They are derived rather from a spiritual essence. Spiritual warmth and light actually draw their essence for a sun that is pure love, and is life itself. Natural warmth and light draw their essence from a sun that is pure fire, that has absolutely no trace of life in it, as stated above.

91. In view of the great difference between the warmth and light of the one world and the other, we can readily see why people who are in one world cannot see people who are in the other. The eyes of

human beings—who see because of natural light—are made of substances from their own world, and the eyes of an angel are made of substances from their own world. In each case, they are formed to receive their own light effectively.

We can see from this how people think from ignorance who will not allow into their faith the notion that angels and spirits are people because they have not seen them with their eyes.

92. Until now, people had not realized that angels and spirits were in a wholly other light and other warmth than people are. They did not even know that another light and another warmth existed.

People had not, in their thinking, actually delved any deeper than the more inward and purer levels of nature. So, many people have set the homes of angels and spirits in the ether, while some have set them in the stars—within nature, that is, and not above or beyond it. Yet angels and spirits are completely above, or beyond, nature, in their own world which is under another sun.

And since spaces in that world are appearances, as set forth above, we cannot say that they are in the ether or the stars. They are actually right with us, bonded to the affection and thought of our spirits; for a human being is a spirit. This is how we can think and intend. So the spiritual world is where people are, and not in any way at a distance from them.

In brief, every individual, as far as the more inward elements of his or her mind are concerned, is in that world, surrounded by angels and spirits there—thinking because of its life, and loving because of its warmth.

THAT SUN IS NOT GOD: IT IS RATHER AN EMANATION FROM GOD-MAN'S DIVINE LOVE AND DIVINE WISDOM. IT IS THE SAME WITH WARMTH AND LIGHT FROM THAT SUN

93. We do not understand that sun which angels see, the source of their warmth and light, to be the Lord Himself, but rather to be a first emanation from Him which is the zenith of spiritual warmth. The zenith of spiritual warmth is spiritual fire, which in its primary correspondence is divine love and divine wisdom.

This is why that sun both looks and is fiery to angels, though not to people. The fire which people experience as fire is not spiritual but natural, the difference being like that between something alive and something dead.

So the spiritual sun makes spiritual people alive and refreshes spiritual things with its warmth, while the natural sun does the same for natural people and things. The natural sun, however, does not do this on its own, but by means of an inflow of spiritual warmth; it provides an auxiliary resource for that inflow.

94. This spiritual fire (which also contains light in its original form) becomes spiritual warmth and light which lessen as they emanate. The lessening occurs by levels, which will be discussed below.

This was portrayed by early people by means of ruddy halos of fire and light gleaming around God's head. This is a usual portrayal today as well, when God is presented as a person in paintings.

95. Experience itself makes it clear that love produces warmth and wisdom produces light. When a person loves, he grows warm, and when he thinks from wisdom he sees things in the light, so to speak. We can see from this that the first emanation of love is warmth and the first emanation of wisdom is light.

We can see that these are correspondences as well. For warmth does not emerge within the love itself, but from it—in intentionality and thereby in the body. And light does not emerge within wisdom, but in discerning thought, and thereby in speech.

So love and wisdom are the essence and life of warmth and light. Warmth and light are emanations. And because they are emanations, they are also correspondences.

96. Anyone who pays attention to the thoughts of his or her own mind may know that spiritual light is completely distinct from natural light. For while a mind is thinking, it sees its objects of vision in light; and people who think spiritually see true things, just as well in the night as in the day.

This is why we attribute light to discernment, and say that discernment sees. For when someone else is talking about various matters, we sometimes say we "see" that it is true, meaning that we understand.

Since discernment is spiritual, it cannot therefore see from natural light. Natural light does not in fact remain engaged; it disappears with the sun. We can see from this that discernment enjoys a different light than the eyes do, and that this light comes from another source.

97. Everyone should be careful not to think that the spiritual world's sun itself is God. God Himself is a person. The first emanation from Him is something fiery and spiritual which looks like a sun to angels. So when the Lord does make Himself visible to angels in person (*Persona*), He makes Himself visible as a person (*Homo*) —sometimes within the sun, sometimes outside it.

98. This correspondence is the reason why in the Word the Lord is called not only "the sun," but "fire" and "light" as well. "The sun" means the Lord in respect to divine love and divine wisdom together, "fire" means the Lord in respect to divine love, and "light," the Lord in respect to divine wisdom.

IN EMANATING FROM THE LORD AS THE SUN, SPIRITUAL WARMTH AND LIGHT MAKE ONE, THE WAY HIS DIVINE LOVE AND DIVINE WISDOM MAKE ONE

99. We have described in Chapter I how divine love and divine wisdom make one in the Lord. Warmth and light make one in the same way because they emanate; the things that emanate make one by correspondence. Warmth does in fact correspond to love, and light to wisdom.

This then follows: just as divine love is divine reality and divine wisdom is divine emergence (nn. 14-16 above), spiritual warmth is the divine that emanates from divine reality and spiritual light is the divine that emanates from divine emergence. Therefore, just as divine love belongs to divine wisdom and divine wisdom to divine love by virtue of that union (see above, nn. 34-39), spiritual warmth belongs to spiritual light and spiritual light is spiritual warmth. Because this kind of oneness exists, it follows that warmth and light, as they emanate from the Lord as the sun, are one.

We will however see below that they are not received as one by angels and people.

100. The warmth and light that emanate from the Lord as the sun are what we call "the spiritual" because of their supreme worth, and we refer to them as "the spiritual" in the singular number because they are one. So in subsequent pages, when mention is made of "the spiritual," it means both together.

This "spiritual" is why that whole world is called spiritual. All elements of that world find their source through that spiritual, and are therefore named after it as well.

The reason that warmth and that light are called "the spiritual" is that God is called a Spirit, and God as Spirit is that emanation.

From his very own essence, God is called Jehovah. But it is by means of this emanation that He gives life and light to angels of heaven and people of the church. This is why we say that giving life and light are done through the spirit of Jehovah.

101. The oneness of warmth and light (that is, of the spiritual that emanates from the Lord as the sun) can be illustrated by using the warmth and light that emanate from the natural world's sun. These two things make one as they leave that sun.

Their not making one on earth is not because of that sun but because of the planet. This revolves on its axis once a day, and makes its orbit on the ecliptic once a year. This is why it seems as though warmth and light do not make one. In midsummer there is more warmth than light and in midwinter there is more light than warmth.

It is the same in the spiritual world. But the planet there does not revolve or move in orbit; rather the angels turn more or less toward the Lord. And people who turn less toward the Lord receive more light than warmth.

That is why the heavens (which are made up of angels) are marked off into two kingdoms, one called celestial and the other called spiritual. Celestial angels receive more of warmth, and spiritual angels more of light. The appearance of the lands they live in also depends on their reception of warmth and light. The correspondence is complete, if we simply substitute for planetary motion a changing in the angels' state.

102. We will see below that, seen in their own light, all the spiritual things that arise from the warmth and light of their sun make one in the same fashion, yet if they are seen as emanating from angels' affections, they do not make one.

When warmth and light make one in the heavens, it is spring-like for angels. But when they do not make one, it is either summery or wintery—not like winter in cold latitudes, but like winter in warm latitudes. Acceptance of love and wisdom in equal measure is the essence of angelhood. So an angel is an angel of heaven in proportion to the union of love and wisdom within him. It is the same with the church person if love and wisdom, or charity and faith, make one in him.

THE SPIRITUAL WORLD'S SUN APPEARS AT MEDIAN HEIGHT, AS FAR FROM ANGELS AS THE NATURAL WORLD'S SUN IS FROM US

103. Many people who come from this world bring along a concept in which God is high overhead and the Lord is in heaven, among the angels. The reason they bring a concept of God as high overhead is that God is called "The Most High" in the Word, and it says that He lives "on high." So they lift up their eyes and their hands when they plead and worship, unaware that "most high" means "inmost."

The reason they bring a concept of the Lord as being in heaven among the angels is that they think of Him only as another person, with some thinking of Him as an angel. They are unaware that the Lord is the actual and only God who governs the universe. If He were among angels in heaven, He could not have the universe under His attention, under His command and control. And if He were not shining like the sun toward the people who are in the spiritual world, angels could not have any light. Angels are in fact spiritual beings, and for this reason only a spiritual light is suited to their essence.

We will see below that there is a light in the heavens which is far superior to light on earth.

104. Another fact then, about this sun, the source of light and warmth for angels: it appears at some height above the lands angels live on, about forty-five degrees up, which is the median height. It also seems to be as far from angels as our world's sun is from us. The [spiritual] sun always appears at this height and at this distance; it does not move around.

This is why angels have no time-units divided into days and years, no daily sequence from morning through noon to evening into night, no yearly sequence from spring through summer to autumn into winter. They have rather an unfailing light and an unfailing springtime. So "states" take the place of times there, as stated above.

105. The most important reasons why the spiritual world's sun appears at median height are the following.

First, by this means, the warmth and light that emanate from that sun are at their median level, therefore in equal measure, and thus in proper moderation. For if the sun appeared above median height, [angels] would get more warmth than light; while if it were lower, they would get more light than warmth. It is the same on earth when the sun is above or below heaven's median.

When it is above, warmth becomes greater than light, and when it is below, light becomes greater than warmth. Actually, the light stays the same in summer and in winter, but the warmth increases and decreases in proportion to the sun's degree of height.

The *second* reason why the spiritual world's sun appears at median height over the angelic heaven, is that this provides a constant springtime through all the angelic heavens. As result, angels are in a state of peace, for this state corresponds to springtime on earth.

The *third* reason is that in this way, angels can turn their faces constantly to the Lord and see Him with their eyes. In fact, the east—therefore the Lord—is in front of angels no matter where they turn their bodies. This is a distinctive feature of that world. It could not occur if that world's sun appeared higher or lower than the median, especially if it appeared at the zenith overhead.

106. If the spiritual world's sun did not appear as far from angels as the natural world's sun does from us, the whole angelic heaven would not exist, with hell

beneath it and our globe of lands and seas below them both, under the Lord's attention, command, omnipresence, omniscience, omnipotence, and providence. It is quite like the sun of our world. If it were not as far as it is from the planet where it appears, it could not be present and effective in all lands with its warmth and light. It could not provide its auxiliary resource to the spiritual world's sun.

107. It is most vital to be aware that there are two suns, one spiritual and one natural, a spiritual sun for people who are in the spiritual world and a natural sun for people who are in the natural world. Without this knowledge, no aspect of creation or of humanity—our present topic—can be properly understood. Certain results can be seen, but unless the causes of the results are seen at the same time, the results can only be seen as if at night.

THE DISTANCE BETWEEN THE SUN AND ANGELS IN THE SPIRITUAL WORLD IS AN APPEARANCE WHICH DEPENDS ON THEIR ACCEPTANCE OF DIVINE LOVE AND DIVINE WISDOM

108. All the misconceptions that are dominant among evil people and among simple folk originate in confirmed appearances. As long as appearances remain simply appearances, they are "apparent truths," and anyone may think and talk in terms of them. But once they are accepted as actual truths (which happens when they are confirmed) then these apparent truths become falsities and misconceptions.

For example, it is an appearance that the sun is borne around the earth once a day, and makes its ecliptic cycle once a year. As long as this is not confirmed, it is an apparent truth, and it is all right to think and talk in such terms. It is all right to say that the sun rises and sets, thus causing morning, noon, evening, and night, that the sun is currently in some or other degree of its ecliptic or height, thus causing spring, summer, autumn, and winter. However, when someone makes up his mind that this appearance is the actual truth,then he is thinking and speaking falsity as a result of misconception.

The same holds true for countless other appearances—not just in natural, civic, and moral matters, but even in spiritual ones.

109. The same holds true for the distance of the spiritual world's sun, which sun is the first emanation of the Lord's divine love and divine wisdom.

The truth is that there is no distance. The distance is rather an appearance that depends on angels' acceptance of divine love and divine wisdom in their levels.

Material presented above may serve to show that distances in the spiritual world are appearances. So for example nn. 7-9—The divine is not in space, and nn. 69-72—The divine fills all space without [itself having] space. If there are no spaces, there are no distances. Or (which is the same thing) if spaces are appearances, distances are appearances too, for distances are a matter of space.

110. The reason the spiritual world's sun seems to be at a distance from angels is that divine love and divine wisdom are accepted by them at a suitable level of warmth and light. An angel, being created and finite, cannot in fact accept the Lord at the first level of warmth and light, the way He is in the sun. Obviously, the angel would be annihilated if this happened. So the Lord is accepted by them at the level of warmth and light that corresponds to their own love and wisdom.

We can illustrate this by the following. An angel of the lowest heaven cannot climb up to the angels of the third heaven. If he does climb and enter their heaven, he falls into a kind of faint, and his life seems to be wrestling with death. This is because he has love and wisdom at a lower level, and the warmth of his love and the light of his wisdom are at the same level.

What would happen, then, if an angel were to climb all the way to the sun and enter its fire?

Because of these differences in the way the Lord is accepted by angels, the heavens seem to be marked off from each other. The highest heaven, called the third heaven, seems to be above the second, with this above the first. Not that the heavens *are* apart, they seem to be apart. In fact, the Lord is just as present with people in the lowest heaven as He is with people in the third heaven. What causes the appearances of distance is in the subjects, the angels, and not in the Lord.

111. It is hard to grasp the truth of this with a natural concept, since this involves space; but it can be grasped by a spiritual concept, since this does not involve space. Angels are in this latter kind of concept.

Nevertheless, we can grasp this much with a natural concept—that love and wisdom (in other words, the Lord who is divine love and divine wisdom) cannot travel through space, but occur within each individual depending on his acceptance of them.

The Lord Himself teaches that He is present with everyone (Matthew 28:20), and that He makes his abode with those who love Him (John 14:21, 23).

112. This may seem to be a matter of very lofty wisdom, since we have used heavens and angels to support it, but the same holds true for people on earth. As far as the more inward reaches of their minds are concerned, people are warmed and enlightened by that same sun—warmed by its warmth and enlightened by its light, to the extent that they accept love and wisdom from the Lord.

The difference between angels and people on earth is that angels are under that sun alone, while people on earth are not only under that same sun but under the world's sun as well. For unless they were under that sun, their bodies could not take form and exist. It is different for angels' bodies, because they are spiritual.

ANGELS ARE IN THE LORD, AND THE LORD IS IN THEM; AND SINCE ANGELS ARE RECIPIENTS, THE LORD ALONE IS HEAVEN

113. Heaven is called "God's dwelling" and also "God's throne," and so people do believe that God lives there the way a king lives in his kingdom. But God—the Lord, that is—is in the sun above the heavens, and is in the heavens by the agency of his presence in warmth and light, as we have shown in the two preceding sections. Even though this is the way the Lord is in heaven, He is still there intrinsically, for (as shown just above, nn. 108-112) the distance between the sun and heaven is not a distance but an appearance of distance. This being the case—the distance being only an appearance—it follows that the Lord Himself is in heaven. He is in fact within the love and wisdom of heaven's angels. And since He is within the love and wisdom of all angels, with angels constituting heaven, He is in the whole heaven.

114. The reason the Lord is not only in heaven but is heaven itself, is that love and wisdom make an angel and these two things belong to the Lord in angels. It follows from this that the Lord is heaven.

Actually, angels are not angels because of anything that belongs to them. What belongs to them is exactly like what belongs to a person on earth—evil. The reason this is what belongs to angels is that all angels were people on earth. and this "possession" [*proprium*] clings to them from the cradle. It is merely moved away. And to the extent that it is moved away, the angel accepts love and wisdom, or the Lord, into himself.

Anyone who just raises his discernment a little can see that the Lord can dwell in angels only in what is

His—in what belongs to Him, that is—which is love and wisdom. It is absolutely impossible for Him to dwell in what belongs to angels, which is evil. This is why the Lord is in them, and they are angels, to the extent that what is evil is moved away.

The actual angelic part of heaven is divine love and divine wisdom. This divine is called "angelic" when it is in angels. We can see from this again that angels are angels because of the Lord, not because of themselves. The same is therefore true of heaven.

115. But we cannot grasp how the Lord is in an angel and an angel in the Lord, unless we know what "uniting" [conjunctio] is like. There is a uniting of the Lord with the angel, and a uniting of the angel with the Lord; so there is a reciprocal uniting.

From the angels' point of view, it is like this. Angels perceive only that they are involved in love and wisdom on their own, just as people on earth do, so it seems to each as though love and wisdom belonged to them. Without this perception, there would be no uniting. The Lord would then not be in the angels, nor the angels in the Lord.

It cannot happen that the Lord is in any angel or person unless, when the Lord is in them with love and wisdom, they perceive and feel this as their own. By this means, the Lord is not only accepted, but is kept after being accepted, and is loved in return. So by this means angels become wise and remain wise.

Who can deliberately love the Lord and the neighbor, who can deliberately be wise, without feeling and perceiving that what is loved and learned and gained is his or her own? Who can retain anything within if this is not the case?

If this were not the case, the inflowing love and wisdom would have no seat, they would actually flow right on through without accomplishing anything. The angel then would not be an angel, nor the person a person. Neither would be anything but something virtually inanimate.

We may conclude from this that there must be a reciprocal element if there is to be a uniting.

116. But now let us describe how it happens that angels perceive and feel this as their own, thus accepting and keeping it, when actually it is not theirs. For we have already stated that angels are not angels because of what belongs to them, but because of things from the Lord that are in them.

Basically, this is how things stand. Within every angel there is a freedom, and there is rationality. These two characteristics are within them in order that they may be able to accept love and wisdom from the Lord.

But neither of these—the freedom or the rationality—belongs to the angels; both within them belong to the Lord.

Nevertheless, since these two characteristics are intimately united to their life—so intimately that we could call them integral parts [*injuncta*] of their life—it seems as though they were their own possessions. Angels can think and intend from them, can talk and act from them. And whatever they do think or intend or say or do from them, seems as though it comes from them. This makes the reciprocal element that is needed for uniting.

However, to the extent that angels believe that love and wisdom are within them and thereby claim them for themselves, as belonging to them, there is nothing angelic in them. To this same extent, then, they have no bond with the Lord. They are not actually involved in truth; and since truth makes one with heaven's light, they cannot, to this same extent, be in heaven. In fact, this leads them to deny that they live from the Lord, and to believe that they live on their own, which would mean that they had a divine essence.

The life which is called angelic and human consists of these two characteristics—freedom and rationality. We may therefore conclude that angels have this reciprocal element for uniting with the Lord, but that, seen in its own capability, this reciprocal element belongs not to the angels, but to the Lord. This is why angels lapse from angelhood if they misuse this reciprocal element, which enables them to perceive and feel the Lord's possessions as their own, by giving themselves credit for it.

The Lord Himself teaches that uniting is reciprocal in John (14:20-24; 15:4-6), and that the Lord's uniting with a person, and the person's with the Lord, occurs within things that belong to the Lord, which are called "his words" (John 15:7).

117. There are people who suppose that Adam was in a kind of freedom or free choice that enabled him on his own to love God and be wise. They suppose further that this free choice was destroyed in his descendants. This, however, is wrong. The human being is not life, but a recipient of life (see above, nn. 4-6, 54-60). And anyone who is a recipient of life cannot love and be wise on the basis of what belongs to him. So even Adam, when he decided to be wise and to love on his own, fell from wisdom and love, and was cast out of paradise.

118. What we have just said about individual angels, we must also say about the heaven that consists of angels, since the divine is the same in greatest things and in smallest things (as shown above in nn. 77-82 above); and what we have said about individual angels and about heaven, we must also say about individuals on earth and the church, since the angel of heaven and the church person act in unison by means of a uniting. Then too, as far as the more inward aspects of his mind are concerned, the church person is an angel. But by "church person," we mean the person who has the church within.

Divine Love

IN THE SPIRITUAL WORLD, THE EAST IS WHERE THE LORD APPEARS AS THE SUN, AND THE OTHER REGIONS DEPEND ON THIS

119. Having discussed the spiritual world's sun and its essence, its warmth and light as well, and the Lord's consequent presence, we shall now proceed to discuss that world's major regions. The reason for discussing that sun and world is that we are discussing God, and love and wisdom. To discuss these latter without beginning at their source would be to start the discussion from effects and not from causes. However, effects are instructive only about effects. If these alone are examined, they do not reveal any cause at all—rather the causes reveal the effects. Knowing effects from causes is being wise; but investigating causes from effects in not being wise, since misconceptions then get in the way, misconceptions which the investigator calls causes. This means that wisdom is deluded.

Causes are prior, and effects later. We cannot see prior things from later ones, but we can see later things from prior ones. This is the pattern of things. This is why in the present work we are dealing with the spiritual world first; that is where all causes exist. Later we shall deal with the natural world, where all visible phenomena are effects.

120. Now let us discuss the major regions in the spiritual world. There are regions there, just as there are in the natural world. But the spiritual world's regions, like that world itself, are spiritual, while the natural world's regions, like that world itself, are natural. They are therefore so different that they have nothing in common.

There are four major regions in each world, called the East, the West, the South, and the North. In the natural world, these regions are fixed, determined by the sun at noon. The North is behind, with the East on one side and the West on the other. No matter where one stands, these regions are determined by the noonday position, and the position of the sun at noon is the same in every location, and is therefore fixed.

It is different in the spiritual world. The regions there are determined by the sun there, which unfailingly appears in its own place; and the place where it appears is the East. As a result, the placing of the major regions is not from the South, the way it is in the natural world, but from the East. The West is behind, with the South on one side and the North on the other.

We shall see below, however, that the source of these regions is not from the sun there, but from the people who live in that world.

121. Since these regions are spiritual (because of their origin, which is the Lord as the sun), the places where angels and spirits live are spiritual as well, being dependent on those regions. Another reason for their being spiritual is that angels and spirits have residence according to their acceptance of love and wisdom from the Lord.

People involved in a higher level of love live in the East, people involved in a lower level of love in the West; people who are involved in a higher level of wisdom live in the South, people involved in a lower level in the North.

This is why in the Word, "the East" in the highest sense means the Lord, while in a reflective [respectivo] sense, it means love for Him. "The West" means a lessening love for Him; "the South" means wisdom in the light, and "the North" means wisdom in the shade. The meaning may vary somewhat depending on the state of the people involved.

122. Granting that the East determines all the major regions in the spiritual world, and that in the highest sense "the East" means the Lord, and also means divine love, we can see that it is the Lord and love to

Him that is the source of everything. We can also see that to the extent that a person is not involved in that love, he is moved away from the Lord, and lives in the West or the South or the North, the distance depending on the acceptance of love.

123. Since the Lord as the sun is always in the East, the early people (for whom all aspects of worship were symbolic of spiritual things) turned their faces toward the East when they prayed. And in order to do this in all their worship, they faced their temples in this same direction, which is why churches today are built in the same way.

THE SOURCE OF THE REGIONS IN THE SPIRITUAL WORLD IS NOT THE LORD AS THE SUN, BUT IS THE ANGELS, DEPENDING ON THEIR ACCEPTANCE

124. It seems as though this variety of habitats stems from the Lord as the sun; however, it stems from the angels. The Lord is not subject to any greater or lesser levels of love and wisdom; that is, He as the sun is not in any greater or lesser level of warmth and light for one individual or another. He is actually the same everywhere. But He is not accepted on the same level by different individuals. This makes angels seem to themselves to be closer to Him or farther away from Him, and also to vary as to regions.

It follows from this that the regions in the spiritual world are nothing but different "acceptances" of love and wisdom, and therefore of warmth and light from the Lord as the sun.

We can see the truth of this from the matters presented above (nn. 108-112), to the effect that distances in the spiritual world are appearances.

125. Since the regions are different "acceptances" of love and wisdom by angels, let us discuss the variety that gives rise to their appearance.

The Lord is in the angel, and the angel in the Lord, as we have shown in the last chapter. But since it seems as though the Lord as the sun is outside the angel, it also seems as though the Lord is seeing the angel from the sun and the angel seeing the Lord in the sun—almost the way an image appears in a mirror.

So if we are to verbalize these matters in keeping with the appearance, it comes out like this: the Lord sees and examines everyone face to face, but the angels do not do the same in return. People involved in a love to the Lord, from the Lord, see Him straight ahead, and are therefore in the East or the West. People who are involved in wisdom to a greater degree see the Lord off to the right, though, while people who are involved in wisdom to a lesser degree see Him off to the left. These latter two groups are in the South and the North respectively.

The reason these latter have an offset view is that love and wisdom emanate from the Lord as a single entity, as we have previously said. Any wisdom which is in excess of love does seem to be wisdom, but it nevertheless is not, because the excess of wisdom does not have within it life from love.

We can see from this the reason for the variety of acceptance, in keeping with which angels seem to live in distinct regions in the spiritual world.

126. We can support the proposition that a distinctive acceptance of love and wisdom makes a region in the spiritual world by observing that angels may change their region depending on the increase or decrease of love within them. We can see from this that the region does not stem from the Lord as the sun, but from the angels, in keeping with their acceptance.

As far as their spirits are concerned, they are in the appropriate regions in the spiritual world, no matter what region of the natural world they are in. For as we have already said, the spiritual world's regions have nothing in common with the natural world's regions. People are in earthly regions as far as their bodies are concerned, but in spiritual regions as far as their spirits are concerned.

127. Just as love and wisdom make a single entity in an angel or a person on earth, so there occur pairs throughout the human body—eyes, ears, and nostrils are pairs; hands, loins, and feet are pairs. The brain is divided into two hemispheres, the heart into two chambers, the lungs into two lobes, and the same holds true elsewhere.

So angel and human alike have a right side and a left. All their right-hand parts go back to love which is wisdom's source, and all left-hand parts to wisdom stemming from love. Or in other words, all right-hand parts go back to the good which is the source of the true, and all left-hand parts to the true stemming from the good.

Angel and human have these pairs so that love and wisdom, or what is good and what is true, may act as one and may as one focus on the Lord. But more on this below.

128. This enables us to see how caught in deception and therefore in falsity people are who think that the Lord bestows heaven arbitrarily, or arbitrarily makes one person more wise and loving than another. In fact, the Lord wants every individual to be wise, to be saved, each one as much as any other. He provides everyone with the resources. As individuals accept these resources and live by them, they are wise and are saved; the Lord is in fact the same for one as for another. But the recipients, the angels and humans, are different because of their different acceptance and life.

We can support the truth of this with the statements just made about regions and about angels living in regions, noting particularly that this variety does not stem from the Lord, but from the recipients.

ANGELS CONSTANTLY TURN THEIR FACES TOWARD THE LORD, AND THEREFORE HAVE THE SOUTH TO THEIR RIGHT, THE NORTH TO THEIR LEFT, AND THE WEST BEHIND THEM

129. Having now said all these things about angels and about the way they turn toward the Lord as the sun, we need to understand that they apply to people on earth, as far as their spirits are concerned. For as far as our minds are concerned, we are spirits; and if we are involved in love and wisdom, we are angels.

Since angels constantly turn their faces toward the rising of the sun—toward the Lord, that is—we refer to the person who is involved in love and wisdom from the Lord as seeing God, as focusing on God, as having God before the eyes, which means living like an angel.

We say things like this in this world both because they actually occur in heaven and because they actually occur in our spirits. Who is not facing God during prayer, no matter what earthly region he or she is facing?

130. The reason angels constantly turn their faces toward the Lord as the sun, is that angels are in the Lord, and the Lord is in them, inwardly guiding their affections and thoughts and ever turning them toward Himself. So they cannot help looking toward the east, where the Lord appears as the sun.

We can see from this that angels do not turn themselves toward the Lord; the Lord turns them toward Himself. Actually, when angels think more deeply about the Lord, they think about Him only as though He were within them. This more inward thought does not produce a distance; distance is produced by a more outward thought, that works together with eyesight. This is because the more outward thought is involved in space, while the more inward is not. Even where the more outward thought is not involved in space, as is the case in the spiritual world, it is still involved in the appearance of space.

But this can hardly be understood by anyone who thinks about the Lord on the basis of space. God is actually everywhere, and yet not in space. He is both within angels and outside them, so angels can see God—the Lord—both within and outside themselves. They see Him within themselves when they are thinking *from* love and wisdom, and outside themselves when they are thinking *about* love and wisdom. But we will deal with this in greater detail in a work on *The Lord's Omnipresence, Omniscience, and Omnipotence.*[1]

Let everyone take care not to slip into the damnable heresy that would have God pouring Himself into people as to be in them and no longer in Himself. Rather, God is everywhere, both within us and outside us; He is in fact in all space without [being bound by] space (as presented above, nn. 7-10, 69-72). For if God were [exclusively] within us, He would be not only divided but even bounded by space. Then we could even think that we ourselves were God.

This heresy is so detestable that in the spiritual world it stinks like a corpse.

131. Angels turn toward the Lord in such a manner that wherever their bodies turn, they are looking at the Lord as the sun in front of them. Angels can turn completely around, seeing the different things that are on all sides, yet the Lord as the sun appears in front of them throughout. This may seem strange, but it is the truth.

I have been enabled to see the Lord as the sun this way. I see Him in front of me. I have seen Him there for many years, no matter what direction I might be facing on earth.

[1]This work was never written as such. The topics are discussed in nn. 50-70 of *True Christian Religion.*

132. Since the Lord as the sun is in front of every angel of heaven, as is the east, it follows that south is to their right, north to their left, and west behind them. This holds true no matter where they turn their bodies. For as we have stated above, all the regions or directions in the spiritual world are marked off from the east. So the people who have the east before their eyes are engaged in these directions—indeed, they themselves determine them. For as presented above (nn. 124-128), the regions do not stem from the Lord as the sun, but from the angels, depending on their acceptance.

133. Now since heaven is made up of angels, and this is what angels are like, it follows that the whole heaven turns toward the Lord, and that by this means heaven is governed by the Lord as though it were a single person—which in the Lord's sight it is. The reader may see in the book *Heaven and Hell*, nn. 59-87, that heaven looks like a single person in the Lord's sight. This is also a source of heaven's regions.

134. Since the regions or directions are virtually engraved on each angel and on the whole heaven, angels, unlike people on earth, know their homes and their dwelling places, wherever they may travel. The reason we do not know our homes and dwelling places from an intrinsic orientation is because we think on the basis of space. This means thinking on the basis of the natural world's regions, which have nothing in common with the regions of the spiritual world.

Birds and animals, though, do have this kind of inherent knowledge. It is actually instinctive with them to know their homes and habitats spontaneously [*ex se*], as we know from an abundance of evidence. This is a clue to the situation in the spiritual world. For all the things that happen in the natural world are results, and all the things that happen in the spiritual world are the causes of the results. No natural phenomenon occurs that does not have its cause in something spiritual.

ALL THE MORE INWARD COMPONENTS OF ANGELS' MINDS AND BODIES ARE TURNED TOWARD THE LORD AS THE SUN

135. Angels have discernment and intentionality, and they have faces and bodies. Further, there are more inward aspects both of discernment and intentionality and of faces and bodies. The more inward aspects of discernment and intentionality are elements of deeper affection and thought. The more inward aspects of the face are the brains, and the more inward aspects of the body are the inner organs, the most important of which are the heart and the lungs.

In short, angels have each and every part that people on earth have, which is why angels are people. The outer form without these inner parts does not make them people; it is rather the outward form together with these parts, actually deriving from them. Otherwise, they would be only images of people, with no life in them because there was no form for life within them.

136. We know that intentionality and discernment govern the body at will. In fact, what discernment thinks, the mouth speaks, and what intentionality intends, the body does. We can see from this that the body is a form which answers [correspondens] to discernment and intentionality. And since form is predicated of discernment and intentionality, we can see that the form of the body answers to the form of discernment and intentionality. But it is not our present task to describe what each form is like. There are countless elements in each, and the countless elements in each act as one because they answer to each other.

This is why the mind, or intentionality and discernment, governs the body at will, exactly as though it were governing itself.

It follows from this that the more inward parts of the mind act as one with the more inward parts of the body, as do the more outward parts of the mind with the more outward parts of the body. We shall discuss the more inward parts of the mind below, after discussing levels of life, and will then treat of the more inward parts of the body.

137. Since the more inward aspects of mind make one with the more inward aspects of body, it follows that when these inward aspects of mind turn to the Lord as the sun, the inward aspects of body do the same. And since the outward aspects of both mind and body depend on the inward ones, they too do the same thing. Whatever the outward does, it does from inner things, since an inclusive entity derives everything it has from the details that constitute it.

We can see from this that because angels turn their faces and bodies toward the Lord as the sun, all the more inward aspects of their minds and bodies have been turned in the same direction.

The same holds true for people on earth if they constantly have the Lord in view, which happens if they are involved in love and wisdom. They then focus on the Lord not only with their eyes and faces, but with their whole mind and their whole heart (that is, with all aspects of intentionality and discernment), and with all aspects of their bodies at the same time.

138. This turning toward the Lord is a real turning; it is a kind of lifting up. People are actually lifted into the warmth and light of heaven, which is accomplished by the opening of their more inward aspects. When these are opened, love and wisdom flow into the inward levels of mind, and heaven's warmth and light into the more inward levels of body. This results in a lifting up which is like coming from a cloud into clear air or from air into the ether. Further, love and wisdom, together with their warmth and light, are the

Lord with the person who, as described above, turns to Him.

The opposite holds true for people who are not involved in love and wisdom, especially for people who are opposed to love and wisdom. The more inward levels of their minds and their bodies alike are closed off; and when they are closed off, the more outward levels react against the Lord, for this is inherent in their nature.

This is why they turn their backs to the Lord, and turning the back is turning toward hell.

139. This actual turning to the Lord stems from love and wisdom both—it is not just from love or just from wisdom. Love alone is like reality without presence, since love does become present in wisdom. And wisdom without love is like presence without reality, since wisdom becomes present from love.

Love does indeed occur apart from wisdom, but this love is characteristic of human beings, not of the Lord. Wisdom too occurs apart from love, and while this wisdom is from the Lord, it does not have the Lord within it. It is like winter's light, which does indeed come from the sun, and yet the essence of the sun, which is warmth, is not within it.

EACH INDIVIDUAL SPIRIT, WHATEVER HIS OR HER QUALITY, TURNS IN THIS SAME WAY TOWARD HIS OR HER OWN RULING LOVE

140. Let us first define "angel" and "spirit." All individuals arrive after death in the world of spirits, which is halfway between heaven and hell, where they work through their times or their states, and according to their lives are prepared for heaven or for hell. As long as they stay in that world, they are called "spirits." All the people who are raised from that world into heaven are called "angels," while all who are thrown down into hell are called "satans" or "devils."

As long as these types are in the world of spirits, the ones who are being prepared for heaven are called angelic spirits and the ones who are being prepared for hell are called hellish spirits. During this interim period, an angelic spirit is united with heaven, and a hellish spirit with hell.

All the spirits who are in the world of spirits are attached to people on earth, because these latter, as far as the more inward aspects of their minds are concerned, are likewise between heaven and hell. Through these spirits they are in touch with heaven or hell, depending on their life.

It must be realized that the *world of spirits* and the *spiritual world* are two different things. The world of spirits is the one we have just been discussing, while the spiritual world comprises that world and heaven and hell.

141. We must also discuss loves, since we are dealing with the fact that because of their loves, angels and spirits turn toward their loves.

The whole heaven is divided into communities according to all the distinct kinds of love; and the same holds true for hell and for the world of spirits. Heaven, however, is divided into communities according to distinct kinds of heavenly love, while hell is divided into communities according to distinct kinds of hellish love. The world of spirits is divided according to distinct kinds of both heavenly and hellish love.

There are two loves which are chief over all others. One chief love—the one all other heavenly loves go back to—is love to the Lord. The other chief love—the one all hellish loves go back to—is a love of being in charge as a result of self-love. These two loves are exact opposites.

142. Since these two loves (love to the Lord and the love of being in charge as a result of self-love) are exact opposites, and since people who are involved in

love to the Lord turn toward the Lord as the sun (as described in the preceding section), we can conclude that everyone involved in the love of being in charge as a result of self-love, turns away from the Lord.

The reason they turn in opposite directions is that for people involved in love to the Lord, there is nothing they love more than being led by the Lord. But for people involved in a love of being in charge as a result of self-love, there is nothing they love more than leading themselves, and they want to be the only ones in power.

We use the phrase "the love of being in charge as a result of self-love" because there is a love of being in charge as a result of a love of doing what is useful. Since this love fits perfectly with love toward the neighbor, it is a spiritual love. Actually though, this love cannot be called a love of being in charge, but rather a love of doing what is useful.

143. The reason all spirits, whatever their quality, turn toward their ruling love, is that love is the life of each individual (as shown in nn. 1-3 of Chapter 1); and a love turns its recipient vessels (called members, organs, and viscera—the whole person, that is) toward the community that is involved in a love like its own, where its own love is, then.

144. Since the love of being in charge as a result of self-love is the exact opposite of love to the Lord, spirits involved in the love of being in charge turn their faces away from the Lord. So their eyes are looking toward that world's west. Since this turns their bodies backwards, the east is behind them, north to their right, and south to their left. The east is behind them because they hate the Lord. The north is to their right because they love deceptions and therefore falsities. The south is to their left because they despise the light of wisdom.

They can turn this way and that, but everything they see around them looks like their love. All of them are natural, sense-oriented. Some of them even believe they are the only people who are alive, and view others as imaginary. They believe they are wiser than anyone else, even though they are insane.

145. There are visible roads in the spiritual world, paved like roads in the natural world. Some of them lead to heaven, and some to hell. However, the roads that lead to hell are not visible to people who are on their way to heaven, nor are the roads that lead to heaven visible to people who are on their way to hell.

There are countless roads like this. In fact, there are roads leading to each particular community in heaven and to each particular community in hell. Each individual spirit sets out on the road that leads to the community of his or her own love, and does not see other roads. This is why each individual spirit makes progress in the course of turning toward his or her own ruling love.

THE DIVINE LOVE AND WISDOM WHICH EMANATE FROM THE LORD AS THE SUN AND MAKE WARMTH AND LIGHT IN HEAVEN ARE THE EMANATING DIVINE WHICH IS THE HOLY SPIRIT

146. We have explained in *The Doctrine of the Lord* that God is one in person and essence, containing a trinity, and that this God is the Lord. We have further explained that His trinity is called Father, Son, and Holy Spirit—the Divine as the source being called the Father, the Divine-Human being called the Son, and the Divine-Emanating being called the Holy Spirit.

We refer to the Divine-Emanating, and yet no one knows why we refer to it as emanating. The reason no one knows this is that people have until now been unaware of the fact that the Lord appears to angels as a sun, and that there emanates from that sun a warmth which is essentially divine love and a light which is essentially divine wisdom. As long as people are unaware of these facts, they cannot help "knowing" that the Divine-Emanating is divine in its own right. This led to the statement in the Athanasian doctrine of the trinity that the Father is one Person, the Son another, and the Holy Spirit another.

However, once it is realized that the Lord appears as a sun, it is possible to have a proper concept of the Divine-Emanating which is called the Holy Spirit—that it is one with the Lord, but that it emanates from Him the way warmth and light emanate from a sun. This is also why angels are in divine warmth and divine light to the extent that they are involved in love and wisdom.

Without a realization that the Lord appears as a sun in the spiritual world, with His Divine emanating as described, there is no way of knowing what "emanating" means. One might suppose, for example, that it meant simply communicating what belongs to the Father and the Son, or simply enlightening and teaching. However, it does not accord with enlightened reason to grant this emanation divinity in its own right, call it God, and mark it off, especially once it is realized that God is both one and omnipresent.

147. We have explained above that God is not within space, and that this is how He is omnipresent. We have further explained that He is the same everywhere, with His apparent differences being in the angels because of the way they accept Him. Now, since the Divine that emanates from the Lord as the sun is within light and warmth, and since light and warmth flow first into the universal recipients which in this world are called atmospheres, which hold clouds, we can conclude that the way these clouds surround the more inward elements of discernment—mortals' or angels'—determines the way the discernment is a recipient of the Divine-Emanating.

By clouds we mean spiritual clouds, or thoughts, which agree with divine wisdom if they stem from things that are true, but disagree if they stem from things that are false. This is why in the spiritual world, when thoughts from true sources are made visible, they look like bright clouds, while thoughts from false sources look like black clouds.

We can therefore conclude that the Divine-Emanating has the same nature in every individual, but is obscured by each one in his or her own particular way.

148. Since the actual Divine is present in angels and mortals by means of spiritual warmth and light, when people involved in and moved by true elements of divine wisdom and good elements of divine love are thinking affectionately about and from these elements, we say that they are *growing warm with God*. Sometimes this phenomenon even reaches perception and sensation, as when a preacher is speaking with zeal.

We refer to these same people as *enlightened by God* as well, because the Lord, through His Divine-Emanating, not only kindles intentionality with spiritual warmth, but also enlightens discernment with spiritual light.

149. From the following passages in the Word we can see that the Holy Spirit is the same as the Lord, and is the actual truth from which people receive enlightenment.

> Jesus said, "When the spirit of truth has arrived, he will lead you into all truth. He will not... speak on his own, but will speak what he has heard."
>
> (John 16:13)
>
> He will glorify me because he will receive from what belongs to me, and will proclaim it to you.
> (John 16:14-15)

He will be with and within the disciples.

(John 15:26)

Jesus said, "The things I tell you are spirit . . . and life."

(John 6:63)

We can see from these passages that the actual truth which emanates from the Lord is called "the Holy Spirit," which gives enlightenment because it is in light.

150. The enlightenment ascribed to the Holy Spirit, while it is in people from the Lord, occurs through the agency of spirits and angels. At this point we cannot describe the nature of this agency. We can mention only that it is utterly impossible for angels or spirits to enlighten people on their own, since they, like mortals, are enlightened by the Lord. Since they are enlightened in the same way, it follows that all enlightenment is from the Lord alone. The reason for the agency of angels or spirits is that the person in enlightenment is placed among the kind of angels and spirits who more than others are receiving enlightenment from the Lord alone.

THE LORD CREATED THE UNIVERSE AND EVERYTHING IN IT BY MEANS OF THE SUN WHICH IS THE FIRST EMANATION OF DIVINE LOVE AND DIVINE WISDOM

151. "The Lord" means God from eternity or Jehovah, called "Father" and "Creator," because (as explained in *The Doctrine of the Lord*) He is the same as the Lord. So in the material below, when we discuss creation, we use the name, "the Lord."

152. In Chapter 1, we explained at some length that everything in the universe was created by divine love and by divine wisdom (see specifically nn. 52 and 53). Now our topic is the agency of the sun which is the first emanation of divine love and divine wisdom.

If people can see results flowing from causes, and then results (from causes) in their arrangement and in sequence, they cannot deny that the sun is the first step in creation, since everything in a sun's world does in fact endure by reason of that sun. Since things endure by reason of it, they emerged from it—the one fact confirms and witnesses to the other. Everything is actually in the sun's view, because it has arranged things that way. Keeping them in view means constantly placing them in view. This is why we say that enduring is a perpetual emerging. If anything were completely removed from the inflow of the sun through atmospheres, it would instantly disintegrate. In fact, the atmospheres, of different degrees of purity, energized by the sun, hold everything together.

Now since the enduring of the universe and everything in it depends on the sun, we can see that the sun is the first step of creation, the source. We speak of "depending on the sun," but we mean "depending on the Lord through the sun," since the sun too was created by the Lord.

153. There are two suns which the Lord used to create everything, a sun of the spiritual world and a sun of the natural world. Everything was created by the Lord through the sun of the spiritual world; but not everything was created through the sun of the natural world since this latter sun lies far below the former one. It is halfway—above it is the spiritual world and below it is the natural world. Further, the sun of the natural world was created to serve as an auxiliary, which we will discuss below.

154. The reason the Lord used the spiritual world's sun to create the universe and everything in it is that this sun is the first emanation of divine love and divine wisdom, and as explained above (nn. 52-82), everything comes from divine love and divine wisdom.

Every created entity, regardless of size, contains three things—purpose, means, and result [or end, cause, and effect]. No created entity occurs which does not contain these three. On the greatest or universal scale, these three occur in the following arrangement. The purpose of everything is in that sun which is the first emanation of divine love and divine wisdom. The means to everything are in the spiritual world; and the results of everything are in the natural world. However, we will explain below how these three occur in primary and in ultimate phenomena.

Since then no created entity occurs which does not contain these three, it follows that the universe and everything in it was created by the Lord through the sun where the purpose of everything is.

155. Creation itself cannot be brought into the mind's grasp unless space and time are removed from thought; but if they are removed, creation can be understood.

If you can (or as much as you can) remove them and can hold your mind in a non-spatial, non-temporal concept, then you will perceive that there is no difference between the greatest and the smallest units of space. Then you cannot help having the same concept of the creation of the universe as you have of the creation of any particular item in the universe. You will perceive that the diversity in things created stems from the presence of infinite things with the God-Man, with consequent unlimited things in the sun which is the first emanation from Him, and these unlimited things coming out like a reflection in the created universe.

This is why nothing can occur anywhere which is the same as something else. This is the source of the variety of everything presented to our eyes spatially in the natural world and in apparent space in the spiritual world. This variety applies to broad categories and to particular items.

These are matters explained in Chapter 1. For example, [we have there presented] that in the God-Man, infinite things are distinguishably one (nn. 17-22); that everything in the universe was created by divine love and divine wisdom (nn. 52-53); that everything in the universe is a recipient of the God-Man's divine love and divine wisdom (nn. 54-60); that the Divine is not in space (nn. 7-10); that the Divine fills all spaces without [being bound by] space (nn. 69-72); and that the Divine is the same in the greatest and the smallest things (nn. 77-82).

156. We cannot say that the creation of the universe and everything in it happened from one space to another or from one time to another—by stages and in sequence, that is—but from the eternal and from the infinite. This is not from an eternity of time, since there is no such thing. It is rather from a timeless eternity which is the same as the Divine. Nor is it from an infinity of space, since there is no such thing. It is rather from a spaceless infinity which is the same as the Divine.

157. Not one shred of creation itself can be ascribed to the sun of the natural world; everything is ascribed to the sun of the spiritual world. This is because the natural world's sun is quite lifeless, while the spiritual world's sun is alive. It is in fact the first emanation of divine love and divine wisdom. A lifeless thing does not act upon anything independently; it is acted upon. So ascribing any part of creation to it would be like ascribing the work of a craftsman to the tool used by the craftsman's hands.

The sun of the natural world is pure fire, with every trace of life removed, but the sun of the spiritual world is a fire which contains divine life. The angelic concept of the fire of the natural world's sun and the fire of the spiritual world's sun is as follows: divine life is within the fire of the spiritual world's sun, but it is outside in relation to the fire of the natural world's sun.

We can see from this that the reality of the natural sun is not intrinsic to it [a se], but is derived from a living force that emanates from the sun of the spiritual world. So if the living force of this latter sun were withdrawn or taken away, the former sun would collapse.

This is why sun worship is the lowest of all forms of worship of God. In fact, it is as dead as the sun itself, which is why sun worship is called "an abomination" in the Word.

158. Since the natural world's sun is pure fire and is therefore lifeless, the warmth that emanates from it is also lifeless, and so is the light that emanates from it. The same holds true for the atmospheres which are called ether and air and which receive that sun's warmth and light in their mass and transmit it; they too are lifeless. Since they are lifeless, so too each and every planetary thing called an earth is lifeless.

Nevertheless, each and every earth is surrounded by spiritual things which emanate and flow out from the sun of the spiritual world. If they were not surrounded by these things, the earths could not be energized, could not bring forth the forms of use we call plants or the forms of life we call animals, nor could they proffer the materials which enable humanity to emerge and to endure.

159. Now, since nature begins with that [natural] sun, and since we refer to everything that emerges and persists from it as "natural," it follows that nature, with each and every part of it, is lifeless. The reason nature seems to be alive in people and animals is found in the life which accompanies and energizes it.

160. Because the lowest elements of nature, constituting the earths, are lifeless, not plastic and variable in keeping with states of affection and thoughts as in the spiritual world, but changeless and fixed, there are units of space in nature, and spatial

distances. Natural things are like this because creation has come to a close in them, has come to its standstill.

We can see from this that units of space are proper to nature; and since these units of space are not appearances of space that respond to states of life, they can also be called lifeless.

161. Units of time, being similarly fixed and invariant, are also proper to nature, for the length of a day is invariably twenty-four hours and the length of a year is invariably three hundred and sixty-five and a quarter days. The very conditions of light and darkness, of warmth and cold, which bring variety to these units of time, keep constantly coming back. The conditions that come back each day are morning, noon, evening, and night, while the yearly ones are spring, summer, fall, and winter. Year-conditions constantly affect day-conditions.

All these conditions, since they are not states of life, as in the spiritual world, are also lifeless. For in the spiritual world there is a constant light and a constant warmth, with the light corresponding to a state of wisdom and the warmth to a state of love for the angels, which is why these states are alive.

162. This enables us to see the idiocy of people who give nature credit for everything. People who decide in favor of nature have taken on a state in which they no longer want to raise their minds above nature. So their minds are closed on top and open below, and they become nature-centered and sense-centered people—spiritually lifeless. And since these people do their thinking only on the basis of the kind of thing they get from their physical senses (or through them, from the world), they actually deny God at heart.

Then, since the tie with heaven has been broken, a tie with hell ensues. All that is left is an ability to think and intend—an ability to think from rationality, and an ability to intend from freedom—which two abilities are given by the Lord to every individual and not taken away. Devils and angels alike have these two abilities, but devils use them to be insane and to do evil things, while angels use them to be wise and to do good things.

WITHOUT THIS PAIR OF SUNS, ONE ALIVE AND ONE LIFELESS, THERE WOULD BE NO CREATION

163. The universe is divided overall into two worlds, a spiritual one and a natural one. In the spiritual world, we find angels and spirits; in the natural world we find mortals [homines].

The two worlds are exactly alike in their outward appearance—so much so that one cannot tell them apart; but in their inward appearance they are quite unlike. The people who are in the spiritual world (who are called angels and spirits, as we have just stated) are themselves spiritual. Being spiritual, they think spiritually and talk spiritually. But the people who are in the natural world are natural, and therefore think naturally and talk naturally. Now, spiritual thought and speech have nothing in common with natural thought and speech.

We can see from this that these two worlds, the spiritual and the natural, are wholly distinct from each other, to the point that they can in no way be merged [simul esse].

164. Now since these two worlds are so distinct, two suns are necessary—one the source of everything spiritual and the other the source of everything natural. And since everything spiritual is alive by origin, and everything natural is lifeless by origin, and the suns are the origins, it follows that the first sun is alive and the second sun dead. It follows further that the dead sun was created by the Lord by means of the living sun.

165. A dead sun was created so that everything in the lowest realms would be fixed, stable, and constant, and so that things could emerge which would be recurrent and lasting. This is the only way creation is given a foundation.

The globe of lands and seas which has this kind of thing in and on and around it, is like a solid platform or foundation, for it is the final work into which everything settles, on which everything comes to rest. Later, we will be saying that it is also like a matrix out of which are produced the results which are the goals of creation.

166. We may conclude that everything was created by the Lord by means of the living sun—nothing by means of the dead sun—because what is living arranges what is dead at will, and forms it for uses which are its goals. This does not happen in reverse order.

Only a person whose rational capacity is beclouded can think that everything, even life, comes from nature. Such a person does not know what life is. Nature cannot arrange life for any purpose; intrinsically, nature is totally inert. The notion that something dead activates something living (that is, that something natural activates something spiritual) is wholly disorderly, and thinking on this basis violates the light of sound reason. There are many ways in which something dead or natural can be altered or changed by things impinging on it from the outside, but it still cannot activate life. Rather, life activates it in keeping with any change imposed on its form.

The same principle applies to the notion of a physical inflow into the spiritual workings of the soul. It is recognized that this does not occur because it is an impossibility.

THE GOAL OF CREATION—THE RETURN OF EVERYTHING TO THE CREATOR, AND THE EXISTENCE OF A UNION—TAKES FORM IN THE LOWEST THINGS

167. We need first to discuss goals [*fines*]. There are three things which follow in sequence, called first end, intermediate end, and last end. They are also called purpose [or goal] [*finis*], means [*causa*], and result [*effectus*].

If any entity is to have real existence, these three must be simultaneously present within it, since a first end does not occur without an intermediate end, and a last end as well. In other words, a purpose does not occur by itself, without means and result. In the same way, a means does not occur by itself without a purpose behind it and a result surrounding it; nor does a result occur by itself, a result without a means and its purpose.

We can grasp the truth of this if we reflect that a purpose without result, or separated from result, is not something that takes form [*existens*], so it is nothing but a word. If a purpose is to be a purpose in fact, it must have limits; it has limits in its result, and here for the first time we call it an "end" because it is an end.

It looks as though the active or effective force had intrinsic form, but this is an appearance caused by its presence within a result. If it is separated from the result, it vanishes instantly. We can therefore see that these three things—purpose, means, and result—must be present in every entity if it is to have real existence.

168. We need also to be aware that the purpose is wholly within the means and wholly within the result as well. This is why purpose, means, and result are called first, intermediate, and last end. But for a purpose to be wholly within a means, there must be something derived from the purpose in which the

purpose must be. And for a purpose to be wholly within a result, there must be something derived from the purpose through the means, in which the purpose must be. In fact, a purpose cannot exist within itself alone; it must be within something that emerges from itself, which it can dwell in with all its properties and which it can produce by its activity, as long as it lasts. The entity in which it lasts [*subsistit*] is the last end, called the result.

169. In both the greatest and the smallest aspects of the created universe, these three things—purpose, means, and result—are present. The reason these three things are present in the greatest and the smallest aspects of the created universe is that these three are present in God the Creator, who is the Lord from eternity. However, since He is infinite, and since in an infinite being infinite things are distinguishably one (as explained above, nn. 17-22), these three things are distinguishably one in Him and in His infinite things.

This is why the universe, created from His own reality, and (functionally regarded) an image of Him, has these three things in its each and every part.

170. The universal purpose, or the purpose of all creation, is that there be an eternal union [*conjunctio*] of the Creator with the created universe. This does not happen unless there are "subjects" in which His divine can live and dwell as though it were in itself. If these subjects are to be His homes and dwellings, they must be apparently independent recipients of His love and wisdom, who will then, apparently independently, lift themselves toward the Creator and unite themselves to Him. Without this element of reciprocity, no union would occur. These subjects are people who can raise and unite themselves in apparent independence. We have explained above, several times, that people are this kind of subject and

that they do accept what is divine with apparent independence.

Through this union, the Lord is present in every work He has created. For in the last analysis, every created thing is for the sake of humanity. So the uses of all created things climb step by step from the lowest things to the human, and on through the human to God the Creator, their source, as we have explained above (nn. 65-68).

171. Creation progresses steadily toward this final goal [*finem ultimum*] by means of these three things—purpose, means, and result—because these three are in the Lord the Creator, as we have just stated. Further, the Divine is within all space without [being bound by] space (nn. 69-72), and is the same in greatest and smallest things (nn. 77-82). We can see from this that in the overall progression toward the final goal, the created universe is relatively an intermediate end. In fact, forms of uses are being constantly raised up from the earth by the Creator Lord, in a sequence that culminates in the human being, who, physically regarded, is derived from the earth. Then the person is raised up by accepting love and wisdom from the Lord. All kinds of means are provided for our acceptance of love and wisdom; and we have been so fashioned that we can accept them if only we want to.

On the basis of what has now been presented, we can see (albeit only in a general way) that the goal of creation—the return of everything to the Creator and the existence of a union—emerges in the lowest things.

172. There is another ground for concluding that these three things—purpose, means, and result—are present in each and every created thing. This is the fact that all results (or "last ends") become afresh "first ends" in an unbroken sequence from the First, who is the Creator Lord, all the way to the last, which is the uniting of humanity with Him.

Wisdom

We can see that last ends become afresh first ends from the fact that nothing occurs which is so inert and lifeless that there is no effective force whatever within it. Even from sand, something exhales which offers a resource for productivity, that is, toward accomplishing something [*ad efficiendum*].

CHAPTER 3

[THE STRUCTURE OF CREATION]

THERE ARE ATMOSPHERES, LIQUIDS, AND SOLIDS IN THE SPIRITUAL WORLD JUST AS THERE ARE IN THE NATURAL WORLD. HOWEVER, THE FORMER ARE SPIRITUAL, WHILE THE LATTER ARE NATURAL.

173. We have stated above, and explained in the book *Heaven and Hell*, that the spiritual world and the natural world are alike, the only difference being that each and every entity in the spiritual world is spiritual, while each and every entity in the natural world is natural. Since these two worlds are similar, there are atmospheres, liquids, and solids as the general materials, the means and substances for the formation of each and every entity, in infinite variety.

174. As for atmospheres, called ethers and gases, these occur in similar form in both worlds, the difference being that the ones in the spiritual world are spiritual and the ones in the natural world are natural.

The former are spiritual because they arise from the sun which is the first emanation of the Lord's divine love and divine wisdom. From that sun they receive into themselves the divine fire which is love and the divine light which is wisdom, and they bring both of these down to the heavens where angels live. They effect the presence of that sun in everything, great and small.

Spiritual atmospheres are separate substances or irreducible forms arising from the sun. And since they receive the sun in their own characteristic ways, the sun's fire is separated into as many substances or forms [as there are atmospheres]. It is, so to speak, folded in; and by being folded in, it is tempered, becoming a warmth which eventually is suited to the love of angels in heaven and of spirits below heaven. The same holds true for the sun's light.

In this respect the natural atmospheres are similar to the spiritual atmospheres, being also separate substances and irreducible forms which arise from the sun of the natural world. They too receive the sun in their own characteristic ways, conceal its fire within themselves, temper it, and bring it down as warmth to the earth where people live. The same holds true for light.

175. The difference between spiritual atmospheres and natural atmospheres is that spiritual atmospheres are recipients of divine fire and divine light—of love and wisdom, that is. They actually hold these within themselves. But natural atmospheres are not recipients of divine fire and divine light. Rather, they are recipients of the fire and light of their own sun, which, as we have explained above, is intrinsically lifeless. So there is nothing within them from the sprital world's sun, though they are surrounded by the spiritual atmospheres derived from that sun.

This difference between spiritual atmospheres and natural atmospheres comes from angelic wisdom.

176. We may establish the existence of atmospheres in the spiritual world (just as they exist in the natural world) on the grounds that angels and spirits breathe

and speak and hear just the way people in the natural world do. Breathing, like speech and hearing, uses the lowest atmosphere called air. We may also use the grounds that angels and spirits see just the way people in the natural world do, and sight does not occur without an atmosphere more pure than air. We may also use the grounds that angels and spirits think and are moved just the way people on earth are, and thought and affection do not occur except by means of still purer atmospheres. Finally, we may cite the grounds that all the bodily parts of angels and spirits, both outward and inward, are held together. The outward ones are held together by the airy atmosphere, the inward ones by the ethereal atmospheres. We can see that the outward and inward bodily forms would collapse if it were not for the surrounding pressure and force of these atmospheres.

Since angels are spiritual, and since absolutely all their bodily parts are held together in their form and design by atmospheres, it follows that these atmospheres are spiritual. They are spiritual because they arise from a spiritual sun which is the first emanation of the Lord's divine love and divine wisdom.

177. We have stated above, and explained in the book *Heaven and Hell*, that there are liquids and solids in the spiritual world just as there are in the natural world, the difference being that the liquids and solids of the spiritual world are spiritual. Being spiritual, they are energized and changed by the light of the spiritual sun, by means of its atmospheres, just the way liquids and solids in the natural world are by the warmth and light of their own sun, through its atmospheres.

178. We mention atmospheres, liquids, and solids at this point because these three are the general materials through which and out of which all things take form, with infinite variety. Atmospheres are the

active forces, liquids the intermediate forces, and solids the passive forces, out of which all results emerge. The sole reason these three forces exist in their sequence is the life that emanates from the Lord as the sun, and which arranges for them to be active.

THERE ARE LEVELS OF LOVE AND WISDOM, RESULTANT LEVELS OF WARMTH AND LIGHT, AND FINALLY LEVELS OF ATMOSPHERES

179.   If the reader does not know that levels [*gradus*] exist, does not know what they are and what their nature is, what follows will be incomprehensible, since there are levels within every created thing and therefore in every form. So in this part of the present work, we must discuss levels.

We can establish clearly the existence of levels of love and wisdom through angels of the three heavens. Angels of the third heaven so surpass angels of the second heaven in love and wisdom, and these latter so surpass angels of the lowest heaven, that they cannot live together. The levels of love and wisdom distinguish and separate them.

This is why angels of lower heavens cannot climb up to angels of higher heavens; and if they are allowed to climb up, they do not see them or anything around them. The reason they do not see them is that the love and wisdom of the higher angels is on a higher level, which transcends their perception. Each individual angel actually is his or her love and his or her wisdom. Further, love united to wisdom is a person in its form because God, who is love itself and wisdom itself, is a person.

I have sometimes been allowed to see angels of the lowest heaven climb up to angels of the third heaven. And when they had arrived, I heard them complain that they did not see a single person, even though they were surrounded by them. Afterwards, they were taught that the higher angels had been invisible because their love and wisdom were beyond their perception, and that love and wisdom make an angel look like a person.

180. We can see even more clearly that levels of love and wisdom occur if we compare angels' love and wisdom to human love and wisdom. It is recognized that angels' wisdom is indescribable by comparison. We shall see below that it is also incomprehensible to us as long as we are involved in natural love. The reason it seems indescribable and incomprehensible is that it is on a higher level.

181. Because there are levels of love and wisdom, there are levels of warmth and light as well. By warmth and light, we mean spiritual warmth and light—the kind angels have in the heavens and the kind we have in the more inward regions, regions of our minds. For we have a warmth of love and light of wisdom like that of angels.

The situation in the heavens is like this. The amount and quality of angels' love determines the amount and quality of their warmth. Their light bears the same relationship to their wisdom. The reason is that, as already explained, love for them is within warmth, and wisdom within light.

The same holds true for people on earth; but there is the difference that angels feel this warmth and see this light, while we do not. This is because we are involved in natural warmth and light, and as long as we are, we feel spiritual warmth only through a kind of pleasant sensation of love, and see spiritual light only through the perception of something true.

Now, since we have no awareness of the spiritual warmth and light within us as long as we are involved in natural warmth and light, and since the only means to awareness is experience from the spiritual world, we must first of all discuss the warmth and light that surround angels and their heavens. In this way alone will light be shed on the subject.

182. However, levels of spiritual warmth cannot be described from experience, because the love to which spiritual warmth corresponds will not fit into thought-concepts. Levels of spiritual light, though, can be described, because light, being in fact a property of thought, does fit. On the basis of levels of light we can understand levels of spiritual warmth, since the levels actually go hand in hand.

Turning then to the spiritual light angels are involved in, I have been allowed to see it with my own eyes. The light for angels of the higher heavens is so brilliant that it can be described only by the brilliance of new snow—yet it is so rich that it still cannot be described, not even in terms of the glory of our world's sun. In short, this light surpasses a thousandfold our noonday light on earth. But the light for angels of the lower heaven can be described in some measure by comparisons, though it still surpasses the fullest light of our world.

The reason no one can describe the light of angels of the higher heavens is that their light is the same as their wisdom. And since their wisdom, compared to our wisdom, is indescribable, so too is their light.

We can determine from these few considerations that levels of light do exist. And since wisdom and love occur on similar levels, it follows that there are similar levels of warmth.

183. Since the atmospheres are receiving and containing vessels for warmth and light, it follows that there are as many levels of atmosphere as there are of warmth and light—as many also as there are levels of love and wisdom.

I have been able to see, on the basis of a great deal of experience in the spiritual world, that there are many atmospheres, distinguished from each other by level. The prime witness to this is the fact that angels of lower heaven cannot breathe in the realm of angels of higher heavens, seeming to labor for breath like creatures raised from the air into the ether, or from water into the air. Then too, the spirits underneath the heavens look as though they were in a cloud. On the existence of several atmospheres, distinguished from each other by levels, see above (n. 176).

THERE ARE TWO KINDS OF LEVELS, VERTICAL LEVELS AND HORIZONTAL LEVELS

184. A knowledge of levels is like a key for unlocking the causes of things and getting inside them. Without this knowledge, we can know hardly anything about cause. In fact, the objects and subjects of both worlds seem so very simple, as though they contained nothing more than meets the eye. Yet actually the ratio between this and what lies within is on the order of one to a thousand or one to tens of thousands.

The invisible inward matters cannot be unveiled unless one knows about levels. Actually, the more outward things progress to more inward ones, and through them to inmost things, all by levels—not by gradient levels, but by distinct levels. We use the term "gradient levels" to refer to losses or decreases—coarser to finer or denser to thinner—or better yet, to additions or increases—finer to coarser or thinner to denser—like levels of light progressing to darkness or levels of warmth progressing to cold.

Distinct levels, though, are quite different. They are like earlier, later, and last things, like purpose, means, and result. We call these "distinct levels because the earlier entity exists in its own right, the later in its own right, and the last in its own right; and yet if they are taken together, they constitute a single entity.

The atmospheres called ethers and airs, from top to bottom, from the sun to the earth, are distinguished by levels of this sort. There are simple elements, so to speak, made up of combining these atmospheres; and by combining these elements, we form what are known as compounds.

These latter levels are distinct because they arise separately. They are the ones we mean by "vertical levels." The former levels are gradient levels because they involve increase along a continuum. They are the ones we mean by "horizontal levels."

185. Each and every phenomenon that arises in either the spiritual or the natural world arises from both distinct and gradient levels together, or from both vertical and horizontal levels. The dimension determined by distinct levels is called "height," while the dimension determined by gradient levels is called "width." Their orientation relative to the eye's viewpoint does not alter the terminology.

Unless these levels are recognized, one cannot know anything about the division into three heavens, the distinction between the love and the wisdom of the angels there, the distinction between the warmth and the light they are involved in, or the distinctions in the atmospheres which surround and envelop them.

Further, unless these levels are recognized, one cannot know anything about distinctions in the more inward faculties of mind in people on earth, or therefore anything about their state in terms of reformation and regeneration. Nor can one know anything about distinctions within the more outward faculties which pertain to the bodies of angels and of people on earth alike. And one can know absolutely nothing about the distinction between what is spiritual and what is natural, and nothing therefore about the distinction of life between humans and animals or the distinction between more and less perfect animals or the distinction between the forms of the vegetable kingdom and the substances of the mineral kingdom.

This enables us to conclude that people who do not know about these levels cannot by exercise of sound judgment see causes. They see the results only, and judge causes on this basis. In most cases, this is done by applying the process of induction, along a continuum, to results. Yet causes do not produce results on a continuum, but by a discrete step. The cause is one thing, the result is another. The distinction is like that between prior and posterior, or between what actively forms and what is formed.

186. For a better grasp of the nature and quality of distinct levels and the difference between them and continuous levels, let us use the angelic heaven as an illustration.

There are three heavens, and they are marked off by vertical levels. This means that one heaven is underneath another. They communicate only by an inflow which comes from the Lord alone through the heavens in proper sequence to the lowest heaven, not the other way around.

But each heaven is itself marked off not by vertical levels but by horizontal levels. People in the middle or at the center are in wisdom's light, while people who are at the circumference or at the boundaries are in wisdom's shadow. So wisdom declines into ignorance the way light declines into shadow—along a continuum.

It is the same with people on earth. The more inward realms of their minds are marked off into the same number of levels as is the angelic heaven, with one of these levels being above another. So the more inward realms of people's minds are marked off by distinct or vertical levels. This is why individuals can be involved in their lowest level or a higher level or their highest level, depending on the level of their wisdom. This is why, when they are involved in their lowest level only, the higher level is closed, and why this latter is opened as they accept wisdom from the Lord.

There are also continuous or horizontal levels in people on earth, just as there are in the heavens. The reason for the similarity between an individual and the heavens is that individuals are heavens in miniature, as far as the more inward realms of their minds are concerned, to the extent that they are involved in love and in wisdom from the Lord. On our being heavens in miniature as far as the more inward elements of our minds are concerned, see nn. 51-58 in the book, *Heaven and Hell*.

187. These few considerations enable us to conclude that if people do not know anything about distinct or vertical levels, they cannot know anything about the human state in terms of reformation and regeneration, processes which occur by acceptance of love and wisdom from the Lord and by a consequent opening of the mind's more inward levels in their proper sequence. Nor can they know anything about the inflow that comes through the heavens from the Lord, or about the design by which they have been created. If they ponder these matters on the basis of continuous or horizontal levels rather than distinct or vertical levels, all they can see about them is based on effects, nothing is based on causes. And sight based solely on effects is based on deceptions, which give rise to one error after another. These can be so multiplied by steps in inductive reasoning that ultimately monstrous falsities are called truths.

188. I am not aware that to date anything has come to light about distinct or vertical levels, only about continuous or horizontal levels. Yet unless both kinds of level are recognized, nothing can come to light about causes in their true nature. So this is the subject of this whole Chapter, since the purpose of the present book is to uncover causes and to see effects on their basis,

thereby dispelling the darkness that envelops church folk on the subject of God, of the Lord, and in general of those divine things which we call "spiritual matters."

I can tell you this—that angels are caught in sadness over the darkness on our planet. They tell me that scarcely anywhere do they see light, that people have seized on falsities and confirmed them and so have multiplied falsity on falsity. They tell me that in order to confirm these falsities, people have used logic based on false premises and falsified true premises to probe into matters which, owing to darkness about causes and ignorance of truths, cannot be dispelled.

They are deeply grieved over people's confirmations of faith separated from charity and justification by such faith, over people's concepts of God, angels, and spirits, and over people's ignorance of the nature of love and wisdom.

VERTICAL LEVELS ARE COMPATIBLE, WITH ONE DERIVED FROM ANOTHER IN A SEQUENCE LIKE PURPOSE, MEANS, AND RESULT.

189. Whereas horizontal or continuous levels include such examples as light to shade, warmth to cold, hard to soft, dense to rare, coarse to fine, and so on, and these levels are familiar from sense experience and visual observation, while vertical or distinct levels are not, we need to give particular attention to these latter levels in the present Chapter; for unless these levels are recognized, we cannot discern causes.

People do not admit that purpose, means, and result follow in a sequence like the prior, the posterior, and the last. They do admit that the purpose must produce the means, and must produce the result through the means, in order for the purpose to emerge; and they make many other admissions about these subjects.

But knowing these things without seeing them by application to concrete instances is knowing only abstractions, which last only as long as analytic matters are held in thought against a metaphysical background.

This is why little if anything is known in the world about distinct levels, even though purpose, means, and result progress by these levels. Actually, a recognition only of abstractions is like something airy, something elusive. But if the abstractions are applied to the kinds of thing that exist in this world, they are like something carefully observed by eyesight on our planet, which stays in the memory.

190. Everything in this world that comes to view, which we call "three-dimensional" or "compound," is made up of vertical or distinct levels. But let some examples illustrate this.

It is acknowledged from visual observation that each muscle in the human body is made up of minute fibers, that these are compounded in layers, make up larger fibers called motor fibers, and that from these bundles arises another complex which is called a muscle. It is the same with the nerves. In nerves, minute fibers are joined together into larger ones which look like threads. By gathering and joining these together, a nerve is formed.

The same holds true in other ways of joining and layering and gathering which result in bodily organs and viscera. These are compounds of fibers and vessels assembled in different ways, with the same levels. The same holds true in each and every menber of the vegetable kingdom and in each and every member of the mineral kingdom. In wood, little threads are joined together in a threefold design; in metals and in stones there are aggregates of parts, again in a threefold design.

We can see from this what distinct levels are like— namely that one thing derives from another, and a third, called a compound, from that, and each level is distinct from the others.

191. On this basis, we can draw conclusions about things not visible to the eye, because the situation is similar for them. We may cite as examples the organic substances which are the recipients and abodes of thoughts and affections in the brains, or the atmospheres, or warmth and light, or love and wisdom. The atmospheres are recipients of warmth and light, and warmth and light are recipients of love and wisdom. So since there are levels of atmosphere, there are similar levels of warmth and light as well, and similar levels of love and wisdom. The relationships of levels of the latter are exactly the same as those of the former.

192. We can conclude from what has just been presented that these levels are compatible—that is, that they have the same character and nature. The smallest, larger, and largest motor fibers are compatible; the smallest, larger, and largest nerve fibers are compatible; wood fibers are compatible from the smallest to their compounds. the same holds true for the various kinds of stone and metal.

The organic substances which are recipients and abodes of thoughts and affections are compatible from the very simplest to the general aggregate which is the brain. The atmospheres, from pure ether to air, are compatible. Levels of warmth and light in the sequence that depends on levels of atmosphere are compatible; and therefore levels of love and wisdom are compatible.

Things which are not of the same character and nature are incompatible, and do not harmonize with compatible things. So compatible things cannot form distinct levels with incompatible ones—only with their own ilk, with things of the same character and nature, with which they are compatible.

193. We can see that these things are in their proper pattern, like purposes, means, and results, since the first element—the smallest—achieves its means through an intermediate and its result through a last.

194. It should be realized that each level is marked off from others by its own proper covering, and that all the levels together are marked off by a general covering. Further, it should be realized that the general covering communicates with more inward and most inward things in their order. As a result, there is a uniting and a unanimous activity of all things.

THE FIRST LEVEL IS THE SUM AND SUBSTANCE OF ALL LATER LEVELS

195. This is because the levels of any subject or entity are compatible; and they are compatible because they have been brought forth by the first level. For their formation is of a particular nature, the first uses layering and aggregating—gathering, in a word—to bring forth a second, and using this second level to bring forth a third. Each one is marked off from the others by a surrounding covering.

We can see from this that the first level is the chief, and distinct, the governing one in subsequent levels; and we can see further that the first level is the sum total of all subsequent levels.

196. We have stated that this is the nature of the levels as they relate to each other, but we mean that this is the nature of the substances within their levels. To talk in terms of levels is to talk in abstract terms, whose universality allows application to any given subject or entity existing in these same levels.

197. We can apply these terms to all the things listed in the preceding section—to muscles, for example, to nerves, to materials and components of both the vegetable and the mineral kingdoms, to the organic

substances which are the subjects of thoughts and affections in people, to the atmospheres, to warmth and light, and to love and wisdom. In each of these, there is a first, distinctive element ruling within subsequent elements; there is in fact something unique within each. And because it is the unique element within them, it totally constitutes them.

We can see the truth of this from principles already recognized, namely that the purpose totally constitutes the means, and through the means totally constitutes the result. For this reason, purpose, means, and result are called first, intermediate, and last ends. We may also cite the principles that the cause behind a cause is also the cause of whatever is caused, that there is nothing essential within a cause except a purpose and nothing essential in motion except effort [*conatus*], and finally that a unique substance is one which is intrinsic substance.

198. On the basis of the foregoing, we can see clearly that the divine, being intrinsic substance or unique and exclusive substance, is the substance from which each and every thing was created, that God therefore wholly constitutes the universe, in keeping with the matters presented in Chapter 1, including these: divine love and divine wisdom are substance and form (nn. 40-43); divine love and divine wisdom are intrinsic substance and form, and are therefore authentic and unique (nn. 44-46); everything in the universe was created by divine love and divine wisdom (nn. 52-60); the universe is therefore a reflection of Him (nn. 61-65); and the Lord alone is heaven, where angels live (nn. 113-118).

ALL TYPES OF PERFECTION INCREASE AND RISE BY LEVELS AND IN KEEPING WITH LEVELS

199. We have already explained (nn. 184-188) that there are two kinds of level, horizontal and vertical. We

have explained that horizontal levels are like levels of light tending toward shade, or of wisdom tending toward ignorance, while vertical levels are like purpose, means, and result or like prior, posterior, and last.

We describe these latter levels as rising and falling, since they are vertical, while we describe the former as increasing and decreasing, since they are horizontal. Vertical levels are so different from horizontal ones that they have nothing in common. So they must be perceived separately, and not at all confused.

200. The reason all types of perfection increase and rise by levels and in keeping with levels is that all attributes are secondary to their subjects, and perfection and imperfection are general attributes. They are in fact predicated of life, of forces, and of forms.

Perfection of life is perfection of love and wisdom. And since intention and discernment are their recipient vessels, perfection of life is perfection of intention and discernment as well, and is therefore also perfection of affections and thoughts. Further, since spiritual warmth is a containant of love and spiritual light a containant of wisdom, their perfection too can be traced back to perfection of life.

Perfection of forces is a perfection of everything that is activated and set in motion by life, but which itself contains no life. The atmospheres, as far as their activities are concerned, are forces of this kind, and so are the organic substances, both inner and outer, of the human being, and even of all sorts of animal. So too are all the things in the natural world which, directly or indirectly, are impelled to activity by the sun.

Perfection of form and perfection of forces are one and the same thing, for the nature of forms depends on the nature of forces. The only difference is that forms are substantial, while forces are their activities. Consequently, the levels of perfection are the same for both. Forms which are not also forces also have a perfection that depends on their level.

201. At this point we will not be discussing perfections of life, forces, and forms as they increase or decrease by horizontal or continuous levels, since these levels are familiar to the world. We will be discussing rather perfections of life, forces, and forms as they rise and fall by vertical or distinct levels, because these levels are not familiar to the world.

Just how perfections rise and fall by these levels, though, is hard to recognize using things visible in the natural world, but it is clearly recognizable using things in the spiritual world. Using things visible in the natural world, we discover only that more marvelous things happen the deeper we look—for example, in the eyes, ears, tongue, muscles, heart, lungs, liver, pancreas, intestines, and other inner organs, also in seeds, fruits, and flowers, and then again in metals, minerals, and gems.

We are aware that more marvelous things happen in all these entities the deeper we look. Notwithstanding, there is little awareness on this basis that they are more deeply perfect according to vertical or distinct levels: an ignorance of these levels has hidden this fact. But because these same levels are quite obvious in the spiritual world (that whole world being in those levels from top to bottom), we can use it to gain acquaintance with these levels. This can then enable us to draw conclusions about kinds of perfection of the forces and forms which exist in similar levels in the natural world.

202. In the spiritual world, there are three heavens arranged by vertical levels. The highest heaven contains angels who in overall perfection surpass angels of the intermediate heaven. The intermediate heaven contains angels who in overall perfection surpass the angels of the lowest heaven. The levels of perfection

are such that angels of the lowest heaven are unable to climb even to the threshhold of perfection of angels of the intermediate heaven, while these latter are unable to climb even to the threshhold of perfection of angels of the highest heaven. This seems paradoxical, but it is the truth nevertheless. It is because they are gathered by distinct levels, not by continuous levels.

It has been borne in on me by an abundance of experience that there is such a difference in affections, thoughts, and therefore speech, between angels of higher and lower heavens, that they have nothing in common. I have also learned that communication takes place only by "correspondences" brought about by the Lord's direct inflow into all the heavens and by His indirect inflow through the highest heaven into the lowest.

This being the nature of these distinctions, they cannot be expressed in natural language nor described, then. Angels' thoughts do not fit into natural concepts, since they are spiritual. They can be expressed and described only by angels themselves, in their own tongues, their own words, and their own writing—not with human ones. This is why people say that indescribable things have been heard and seen in the heavens.

We can grasp the distinctions to some extent in the following way. The thoughts of angels of the highest or third heaven are thoughts about purposes; the thoughts of angels of the intermediate or second heaven are thoughts about means; and the thoughts of angels of the lowest or first heaven are thoughts about results.

We do need to realize that it is one thing to think on the basis of purposes, and another to think about purposes; that it is one thing to think on the basis of means, and another to think about means; and that it is one thing to think on the basis of results, and another to think about results. Angels of the lower heavens do think about means and purposes, but angels of the higher heavens think on the basis of means and purposes. Thinking on this basis is a matter of higher wisdom, thinking about them, a matter of lower wisdom. Thinking on the basis of purposes is a matter of wisdom; thinking on the basis of means is a matter of intelligence; and thinking on the basis of results is a matter of being informed.

We can see from this that all perfection rises and falls by and according to these levels.

203. Since the more inward reaches of people—the realms of their purposing and discernment—are in levels like the heavens, we are actually heavens in miniature, as far as the inner reaches of our minds are concerned. This means that the perfections of these inner reaches are like those of heaven.

These perfections, however, are not visible to people as long as they are living in this world. They are then actually on the lowest level, and higher levels cannot be recognized from the lowest level. After death, though, they are recognized. For at that point, individuals reach the level that answers to their own love and wisdom. They in fact become angels. They think and say things indescribable to their "natural" selves. At that time there is a raising of all their mental elements —not a raising by a simple ratio, but by a triple ratio. Vertical levels follow the latter ratio, horizontal levels the former. But the only people who do ascend, who are raised up by vertical levels, are the ones who were involved with matters of truth in the world, and applied them to life.

204. It looks as though antecedent things were less perfect than subsequent things, or simple things than compounds. However, the antecedents which give rise to things subsequent, the simple things which give

rise to compounds, are actually more perfect. This is because the antecedent or simple things are more naked, less veiled by lifeless material substances. They are more divine, so to speak; and so they are closer to the spiritual sun where the Lord is.

The essence of perfection is of course in the Lord, and consequently in the sun which is the first emanation of His divine love and divine wisdom. Perfection therefore occurs in the things next in the sequence; and so on, in order, all the way to the lowest things, which are more imperfect as they are more remote.

If this kind of primary perfection did not exist in antecedent and simple substances, neither humans nor any animal could emerge from seed, and survive thereafter. Neither could the seeds of trees and fruits sprout and multiply. In fact, the more antecedent an antecedent is, or the simpler a simple substance is, the more immune to harm it is, because it is more perfect.

IN A SEQUENTIAL ARRANGEMENT, THE FIRST LEVEL CONSTITUTES THE HIGHEST AND THE THIRD LEVEL CONSTITUTES THE LOWEST; BUT IN A SIMULTANEOUS PATTERN THE FIRST LEVEL CONSTITUTES THE INMOST AND THE THIRD LEVEL THE OUTMOST

205. There is a sequential and a simultaneous arrangement. The sequential arrangement of these levels is from highest to lowest, or from top to bottom. The angelic heavens are in that arrangement—the third of these heavens is highest, the second is intermediate, and the first is lowest. This is how they are placed in relationship to each other. States of love and wisdom for angels are in the same sequential arrangement; so are states of warmth and light, and of spiritual atmospheres. All the perfections of forms and forces there are in the same arrangement.

When vertical or distinct levels occur in a sequential arrangement, they are comparable to a tower divided into three levels which allow ascent and descent. The most perfect and lovely things are in the upper story, with less perfect and lovely things in the middle one, and still less perfect and lovely things in the lowest one.

However, a simultaneous arrangement comprising these same levels looks different. In this case, the things that were highest in the sequential arrangement, the most perfect and lovely things mentioned above, are in the center; lower things in an intermediate area, and lowest things in the circumference. This is like the situation with a solid object composed of those three levels, with the subtlest elements in its middle or center, less subtle elements surrounding them, and on the surfaces which make the circumference, elements compounded from these others, and therefore coarser. It is as though the tower described above had settled into a plane, with the highest level making up the middle, the intermediate level making up the intermediate area, and the lowest level making up the outside.

206. Since the highest level of a sequential arrangement does become the middle area of a simultaneous arrangement, "higher" in the Word means more inward, and "lower" means more outward. There are similar meanings for "upward" and "downward" and for "high" and "deep."

207. In the last member of any series, these distinct levels are present in simultaneous arrangement. The motor fibers in every muscle, the fibers in every nerve, the fibers and ducts in every viscous and organ, are in this kind of arrangement. At their center are things at once simplest and most perfect; the surface is compounded from these things.

The same arrangement of these levels occurs in every seed and in every fruit, in every metal and mineral as well. This is the nature of their components, which constitute the whole. They are in fact sequential components, or varieties layering and compacting out of the simple elements which are their primary substances or materials.

208. In brief, levels of this kind exist within every "ultimate" [last member of a series], and therefore in every result. For every ultimate consists of antecedents, and these consist of primary things. Too, every result consists of a means, and this consists of a purpose, with the purpose being all there is to the means, and the means being all there is to the result (as explained above). The purpose, then, constitutes the center, the means constitutes the intermediate area, and the result constitutes the surface.

In subsequent pages, we will see that the same arrangements obtain for levels of love and wisdom, of warmth and light, and of the organic forms of affections and thoughts in people. We have dealt with the series of these levels in both sequential and simultaneous arrangements in *The Doctrine of the New Jerusalem Concerning Sacred Scripture* (n. 38 and elsewhere), demonstrating that the same levels exist within each and every detail of the Word.

THE FINAL LEVEL IS THE AGGREGATE, CONTAINANT, AND FOUNDATION OF ANTECEDENT LEVELS

209. The doctrine of levels we are offering in this chapter has thus far been illustrated by various things that occur in the two worlds by levels of the heavens where angels live, levels of their warmth and light, and by levels of atmosphere. We have also used various things in the human body, and in the animal and mineral kingdoms.

But this doctrine is susceptible to further extension. Its scope includes not only natural phenomena, but civil, moral, and spiritual ones as well, in their each and every detail.

There are two reasons why the doctrine of levels reaches out to include matters of this sort. The *first reason* is that there is a trine in everything subject to any predication—a trine called purpose [end], means [cause], and result [effect], with these three interrelated according to vertical levels. The *second reason* is that no civil, moral, or spiritual phenomenon is divorced from substance—rather they are substances. For just as love and wisdom are not abstractions but substances (as explained above, nn. 40-43), so too is every phenomenon which we call civil or moral or spiritual. We can indeed think about these as abstract and insubstantial, but intrinsically they are not abstractions.

Take for example affection and thought, charity and faith, purposing and discernment. It is the same for these as it is for love and wisdom—namely, they do not occur apart from substrata which are substances, but are rather states of these substrata or substances. We will see later on that they are their changes, which make perceptible alterations. Substance means form as well, since no substance occurs apart from a form.

210. Since people can think and have in fact thought about purposing and discernment, affection and thought, and even charity and faith, as abstract, divorced from the substances which are their substrata, the result has been the death of the accurate concept of them, the concept that they are states of substances or forms. This is exactly like sensations and actions, which are not entities divorced from the sensory and motor organs. Divorced or separated from these, they are nothing but rational constructs. They are actually like sight without an eye, hearing without an ear, taste without a tongue, and the like.

211. Since all civil, moral, and spiritual matters go through levels in the same way as natural matters (not just through continuous levels but through distinct levels as well), and since the stages of distinct levels are like stages of purposes moving to means and of means moving to results—because of this, I wanted to illustrate and support the present topic (the final level as the aggregate, containant, and foundation of antecedent levels) with the material cited above. I refer to mentions of love and wisdom, purposing and discernment, affection and thought, and charity and faith.

212. As to the final level being the aggregate, containant, and foundation of antecedent levels, this finds clear support in the motion of purposes and means to results. A result as being the aggregate, containant, and foundation of means and purposes is something an enlightened rational capacity can grasp. But this capacity cannot so clearly grasp the fact that a purpose, with all its properties, and a means, with all its properties, are effectively actually within the result—that the result is their complete aggregate.

We can establish the truth of this from what we have already said in this chapter, with special emphasis on the following points: one entity exists from another in threefold series, and a result is nothing but a purpose in its final [form]; and since the final form is the aggregate, it follows that the final form is the containant and also the foundation.

213. Turning to love and wisdom, then, love is the purpose, wisdom the means through which, and use is the result. Further, use is the aggregate, containant, and foundation of wisdom and love; and use is such an aggregate, and such a containant that all the elements of love and all the elements of wisdom are actually within it—it is their simultaneous presence.

However, we must bear clearly in mind that all the compatible and harmonious elements of love and wisdom are within a use according to the principles stated and explained in the preceding pages (nn. 189-94).

214. Affection, thought, and action exist in the same series of levels, since every affection goes back to love, every thought to wisdom, and every action to use. Charity, faith, and good work exist in the same series, since charity is a matter of affection, faith a matter of thought, and good work a matter of action. Purposing, discernment, and physical activity exist in the same levels, since purposing is a matter of love and therefore of affection, discernment a matter of wisdom and therefore of faith, and physical activity a matter of use and therefore of work.

This means, then, that just as all elements of love and wisdom dwell in use, so all elements of thought and affection dwell in action, all elements of faith and charity dwell in good work, and so on. But all these are of the same type, that is, harmonious.

215. Until now, people have been unaware of the fact that the final member of each series (that is, use, act, work, and physical activity) is the aggregate and containant of everything antecedent.

It does look as though nothing more were present within use, act, work, and physical activity than there is within motion; however, all the antecedent elements are actually present within the former phenomena—so completely present that nothing is missing. The antecedents are enclosed within them like wine in a bottle or furnishings in a house. The reason they are not visible is that we are only looking from the outside; and when we look from the outside, there is nothing but activities and motions.

It is like the situation when arms and hands move, and we are unaware that a thousand fibers are cooperating for each and every one of their motions, and that thousands of elements of affection and thought match the thousand motor fibers, activating those motor fibers. But since they act from within, this is not visible to any physical sense.

It is recognized that nothing is accomplished in or through the body unless it comes from purposing through thought. And since both of these are at work, we cannot doubt that each and every detail of purposing and thought is dwelling within the act—they cannot be divided. This is why people, on the basis of deeds or works, make judgments about the "thought from purpose" which we call "intent."

There is something I have been made aware of. Angels perceive and see simply from a person's deeds or work the whole complex of purposing and thought of the person who is doing the acting. Angels of the third heaven perceive and see the "purpose for which" that is from intention; and angels of the second heaven see the means through which the purpose is working. This is why works and deeds are prescribed so often in the Word, and why it says that people are known by their works and deeds.

216. It is a matter of angelic wisdom that if purposing and discernment (or affection and thought, or thus charity and faith) do not enter and clothe themselves in works or deeds when this is possible, they are nothing but transient vapors, or like airy mirages that vanish; that they first have some permanence within individuals and become part of their life when they perform and do them. The reason is that the final form is the aggregate, containant, and foundation of its antecedents.

Such a vapor, such a mirage is faith divorced from good works, and such too are faith and charity apart from their exercise. The one difference is that people who give status to both faith and charity have the knowledge and power to intend and to do good things, while people involved in a faith divorced from charity do not.

VERTICAL LEVELS ARE FULLY AND EFFECTIVELY PRESENT IN THEIR FINAL LEVEL

217. We explained in the last section that the final level is the aggregate, containant, and foundation of antecedent levels. It follows from this that the antecedent levels are fully present in their final level. They are then actually in their result, and every result is the fulfillment of its means.

218. Now we are proposing that these rising and falling levels (also called prior and posterior, or vertical and distinct levels) are effectively present in their final level. This proposition finds support in all the corroborative examples drawn from sensory and perceptible phenomena in the foregoing sections. At this point, however, I want to support the proposition simply by reference to energy [*conatus*], force, and motion in lifeless and in living entities.

It is recognized that energy by itself accomplishes nothing, but works through forces which respond to it, and that through these forces, energy sets up motion. A corollary is also recognized, that energy wholly accounts for force, and through force, wholly accounts for motion. Since motion is the final level of energy, we recognize that energy realizes its effectiveness through motion.

Energy, force, and motion are united exactly according to vertical levels, whose union is not on a continuum, since they are distinct, but occurs by correspondence. For energy is not force, and force is not motion. Force is rather produced by energy (force is actually "awakened energy"), and motion is produced through force. So there is no effectiveness in energy alone or in force alone—only in motion, which is their product.

This may seem doubtful at this point, since we have not illustrated it by applying it to things we can sense and perceive in nature, but this is nevertheless how these phenomena progress to effectiveness.

219. Let us try applying these premises to living energy, living force, and living motion. The living energy in human beings (who are living entities) are their purposing united to discernment. The living forces in human beings are the inner components of their bodies, all containing motor fibers woven together in various ways. Living motion in human beings is action, which is produced through those forces, by purposing united to discernment.

The more inward elements, which are elements of purposing and discernment, make up the first level; the more inward elements of the body make up the second level; and the whole body, which includes the preceding, makes up the third level.

It is acknowledged that the more inward elements of the mind are powerless except through forces within the body, and that the forces too are powerless except through action of that same body. These three levels do not act on a continuum, but distinctly, and acting distinctly is acting by means of correspondences. The more inward elements of the mind correspond to the more inward elements of the body; and the body's more inward elements correspond to its more outward ones, through which actions take place. So the first two are empowered by means of the more outward elements of the body.

It may seem as though energies and forces are somewhat empowered even though no action occurs—for example in times of sleep and in states of rest. However, at such times the energies and forces find their outward forms in the general motor functions of the body, the heart and the lungs. When their action ceases, the forces cease, and the energies with them.

220. Since the whole—the body—finds outward forms for its effectiveness primarily in the arms and hands, which are outmost, arms and hands in the Word mean power, with "the right hand" meaning a higher power.

This being the way the levels unfold and stretch out into effectiveness, the angels who are with individuals (and are responsive to everything in them) can tell simply from an action done by the hand what individuals are like as far as discernment and purposing are concerned. Then they can tell what they are like as far as charity and faith are concerned, as far, then, as the inner life of their minds and the resultant outer life of their bodies.

I have often been amazed that angels have this insight simply on the basis of physical actions performed by a hand. However, I have been shown this by first-hand experience any number of times. I have been told that this is why ordination into ministry is accomplished by the laying on of hands, why "touching with the hand" means communicating, and so on.

All this has led to the conclusion that the whole of charity and faith is within works, and that charity and faith divorced from works are like rainbows around the sun, which fade away and are obliterated by a cloud. This is why "works" and "doing" are mentioned so often in the Word, why it says that our salvation depends on them. Then too, the person who "does" is called wise, and the person who does not "do" is called foolish.

It needs to be realized, though, that "works" here mean the uses that are in fact accomplished. The whole of charity and faith is within them, and in accord with them. The correspondence mentioned above is with uses, since that correspondence is spiritual; but it occurs by means of substances and materials which are subject entities.

221. At this point, it is possible to unveil two arcana which come within the compass of understanding thanks to the concepts presented above.

The first arcanum is that the Word finds its full expression and its proper power in its literal meaning.

Actually, there are three meanings in the Word, following the three levels. There is a heavenly meaning, a spiritual meaning, and a natural meaning.

Because these meanings exist in the Word in keeping with the three vertical levels, and because their union is accomplished by correspondences, the final meaning, the natural, called the literal meaning, is not simply the aggregate, containant and foundation of the corresponding more inward meanings. No, the Word, in this final meaning, finds it full expression and its proper power. The truth of this has been amply presented and supported in *The Doctrine of the New Jerusalem on the Sacred Scriptures* (nn. 27-35, 36-49, 50-61, 62-69).

The second arcanum is that the Lord entered the world and took on a human nature in order to assume the power to conquer the hells and set everything in order in heaven and on earth. He superimposed this human nature on His own former human nature.

The human nature He superimposed in the world was like the human nature of people in the world, while the other one was divine and therefore infinitely transcended the finite human nature of angels and mortals. And since He completely glorified this natural human nature all the way to its limits, He rose from the dead with His whole body, unlike any mortal.

By taking on this human nature, He assumed a divine power capable not only of conquering the hells and setting the heavens in order, but also of keeping the hells subdued forever, and of saving humanity. This power is meant by His sitting on the right hand of God's power and might.

Since by taking on a natural human nature, the Lord made Himself divine and true in outmost things, He is called the Word, and it says that the Word was made flesh. What is divine and true in outmost things is the Word in its literal meaning. He accomplished this by

124

fulfilling everything about Himself in the Word, in Moses and The Prophets.

All individuals are actually their own good and their own truth: nothing else makes a person human. The Lord, though, by taking on a natural human nature, is the actual Divine-Good and Divine-True, or in other words, actual divine love and divine wisdom, in first and last elements alike. Ths is why He appears as a sun in the angelic heavens with stronger radiance and greater brilliance after his advent than before it.

This is an arcanum that can fall within the grasp of intellect because of the doctrine of levels. We will discuss later His omnipotence before His advent into the world.

BOTH KINDS OF LEVEL EXIST IN THE LARGEST AND SMALLEST OF ALL CREATED THINGS

222. We cannot use visible phenomena to illustrate the fact that the largest and smallest of all things are made up of distinct and continuous (or vertical and horizontal) levels, because the smallest things are not visible to the eye, while the largest visible phenomena do not seem to be separated into levels. So all we can do is use universal principles to present this subject. And since angels are in a wisdom that derives from universal principles, and are consequently in possession of information about details, we may present some of their basic axioms about these matters.

223. The angels' basic axioms on this subject are the following. Nothing occurs, no matter how small, that does not contain both kinds of level. For example, this applies to the smallest part of any animal, the smallest part of any plant, the smallest part of any mineral, and the smallest part of ether and air. Further, since ether and air are receivers of warmth and light, the same applies to the smallest part of warmth and light. Further still, since spiritual warmth and spiritual light

are receivers of love and wisdom, the same applies to the smallest part of these—no matter how small, they all contain both kinds of level.

It also follows from the angels' basic axioms that the smallest element of affection or the smallest element of thought—even the smallest element of a thought-concept—is made up of both kinds of level, that any smallest element which is not so constituted, is nothing. It has in fact no form, and therefore no quality, nor any state which can be altered or varied, which would enable it to have presence.

Angels use the following truth to support this premise. In God the Creator (who is the Lord from eternity) infinite things are distinguishably one. Too, there are infinite things within His infinite things. In these infinitely infinite things, there are both kinds of level, which are also distinguishably one in Him. Since these things are in Him, and since everything was created by Him, with every created thing in some visible aspect going back to things within Him, it follows that there is not the smallest created entity which does not contain these kinds of level.

The reason these levels occur in both the smallest and the largest things is that the divine is the same in things largest and smallest. (On infinite things being distinguishably one in the God-Man, see above nn. 17-22. On the divine being the same in greatest and smallest things, see nn. 77-82. Further examples of these principles may be found at nn. 155, 169, and 171.)

224. We have stated that no element of affection or thought or even of a thought-concept occurs, no matter how small, which does not contain both kinds of level. This is because love and wisdom are substance and form (as presented above, nn. 40-43): the same holds true of affection and thought.

And since (as stated above) no form occurs which does not contain these levels, it follows that the entities named contain these same levels. In fact, to separate love and wisdom, affection and thought then, from substance and form, is to annihilate them. This is because they do not occur outside their proper subjects, perceived by people as they change, and making them effectively present.

225. The largest entities, which contain both kinds of level, are the universe in its entirety, the natural world in its entirety, and the spiritual world in its entirety. We include every empire and every kingdom in its entirety; we include the whole civil aspect of an empire or kingdom, the whole moral aspect, and the whole spiritual aspect in its entirety. We include the whole animal kingdom, the whole vegetable kingdom, and the whole mineral kingdom, each in its entirety. We include the atmospheres of each world taken together, and their appropriate kinds of warmth and light.

We also include less extensive entities, such as humanity in its entirety, each animal species in its entirety, each tree and shrub in its entirety, each stone and metal in its entirety.

In one respect, the forms of these entities are alike, being made up of levels of both kinds. The reason is that the Divine by which they were created is the same in largest and in smallest things (as presented above, nn. 77-82). The details, even the smallest, of these entities are like the more inclusive and most inclusive entities in being forms characterized by both kinds of level.

226. Because both greatest and smallest things are forms characterized by both kinds of level, there is a linking of them from beginning to end; likeness actually unites them. However, there is nothing, no matter how small, that is exactly like anything else, which results in a distinctiveness of everything, down to the last detail.

The reason no smallest entity—in any form, or sharing various forms—occurs exactly like another, is that these same levels exist in the largest entities, which are made up of the smallest ones. Given the existence of these kinds of level in the largest entities, with constant distinctions therefore from top to bottom and from center to circumference, it follows that there are no lesser or least components (which contain the same levels) that are identical.

227. It is a matter of angelic wisdom that the perfection of the created universe stems from the likeness of its most inclusive and its most detailed (or greatest and most minute) parts, as far as these levels are concerned. Given this circumstance, one component actually focuses on another as its like, with which it can be wedded for its every useful activity, manifesting its every purpose in results.

228. But these matters may seem like paradoxes because they have not been set forth with applications to visible phenomena. There is a tendency, though, for matters that are abstract because they are universal, to be understood more readily than they are applied, because the application involved an endless variety, and variety is confusing.

229. Some people teach that there is a substance so simple that it is not a form made up of lesser forms, with secondary substances or compounds arising from that substance by gathering it together, resulting eventually in the substances we call matter.

But these simplest substances do not exist. What actually is a substance without a form? It is of such nature that it can have no attributes, and nothing can be compounded by gathering together some entity which has no attributes. We shall see below, when we discuss forms, that there are countless things within the very first created substances, which are the smallest and simplest substances.

THERE ARE THREE INFINITE AND UN-CREATED VERTICAL LEVELS IN THE LORD, AND THREE FINITE AND CREATED LEVELS IN A HUMAN BEING

230. The reason there are three infinite and uncreated vertical levels in the Lord, is that the Lord is love itself and wisdom itself, as we have already explained. Since the Lord is love itself and wisdom itself, He is also use [roughly, "fruitful activity"] itself, for love has use as its goal, and produces it by means of wisdom. In fact, apart from use, love and wisdom have no end or goal, which means that they have no home of their own. So we cannot say that they exist or take form unless there is a use which contains them.

These three things make up the three vertical levels in living entities. These three things are like the first end, the intermediate end which we call the means, and the final end which we call the result. We have already presented, and amply supported, the proposition that purpose, means, and result make up the three vertical levels.

231. We can determine that these three levels exist within human beings, on the grounds that our minds can be raised all the way to the levels of love and wisdom that involve angels of the second and third heavens. In fact, all angels were born as human beings; and as far as the more inward aspects of our minds are concerned, people are heavens in miniature. So by creation, there are as many vertical levels in us as there are heavens.

Then too, the individual person is an image and likeness of God. So these three levels are engraved in the individual because they are in the God-Man—in the Lord, that is. To determine that these levels are infinite and uncreated in the Lord, and finite and created in us, we may use material presented in Chapter 1—for example, the fact that the Lord is intrinsic love and wisdom, while we are recipients of love and wisdom from the Lord; or the fact that nothing which is not infinite can be predicated of the Lord, while nothing that is not finite can be predicated of us.

232. For angels, these three levels are called heavenly, spiritual, and natural. For angels, the heavenly level is the level of love, the spiritual level is the level of wisdom, and the natural level is the level of uses. The reason for giving these names to these levels is that the heavens are divided into two kingdoms, with one kingdom called heavenly and the other spiritual, and with a third kingdom added, where people in this world are, which is the natural kingdom.

Then too, the angels who make up the heavenly kingdom are involved in love and the angels who make up the spiritual kingdom are involved in wisdom, while people in this world are involved in uses. For this reason, the three kingdoms are united. In the next chapter, we will explain how to understand our being "involved in uses."

233. I have been told from heaven that in the Lord from eternity, who is Jehovah, before He took on a human nature in this world, the first two levels existed in actuality, while the third level existed in potential, just as is the case with angels. But after the Lord took on a human nature in this world, He put this third level (called natural) on over the others, thus becoming a person like people in this world, though with the difference that this level was infinite and uncreated like the first ones, while in angels or people these levels are finite and created.

Actually, the divine that had filled all space without itself being bound by space (nn. 69-72) did penetrate even to the limits of nature, but before the donning of a human nature, the divine inflow into the natural level was indirect, through the angelic heavens, while after the donning of the human nature it was direct, from Him. This is why all the churches in the world before His advent were representative of spiritual and heavenly matters, while after His advent they became "natural-spiritual" and "natural-heavenly," and representative worship was abolished. This is also why after the donning of the human nature, the sun of the angelic heaven (which as we have already stated is the first emanation of His divine love and divine wisdom) blazed out with greater glory and brilliance than before.

This is the meaning of the following words from Isaiah:

> In that day, the light of the moon will be like the light of the sun, and the light of the sun will be multiplied by seven, like the light of seven days (Isaiah 30:26).

This is predicated of the state of heaven and the church after the Lord's coming into the world. And we find in the book of Revelation,

> The Son of Man's face looked like the sun shining full strength (Revelation 1:16).

with similar statements elsewhere (for example, in Isaiah 60:20, II Samuel 23:3,4, and Matthew 17:1,2).

The indirect enlightenment of humanity through the angelic heaven, which obtained before the Lord's advent, is comparable to moonlight, which is an indirect form of sunlight. Since this became a direct enlightenment after His advent, it says in Isaiah that "the light of the moon will be like the light of the sun," and in David, "In His day will the righteous man flourish, and there will be abundant peace even until there is no moon (Psalm 72:7)." This too is about the Lord.

234. The reason the Lord from eternity, or Jehovah, put on this third level over the others, by taking on a

human nature in this world, was that He could not enter this world except by means of a nature like our human nature—only, that is, by being conceived by His own divine [nature] and born of a virgin. So He could take off a nature which was intrinsically dead and yet receptive of the divine, and put on a divine nature.

This is the meaning of the two states which characterized the Lord in this world, called the state of emptiness and the state of glorification, discussed in *The Doctrine of the Lord.*

235. We have said this much in a general way about the threefold ladder of vertical levels. But since these levels occur in both the greatest and the smallest things, as stated in the preceding section, we cannot say anything specific about them at this point. We can say only this, that there are levels like these in each and every element of love, there are levels like these therefore in each and every element of wisdom, and in consequence there are levels like these in each and every element of use. But all of these are infinite in the Lord, while they are finite in angels and in mortals.

However, we cannot describe and unfold how these levels exist in love, wisdom, and uses, except by a long process.

THESE THREE VERTICAL LEVELS ARE WITHIN EACH INDIVIDUAL FROM BIRTH, AND CAN BE OPENED IN SEQUENCE. AS THEY ARE OPENED, THE INDIVIDUAL IS IN THE LORD, AND THE LORD IS IN THE INDIVIDUAL

236. Until now, people have not realized that there are three vertical levels in each individual. This is because they have not recognized the [basic] levels, and as long as the basic levels are unrecognized, they cannot know any levels but continuous ones. And when only these latter levels are known, people can

believe that love and wisdom in human beings increase only along a continuum.

But it needs to be realized that there are three vertical or distinct levels within each individual from birth, one above, or within, the other, and that each vertical or distinct level has horizontal or continuous levels according to which it increases along a continuum. For both kinds of level exist within everything, no matter how large or small, as presented above (nn. 222-229). One kind of level cannot occur without the other.

237. These three vertical levels are called natural, spiritual, and heavenly, as stated above (n. 232). When people are born, they arrive first on the natural level. On this level, they grow along a continuum, gaining information and getting discernment thereby, ultimately reaching that highest level of discernment called "a rational faculty."

This in itself, however, does not serve to open the second level, which is called spiritual. This is opened by a love of useful activities which stems from elements of discernment, provided this is a spiritual love of uses; and this love is love toward the neighbor. This level too grows along a continuum all the way to its peak, and it grows by means of insights into what is good and true—by means of spiritual truths.

Again, though, these in themselves do not serve to open the third level, which is called heavenly. This is opened rather by means of a heavenly love of useful activity, and this love is a love for the Lord. Love for the Lord is nothing but applying the Word's precepts to life; and these precepts essentially are to flee evil acts because they are hellish and devilish, and to do good acts because they are heavenly and divine.

This is how these three levels are opened in an individual, in sequence.

238. As long as people are living in this world, they are unaware of the opening of these levels within themselves. This is because they are at this point involved in the natural level, which is the final one, and are doing their thinking and purposing and talking and acting on the basis of that level. The spiritual level, which is more inward, does not communicate with the natural level along a continuum, but does so by means of correspondences, and communication by means of correspondences is imperceptible.

Once individuals lay aside the natural level, though, which happens when they die, they enter whatever level within them had been opened in this world. A person within whom the spiritual level had been opened enters the spiritual level; a person within whom the heavenly level had been opened enters the heavenly level. People who after death have entered the spiritual level no longer think, purpose, talk, and act naturally; they do so spiritually: and people who have entered the heavenly level think, purpose, talk, and act in keeping with their own level.

Further, since communication across the three levels occurs only by means of correspondences, there exist such kinds of distinction by level in love, wisdom, and useful activity that [the levels] have nothing in common by continuity.

We can therefore see that people are possessed of three vertical levels which can be opened in sequence.

239. Since three levels of love, wisdom, and consequent useful activity exist within us, it follows that there exist within us three levels of purposing and discernment and consequent completion, or definition in useful activity. For purposing is the recipient vessel of love, discernment the recipient vessel of wisdom, and completion is their consequent useful activity. We can see from this that there is within every individual a natural, a spiritual, and a heavenly

purposing and discernment—potentially from birth, and actually when they are opened.

In a word, the human mind (which consists of purposing and discernment) comprises, by creation and therefore from birth, three levels. We can therefore see that we have a natural mind, a spiritual mind, and a heavenly mind, can thereby be raised into angelic wisdom, and can even own this while we are living in this world. Yet we do not become involved in this wisdom except after death, if we become angels; then we say indescribable things, which a natural person cannot grasp.

I knew a man of indifferent learning on earth, and after his death I saw him and talked with him in heaven, perceiving clearly that he talked like an angel, and that the things he was saying were beyond the perception of a natural person. This was because he had in this world applied the precepts of the Word to his life and has worshipped the Lord; and because of this the Lord raised him to the third level of love and wisdom.

It is important to be aware of this raising of the human mind: understanding of the matters following depends on it.

240. There are two God-given abilities within us, which distinguish us from animals. The first is the ability to discern what is true and what is good. This ability is called rationality, and is an ability that belongs to our discernment. The second is the ability to do what is true and what is good. This ability is called freedom, and is an ability that belongs to our purposing. From rationality, we can think whatever we want to—for God or against God, for the neighbor or against the neighbor. We can also intend and do what we think; but if we see something evil and fear its punishment, we can refrain from doing it because of our freedom.

It is because of these two abilities that we are human, and are distinguished from animals. These two abilities belong to us as gifts from the Lord, and are constantly being given by Him. They are not taken away from anyone, for if they were taken away, that person's human quality would die.

The Lord is within these two abilities in each and every individual, good and evil alike. They are the Lord's abode in the human race. This is why every individual, whether good or evil, lives forever. But the Lord's abode within an individual is more intimate as that individual uses these abilities to open the higher levels. By opening them, a person actually enters higher levels of love and wisdom, and therefore comes closer to the Lord.

This may serve to demonstrate that as these levels are opened individuals are in the Lord, and the Lord is in them.

241. We have already noted that the three vertical levels are like purpose, means, and result, and that love, wisdom, and use follow the pattern of these levels. We now therefore need to say a little about love as purpose, wisdom as means, and use as result.

If reason is consulted while it is in light, we can see that a person's love is the purpose in everything, for it is what we love that we think about, decide for, and do, which means that we treat it as our purpose. We can also see from reason that wisdom is the means, since the love which is our purpose seeks out in discernment means by which it may arrive at its goal. It therefore consults its wisdom, and wisdom's intermediaries constitute the means through which [the goal is reached]. It needs no explanation to see that use is the result.

One person's love is not the same as another's, though, which means that one person's wisdom is not the same as another's, and that their uses differ as well. Since these three are of the same nature (see above, nn. 189-194), it follows that the quality of our wisdom and use are determined by the quality of our love. We are here using the word wisdom to mean whatever belongs to our discernment.

SPIRITUAL LIGHT FLOWS INTO PEOPLE THROUGH THREE LEVELS, BUT SPIRITUAL WARMTH DOES SO ONLY TO THE EXTENT THAT A PERSON FLEES EVILS AS SINS AND FOCUSES ON THE LORD

242. The preceding presentation shows that light and warmth emanate from heaven's sun, which is the first emanation of divine love and divine wisdom (treated in Chapter 2). The light comes from its wisdom and the warmth from its love. It also shows that light is recipient of wisdom and warmth recipient of love, and that we come into that divine light to the extent that we come into wisdom, and into that divine warmth to the extent that we come into love.

It further shows that there are three levels of light and three levels of warmth, or three levels of wisdom and three levels of love, and that these levels are formed within us so that we may be recipients of divine love and divine wisdom—recipients of the Lord.

We now need to show that spiritual light flows into us through these three levels, but that spiritual warmth does so only to the extent that we flee evils as sins and focus on the Lord. Another way of saying this is to say that we can accept wisdom all the way to the third level, but not love unless we flee evils as sins and focus on the Lord. Still another way of saying it is to say that our discernment can be raised into wisdom, but that our intentionality cannot be raised unless we flee evils as sins.

243. Experience in the spiritual world has made it quite clear to me that discernment can be raised into

heaven's light or angelic wisdom, and that its love cannot be raised into heaven's warmth or angelic love unless we flee evils as sins and focus on the Lord.

I have often seen and perceived simple spirits, spirits who knew only that God exists and that the Lord was born as a person—practically nothing more than this—understanding subtleties of angelic wisdom fully, almost like angels. They were not the only ones, though. Even many of the devilish crowd understood.

These people, though, understood while they were attentive to others and not while they were thinking privately. While they were being attentive to others, that is, light was coming in from above, but while they were thinking privately, the only light that could come in was the light responsive to their warmth or love. So after they had listened to these subtleties and grasped them, when they turned their attention away, they retained nothing. In fact, the members of the devilish crowd then rejected what they had perceived and completely denied it. The reason was that the fire of their love, and the light of that fire, being deceptive, cast a darkness which stifled heavenly light as it entered from above.

244. The same thing happens in this world. Anyone who is not just plain stupid, or so smug and intellectually arrogant as to be rigid in misconceptions, will understand quite elevated things when people say or write them, and given some affection for knowledge, will retain them and can later confirm them. Bad and good people alike can do this.

Even though bad people may at heart deny the divine matters proper to the church, they can still understand them, talk about them, preach them, and support them in learned treatises. When they are left to themselves in thought, though, their hellish love leads them into contrary ideas, and they deny such principles. We can see from this that discernment can be in spiritual light even when intentionality is not in spiritual warmth.

It also follows from this that discernment cannot lead intentionality, or that wisdom cannot produce love. Wisdom can only teach and show the way, teaching how we are to live and showing the path we are to follow. It follows further that intentionality leads discernment and manages to have it work with it as one, and that the love within discernment calls "wisdom" whatever in discernment agrees with it.

We will see below that intentionality does nothing on its own, apart from discernment. Everything that it does it accomplishes in conjunction with discernment. However, it is intentionality that adopts discernment into alliance with itself by flowing into it. The reverse process does not occur.

245. We must now describe the inflow of light into the three levels of the life of the mind within human beings.

The forms within a person recipient of warmth and light or love and wisdom—which are as stated, threefold or of three levels—are transparent from birth, and let spiritual light through the way clear glass lets natural light through. This is why a person can be raised all the way to the third level as far as his wisdom is concerned. However, these forms are not opened except as spiritual warmth unites itself to spiritual light, or love to wisdom. By means of this union, the transparent forms of the second level are opened.

This is analogous to the light and warmth of this world's sun for plants on earth. Winter light, which is just as bright as summer light, opens nothing in seeds or in trees. But when the warmth of spring unites itself to the light, then it makes things open. The analogy holds because spiritual light corresponds to natural light, and spiritual warmth corresponds to natural warmth.

246. The only way to gain this spiritual warmth is to flee evil deeds as sins, and then to look to the Lord. For as long as a person is involved in evil things, he is involved in a love of them, actually in a craving for them, and the love of what is evil and the craving are, as loves, the opposites of spiritual love and affection. This former love and craving can be put aside only by fleeing from evil deeds as sins. And since people cannot flee from them on their own, but need the Lord, they must look to Him.

So when people, relying on the Lord, do flee from them, then their love of what is evil and its warmth is put aside, and is replaced by a love of what is good and its warmth. By this means, a higher level is opened.

In fact, the Lord flows in from above and opens it, uniting then the love or spiritual warmth to the wisdom or spiritual light. As a result of this bonding, people begin to blossom like trees in springtime.

247. It is by this inflow of spiritual light into all three levels of mind that a human being is differentiated from animals. Beyond what animals can do, humans can think logically, see true things on a spiritual level as well as a natural level, and on seeing them can acknowledge them and can therefore be reformed and regenerated.

The ability to receive spiritual light is what we mean by the rationality discussed above, which is given to everyone by the Lord and never taken away, since if it were taken away, there would be no possibility of reformation. It is in consequence of the ability called rationality that people can not only think, but can even talk on the basis of thought, unlike animals. Then in consequence of their other ability, called freedom (also discussed above), people can do the things they are thinking in their discernment.

248. In the preceding pages, we have shown that there are three levels of the human mind, which are called natural, spiritual, and heavenly, and that these levels within a person can be opened in sequence. Then we have shown that the natural level is opened first, and that later if the individual flees from evil deeds as sins, the spiritual level is opened, and finally—the heavenly level.

Since these levels opened in sequence, depending on a person's life, it follows that the two higher levels may also not be opened, and the person may then stay on the natural level, which is the lowest [*ultimus*].

It is recognized even in this world that there is a natural person and a spiritual person, or an outer person and an inner person. But people do not realize than a natural person becomes spiritual by the opening of some higher level within, that this opening is accomplished by a spiritual life, which is a life in accord with divine precepts, and that, failing a life according to these precepts, the person remains natural.

249. There are three kinds of natural person. The first kind comprises people who do not know anything about divine precepts. The second comprises people who know such precepts exist, but give no thought to living by them. The third comprises people who despise and reject them.

As for the *first category*—the people who do not know anything about divine precepts—they cannot help remaining natural, since they cannot be taught by themselves. Every individual is taught about divine precepts by other people who know them as matters of their religion, and not by direct revelation. On this, see the *Doctrine of Sacred Scripture*, nn. 114-118.

As for the people in the *second category*—the people who know that divine precepts exist, but give no thought to living by them—they too remain natural, concerned only with matters of the world and the flesh. After death, they become attendants and servants depending on the service they can perform for the people who are spiritual. For the natural person is an attendant and servant, while the spiritual person is a master and lord.

As for people in the *third category*—the people who despise and reject divine precepts—they not only remain natural, but become sense-oriented in proportion to their distaste and rejection. Sense-oriented people are the lowest kind of natural people, incapable of thought elevated above the deceptive appearances of the physical senses. After death, they are in hell.

250. Since people in this world do not know what a spiritual person or a natural person is, with many people calling someone spiritual who is only natural and vice versa, we need to discuss the following topics separately.

> (i) *What a natural person is, and what a spiritual person is.*
>
> (ii) *The nature of a natural person in whom the spiritual level has been opened.*
>
> (iii) *The nature of a natural person in whom the spiritual level has not been opened, but has not been closed off.*
>
> (iv) *The nature of a natural person in whom the spiritual level has been completely closed off.*
>
> (v) *Finally, the nature of the distinction between the life of a simply natural person and the life of an animal*

(i)*What a natural person is, and what a spiritual person is.*

251. A person is not a person by virtue of face and body, but by virtue of discernment and purposing. So when we refer to a natural person or a spiritual person, we mean that person's discernment and purposing, specifying them as either natural or spiritual.

In discernment and purposing a natural person is like the natural world, and can even be called a world or a microcosm. Further, in discernment and purposing a spiritual person is like the spiritual world, and can even be called that world, or a heaven. We can see then that a natural person, being a natural world in a kind of image, loves things proper to the natural world, and that a spiritual person, being a spiritual world in a kind of image, loves things proper to that world or heaven.

A spiritual person does, of course, love the natural world too, but only as a master loves his attendant, who enables him to do useful things. It is by useful activities that a natural person comes to resemble a spiritual one, which happens when the natural person feels a delight in useful activity from a spiritual source. This kind of natural person could be called "natural-spiritual."

A spiritual person loves things which are true on a spiritual level. Such a person loves not only to know and discern them, but also intends them. In contrast, a natural person loves to say and do that kind of truth. "Doing something true" is fulfilling a use.

This subordination stems from the bond between the spiritual world and the natural world. For anything visible and occurring in the natural world has its cause in the spiritual world.

We conclude from this that a spiritual person is quite different from a natural person, and that the only kind of communication that occurs between them is that between cause and effect.

(ii) *The nature of a natural person in whom the spiritual level has been opened.*

252. This we can see from the foregoing, adding that a natural person is a complete person once the spiritual level within has been opened. Then he or she is actually associated with angels in heaven, is at the

same time associated with people in this world, and is on both respects living under the Lord's guidance. In fact, the spiritual person draws commandments through the Word from the Lord, and follows them through by means of the natural person.

Natural people whose spiritual level has been opened are not aware of thinking and acting from that spiritual person. It seems as though they are doing this on their own. They are not however doing this on their own, but from the Lord.

Neither do natural people whose spiritual level has been opened realize that, by means of their spiritual person, they are in heaven, even though their spiritual person is surrounded by angels of heaven. Sometimes they are even visible to angels, but since they retreat to their natural person, they disappear shortly.

Neither do natural people whose spiritual level has been opened realize that their spiritual mind is filled with thousands of mysteries of wisdom and thousands of delights of love from the Lord, and that they will become involved in them after their death, when they become angels.

The reason a natural person does not realize all this is that the communication between the natural and the spiritual person occurs by means of correspondences; and communication by means of correspondences is perceived in the discernment only as truths are seen in light, and is perceived in the purposing only as useful activities are carried out because of an affection for them.

(iii)

253. *The nature of a natural person in whom the spiritual level has not been opened, but has not been closed off.*

The spiritual level has not been opened but still has not been closed off in people who have lived a life of

144

some charity, but have been aware of very little that is actually true. The reason is, that this level is opened by the uniting of love and wisdom, or of warmth with light. Spiritual love or warmth alone does not open it, nor does spiritual wisdom or light alone—it takes both, united to each other.

So if there is no awareness of things genuinely true, which are the source of wisdom or light, love has no power to open this level. It only keeps it susceptible to being opened. This is what we mean by its not being closed off. There is a similar situation in the vegetable kingdom, in that warmth alone does not make seeds and trees sprout, but warmth in conjunction with light does so.

We need to realize that everything true is a matter of spiritual light, and everything good a matter of spiritual warmth; also that what is good uses things true to open the spiritual level. For what is good uses things true to accomplish what is useful, and useful activities are the good results of love, drawing their essence from this union of what is good and what is true.

As for the eventual lot after death of people whose spiritual level has not been opened but has not been closed off, since they are natural people finally and not spiritual, they are in the lowest parts of heaven, where they sometimes have a hard time of it. Or they are on the fringes of a somewhat higher heaven, where they live in a kind of twilight. For as already stated, in heaven and in each of its communities, the light lessens as one moves from the center toward the borders. At the center are people especially involved in things divinely true, and at the borders people involved in little of what is true. And people are involved in little of what is true if all they know in religion is that God exists and that the Lord suffered for their sakes. They are aware too that charity and faith are essential elements of the church, but they do not take the trouble to know what faith is and what charity is. Yet essentially, faith is truth, and truth is many-sided; and charity is every act of service which a person does because of the Lord. People do this because of the Lord when they flee from evil deeds as sins.

It is just as we have already said—the purpose wholly accounts for the means, and the purpose through the means wholly accounts for the results. The purpose is charity or the good; the means is faith or the true; and the result is good works or useful activities.

We can see from this that no more of charity can be carried over into deeds than is united to these true things which we refer to as faith. These are the means by which charity enters into deeds, and gives them their quality.

(iv)

254. *The nature of a natural person in whom the spiritual level has been completely closed off.*

The spiritual level is closed off in people who, as to their lives, are involved in evil pursuits, and is even more so in people who are involved in matters of falsity because of their evil pursuits.

There is a similar situation in a small nerve fiber, which contracts at the slightest touch of something alien. There is a similar situation too with each motor fiber of a muscle, a muscle itself, or even the whole body at the touch of something hard or cold. This is what is done within a person to the substances and forms of the spiritual level by evil and false things, which are in fact alien.

Actually, since the spiritual level is in heaven's form, it allows nothing to enter but what is good, or is true because of what is good. These are of congenial nature, while things evil, or false because of what is evil, are alien.

This level contracts, and is closed off by contracting, especially in people who in this world are involved in self-love and in a love of domineering, because this love is the opposite of love for the Lord. It is also closed off in people whose love of the world results in a mad craving to get hold of the goods of other people, but this case is not so severe.

The reason these loves close the spiritual level is that they are the sources of everything evil. The contraction or closing off of this level is like a spiral twisting backwards. This is why, after this level is closed off, it reflects heaven's light back. So below it, there is gloom instead of heaven's light. Accordingly, the truth which is in heaven's light causes [lit. "becomes"] nausea.

In people like this, not only is this level itself closed off, so too is the higher part of the natural level which we call rational. Eventually, only the lowest part of the natural level stands open, the part called sensory. This is next to the world and the outer physical senses, and from then on these senses are the basis for this person's thinking, talking, and calculating.

Natural people who have become sense-oriented by reason of evil deeds and consequent falsities, do not look like people in the spiritual world in heaven's light. They look instead like monsters, with indented noses as well. They have pushed-in noses because a nose corresponds to a perception of what is true. They cannot bear a ray of heaven's light. The only light such people have in their caves is like the light from embers or glowing coals.

We can see from this the identity and nature of the people in whom the spiritual level has been closed off.

(v)

255. *The nature of the distinction between the life of a natural person and the life of an animal.*

We will be discussing this distinction later, when we deal specifically with life. Here we may simply state that the distinction is this. A human being has three levels of mind, or three levels of discernment and purposing. These levels can be opened in sequence. And since they are transparent, people can be raised into heaven's light as far as their discernment is concerned, and see not only civil and moral, but even spiritual truths. From the many things they have seen, they can come to true and orderly conclusions, and keep perfecting their discernment to eternity.

Animals, however, do not have the two higher levels. They have only the natural levels, which, apart from the higher levels, afford no possibility of thinking about any civil, moral, or spiritual subject.

Further, since these natural levels are not susceptible of being opened and therefore raised into a higher light, animals cannot think in a sequential pattern. They think in a simultaneous pattern, which is not really thinking, but is rather acting by a knowledge that corresponds to their love. And since they cannot think analytically and survey their lower thought from some higher vantage point, they cannot talk, but rather make sounds suitable to the knowledge that belongs to their love.

However, sense-oriented people (the lowest kind of natural person) differ from animals only in their ability to fill their memory with data and to think and talk on that basis. This they derive from an ability possessed by every human being, namely the ability to discern what is true if they want to. This is the distinctive ability. Many people though, by misusing this ability, make themselves lower than animals.

SEEN OUT OF CONTEXT [*IN SE*], THE NATURAL LEVEL OF THE HUMAN MIND IS A CONTINUUM, BUT BY CORRESPONDENCE WITH THE TWO HIGHER LEVELS, IT SEEMS, AS IT IS RAISED, TO HAVE DISTINCT LEVELS

256. Even though this is virtually incomprehensible to anyone who does not yet have access to a knowledge of vertical levels, we still need to unveil it because it is a matter of angelic wisdom. Even though this wisdom cannot enter a natural person's thinking the way it does an angel's, it can still be grasped by discernment when this is raised all the way to the level of light angels are involved in. Discernment can actually be raised that far, and enlightened to the extent that it is raised.

The enlightenment of the natural mind, however, does not climb up by distinct levels; it rather increases on a continuous level. Then, as it increases, it is enlightened from within as a result of the light proper to the two higher levels.

To understand how this happens, we need a perception of vertical levels—that one is above another, and that the natural level, the final one, is like a general covering for the two higher levels. As the natural level is raised toward a higher level, then, the higher level exerts itself into the more outward natural level, and enlightens it.

As a result of the light from the higher levels, a kind of enlightenment occurs from within. However, this is received by the natural level, which embraces and surrounds it, along a continuum—brighter and clearer as it rises. That is, the natural level is enlightened from within, as a result of the light of the higher levels, according to distinct levels; but within the natural level itself, this enlightenment occurs on a continuum.

We can therefore see that as long as a person is living in this world and is thereby involved in the natural level, he cannot be raised *into* the actual kind of wisdom that exists in angels, but only into a higher light *up to* [the light of] angels, receiving enlightenment from their light, which flows in and shines from within.

But this I cannot describe any more clearly. It is better grasped by attending to its results, since when there is some prior knowledge of causes, results present causes within themselves in the light, and thereby illumine them.

257. The following are results. (1) The natural mind can be raised up to heaven's light, which surrounds angels, and can perceive in a natural fashion what angels perceive spiritually—can perceive this less fully, that is. Nevertheless, the human natural mind cannot be raised into actual angelic light. (2) By means of an uplifted natural mind, a person can think and even talk with angels. In such cases, though, the thought and speech of the angels flow into the natural thought and speech of the person, and not vice versa. So angels talk with a person in a natural language, the person's own common tongue. (3) This occurs by reason of a spiritual inflow into what is natural, and not by reason of any natural inflow into what is spiritual. (4) Human wisdom—which is natural as long as a person is living in a natural world—can never be raised into angelic wisdom but only into a kind of reflection of it. This is because the raising of the natural mind happens along a continuum, from darkness to light, so to speak, or from cruder to purer. However, people whose spiritual level has been opened do become involved in this wisdom when they die. They can also become involved in it through the quiescence of their physical senses, when there is an inflow from above into the spiritual elements of their minds. (5) The human natural mind is composed of both spiritual and natural substances. Thought occurs because of the spiritual substances, but not because of the natural substances. These latter substances fade away when a person dies; but the spiritual substances do not. So after death, when a person becomes a spirit or an angel, the very same mind retains the same form

it had in the world. (6) The natural substances of this mind, which we have just described as fading away at death, form a skin-like case for the spiritual body which a spirit or angel inhabits. It is by means of this kind of case, derived from the natural world, that their spiritual bodies have permanence, the natural being the final vessel. This is why there is no spirit or angel who was not born human.

We append these secrets of angels' wisdom here in order to provide knowledge about the nature of the natural mind within human beings, which will be further discussed below.

258. Every individual is born with an ability to discern elements of truth all the way to the inmost level, where angels of the third heaven live. In fact, as human discernment rises along its continuum, around the two higher levels, it receives the light of the wisdom of those levels in the manner described above (n. 256).

This is why people can become rational in proportion to their minds' ascent. If their minds are raised up to the third level, they attain a rationality derived from the third level. If they are raised up to the second level, they attain a rationality derived from the second level. And if they are not raised, they are rational on the first level. We say that they attain a rationality from these levels because the natural level is the general recipient of their light.

The reason people do not attain the highest level of rationality is that love, a matter of purposing, cannot be raised up in the same way as wisdom, which is a matter of discernment. Love, a matter of purposing, is raised up only by fleeing from evil deeds as sins, and then by doing good deeds of charity, which are useful activities that the Lord then enables the person to fulfill.

So if love, the matter of purposing, is not raised up at the same time, then no matter how high the wisdom (a matter of discernment) may rise, it will ultimately slide back down to its own love. This is why people are rational only on the first level unless their love is raised into a spiritual level at the same time.

This enables us to conclude that the human rational capacity seems to comprise three levels—a rational capacity from what is heavenly, a rational capacity from what is spiritual, and a rational capacity from what is natural. We may also conclude that rationality, which is an ability that can be raised up, exists within people whether it is raised up or not.

259. We have stated that every individual is born with this ability, namely rationality. We mean, however, every individual whose outward elements have not been damaged by circumstances—be it in the womb or by injury after birth, by head wounds, or by insane love bursting forth and loosening all restraint. For these people, the rational capacity cannot be raised up. Actually, for people like this, the life proper to their purposing and discernment does not have any boundaries to rest in, so arranged that their life can control behavior in an orderly fashion on the most outward level. Life does act within outward limits, but not because of the outward limits. On the impossibility of raising the rational ability of infants and children, see below (n. 266, end).

THE NATURAL MIND, THE ENVELOPE AND VESSEL OF THE HIGHER LEVELS OF THE HUMAN MIND, IS REACTIVE. IF THE HIGHER LEVELS ARE NOT OPENED, IT ACTS COUNTER TO THEM; WHILE IF THEY ARE OPENED, IT COOPERATES WITH THEM

260. In the last section, we showed that the natural mind, being on the final level, surrounds and encloses the spiritual mind and the heavenly mind, which are higher in level. Now it is appropriate to show that the

natural mind reacts to the higher or more inward minds. The reason it reacts is that it does surround, enclose, and contain them, which could not happen without some reaction. For if it did not react, the more inward elements would either remain enclosed and atrophy, or would force their way out and dissipate.

It would be as though the coverings of the human body did not react, and the viscera which are the inner parts of the body fell out and so scattered. Or it would be as though the membranes that envelop a muscle's motor fibers did not react to the force of those fibers as they acted. Not only would the action cease, even the whole inner fabric would unravel.

The same principle applies for every final level of [a series of] vertical levels. It therefore applies for the natural mind relative to the higher levels. For as we have already stated, there are three levels to the human mind—natural, spiritual, and heavenly—and the natural mind is on the final level.

Another reason the natural mind reacts to the spiritual mind is that the natural mind consists of spiritual world substances as well as natural world substances, as already stated (n. 257). Natural world substances react inherently to spiritual world substances. Actually, natural world substances are intrinsically lifeless, and are activated from the outside by spiritual world substances. Lifeless substances which are activated from the outside have an inherent resistance and therefore an inherent reaction.

We can thus conclude that the natural person reacts to the spiritual person, and that there is conflict. It makes no difference whether we refer to the natural and the spiritual person, or to the natural and the spiritual mind.

261. All this enables us to determine that if a spiritual mind has been closed, its natural mind is constantly working against the elements of that

spiritual mind. It is afraid that something will flow in from it and disturb its own states. Everything that flows in through the spiritual mind is from heaven, since the spiritual mind is a heaven in form. Everything that flows into the natural mind is from this world, since the natural mind is a "this world" in form. It therefore follows that when the spiritual mind has been closed, the natural mind reacts against all heaven's influences, and admits only those elements that provide it with means for acquiring and keeping worldly things. And whenever heavenly things are used by a natural mind as means to its own ends, then even though those means appear heavenly, they become natural. The purpose actually changes their quality; they actually become like the data of a natural person, with no trace of life within them.

However, since heavenly things cannot be united to natural ones so as to act as a unit, they separate, and in purely natural people the heavenly things come to rest outside, in a circumference around the natural things within. This is why purely natural people can say and proclaim heavenly matters and even imitate them in behavior, even though they are inwardly thinking contrary to them. This latter they do when they are alone, the former when they are in company. But more on this below.

262. When a natural mind (or person) loves itself and the world supremely, then from an inborn reaction it acts against the characteristics of the spiritual mind or person. It feels pleasure then in all kinds of evil deeds—in acts of adultery, fraud, vengeance, blasphemy, and the like. Further, it then recognizes nature as the creatress of the universe, and confirms everything by its rational capacity. Once this confirmation is accomplished, it takes the good and true elements of heaven and the church and either corrupts or stifles or distorts them, eventually com

ing to avoid them, to hold them in distaste, or to hate them.

This occurs in people's spirits, and shows in their bodies to the extent that they dare to talk with others without fear of losing the reputation they need for prestige and profit.

When people are like this, then step by step their spiritual minds become more and more tightly closed. It is the use of false things to confirm what is evil that primarily effects the closure. This is why the evil and false things that have been confirmed cannot be uprooted. They are uprooted only in this world, by means of repentance.

263. Completely different, though, is the state of a natural mind when its spiritual mind has been opened. Then the natural mind arranges itself in submission to the spiritual mind, and obeys it. In fact, the spiritual mind, from above or within, is acting into the natural mind and taking away the elements there that react. It is adapting itself to the elements which are cooperative. So the excessive reaction is taken away step by step.

We need to realize that action and reaction occur in the greatest and smallest parts of the universe, both the living parts and the dead. This is the source of the balance of all things. It is lost when action exceeds reaction or vice versa.

The same principle applies to the natural mind and the spiritual mind. When a natural mind acts out of the pleasures of its love and the comfort of its thinking (which are intrinsically evil and false), then the reaction of that natural mind sets aside the things proper to its spiritual mind. It blocks the doorway against their entry, it works things so that the source of behavior lies in the kinds of thing that agree with its own reaction. This causes an action and reaction of the natural mind, opposed to the action and reac tion of its spiritual mind. This results in a closing of the spiritual mind like a spiral twisting backwards.

If however, the spiritual mind is opened, then the action and reaction of the natural mind are reversed. In fact, the spiritual mind is then acting from above or within, using all the while the elements within the natural mind that have been arranged in submission to it, from the more inward to the more outward. It re-twists the spiral which the action and reaction of the natural mind are in. Actually, this latter mind is from birth in opposition to the characteristics of its spiritual mind. It derives this genetically from its parents, as is known.

This is what that change of state is like which we call re-formation and re-generation. We may liken the state of a natural mind before reformation to a spiral twisting and bending itself around downwards, while after reformation we may liken it to a spiral twisting and bending itself around upwards. So before reformation, people are looking down toward hell, while after reformation they are looking up toward heaven.

EVIL ORIGINATES IN THE MISUSE OF ABILITIES WHICH ARE PROPER TO HUMAN BEINGS, AND ARE CALLED RATIONALITY AND FREEDOM

264. By "rationality" we mean the ability to discern what is true and hence what is false, and what is good and hence what is evil. By "freedom" we mean the ability to think, intend, and do these things freely.

We can draw several conclusions from material presented above, and we will offer further support for them below. These conclusions are the following. Every individual has these two abilities from creation and therefore from birth, and they come from the Lord. They are not taken away from us. They are the source of the appearance that we think, talk, intend and act, in apparent independence. The Lord lives in these two abilities in every individual. This union is why we live to eternity. These abilities are the means and the only means of our ability to be reformed and regenerated. Finally, it is by these abilities that humans are differentiated from animals.

265. As to the fact that evil originates in the misuse of these abilities, we will discuss it in the following sequence:

(i) *Evil people enjoy these two abilities just as good people do.*

(ii) *Evil people misuse them to support evil and false things, while good people use them to support good and true things.*

(iii) *Evil and false things confirmed within individuals persist, becoming part of their love and therefore of their life.*

(iv) *Things that have become part of the love and the life are born into offspring.*

(v) *All evil things, both inborn and acquired, dwell in the natural mind.*

266. (i) *Evil people enjoy these two faculties just as good people do.*

We have explained in the last section that the natural mind, as far as its discernment is concerned, can be raised all the way up to the light which angels of the third heaven are in, can see truths, recognize them, and then say them.

This enables us to see that, since the natural mind can so be raised, evil people as well as good ones enjoy the ability we call rationality. And since the natural mind can be raised that far, we can see that evil people can also think and say things that are true. As for their ability to intend and do such things, though, even though they may not actually intend and do them, this is witnessed by both reason and experience.

Reason asks, "Who is incapable of intending and doing what he or she is thinking?" If people do not intend and do, perhaps it is because they have no love to intend and do. The ability to intend and do is freedom, which the Lord gives to every individual. The absence of intending and doing when this is possible stems from a love of evil which repels. However, this love can be resisted, and many people do in fact resist it.

I have often had this confirmed *by experience* in the spiritual world. I have listened to evil spirits who were devils inside, who in the world had thrown out the true elements of heaven and the church. When their curiosity (which everyone is involved in from childhood) was aroused by that glory that surrounds every love with a kind of fiery radiance, they perceived mysteries of angelic wisdom, just as well as did those good spirits who were inwardly angels. Not only that, the devilish spirits said that they could even intend and do what these mysteries enjoined, but that they did not want to.

I could see from this that evil as well as good people have the ability called freedom. You may inquire within your own heart, and will observe that this is true. The reason a person can intend is that the Lord, the source of this ability, is constantly granting the possibility. For we stated above that the Lord dwells in these two abilities within each individual—in the ability or power, which is being able to intend.

As far as the ability to understand is concerned which we call rationality, this does not occur in individuals until their mind has reached its maturity. In the meanwhile, it is like a seed in an unripe fruit, which cannot open in the ground or sprout in the field. Nor does this ability occur in the people described in n. 259 above.

267. (ii) *Evil people misuse these abilities to support evil and false things, while good people use them to support good and true things.*

From the cognitive ability called rationality and the voluntary ability called freedom, we derive the ability to support whatever we want to. In fact, natural people can raise their discernment into higher light as far as they want to. But people involved in evil and false concerns do not raise it higher than the upper region of their natural mind, rarely to the region of their spiritual mind.

This is because they are involved in the pleasures of the love of their natural mind, and if they rise above that, they lose the pleasure of its love. If they rise still further, and see the true things that contradict their life pleasures or the premises of their own intelligence, then they may falsify them, or ignore them and set them aside contemptuously, or they may file them in their memory to be of service to their life's love or to the pride of their own intelligence, as tools [*pro mediis*].

We can readily see that natural people can support anything they want to, from the number of heresies in Christendom, each one maintained by its own adherents.

As for the possibility of defending anything evil and false, no matter what kind, who is not aware of this? It can be maintained, and is inwardly maintained by evil people, that God does not exist and that nature is everything and created itself, or that religion is only a tool for keeping simple souls in chains, or that human foresight is everything and that divine providence is nothing more than maintaining the universe in the pattern in which it was created, or that acts of murder, adultery, theft, fraud, and vengeance are quite legitimate, according to Machiavelli and his followers.

Natural people can support these and many similar opinions, nay, they can fill books with supporting arguments. And once they are supported, these false opinions stand forth in their own illusory light, while true ones seem to be in such darkness that they are invisible except as ghosts at night.

In short, take the falsest opinion, put it in the form of a hypothesis, and say to clever people, "Support this," and they will support it to the utter snuffing out of the light of truth. But lay aside the supporting arguments, back off, and look at that same hypothesis on the basis of your own rationality, and you will see its false nature in its own distorted form.

On this basis, we can conclude that people can misuse those two abilities the Lord has placed within them, to support all kinds of evil and false notions. No animal can do this, because no animal enjoys these abilities. So animals are born into their own life pattern and into all the information proper to their natural love, while humans are not.

268. *(iii) Evil and false things confirmed within people persist, becoming part of their love and therefore of their life.*

Acts of supporting what is evil and false are acts of dispersing what is good and true; and if they intensify, they become acts of rejection, since the evil displaces and rejects the good, and the false does the same to the true. As a result, acts of supporting what is evil and false are acts of closing off heaven, for everything good and true flows in from the Lord through heaven. Once heaven is closed, the person is in hell, in a community there where evil and false things of like nature are in control, a hell he or she is thereafter unable to leave.

I have been allowed to talk with some people who centuries ago had inwardly supported the false tenets of their own religions, and have seen them persisting in the same beliefs they were involved in in this world. This is because everything we maintain within ourselves becomes part of our love and of our life. It becomes part of our love because it becomes part of our purposing and discernment, and purposing and discernment make up everyone's life. Once it becomes part of our life, it becomes part not only of our whole mind but of our whole body as well.

We can see, then, that people who maintain themselves in evil and false [attitudes] have this nature from head to toe. And once the whole person has this nature, there is no reverse process by which he or she can be brought back into the opposite state and thereby rescued from hell.

It is possible, on the basis of these facts and others presented earlier in this section, to see what the source of evil is.

269. (iv) *Things that have become part of the love and the life are born into offspring.*

It is recognized that people are born into involvement in evil, and that they derive this by heredity from their parents. Some people do believe that it is not from their parents but through their parents from Adam, but this is wrong. Individuals derive this from their fathers, from whom they derive their soul, which puts on a body within the mother. Actually, the sperm that comes from the father is the first recipient of life, but it is the same kind of recipient that existed within the father. It is in fact in the form of his love, and everyone's love is consistent in its greatest and smallest forms. There is within it a striving toward the human form, which it does gradually realize. It follows from this that the evils we call hereditary come from the fathers—from grandfathers and great-grandfathers in sequence, then, branching off into their descendants.

270. (v) *All evil things, both inborn and acquired, dwell in the natural mind.*

The reason evil and consequent false things dwell in the natural mind is that in form or in reflection, this mind is this world. The spiritual mind, in contrast, is in form or in reflection a heaven. There can be no room in heaven for anything evil. So from birth, this latter mind is not open, but has merely the potentiality of being opened.

Further, the natural mind gets its form in part from the substances of the natural world, but the spiritual mind gets its form from the substances of the spiritual world alone, and is preserved in its purity by the Lord in order that individuals may become human. They are actually born animals, but become people.

The natural mind is curved into spirals from right to left, while the spiritual mind is curved into spirals from left to right, so that the two minds are turned against each other, in reverse. This is a clue that evil dwells in the natural mind, and works from that base against the spiritual mind. Further, spiraling from right to left is downward and therefore toward hell, while spiraling from left to right moves upward, and therefore toward heaven.

The following experience has enabled me to see the truth of this. Evil spirits cannot turn their bodies from left to right, only from right to left, while good spirits have great difficulty turning their bodies from right to left, but easily turn them from left to right. The turning follows the flow of the more inward elements of the mind.

IN EVERY RESPECT, EVIL AND FALSE THINGS ARE DIRECTLY OPPOSED TO THINGS GOOD AND TRUE, BECAUSE EVIL AND FALSE THINGS ARE DEVILISH AND HELLISH, WHILE GOOD AND TRUE THINGS ARE GODLY AND HEAVENLY.

271. When people hear that "evil" and "good" are opposites and that the falsity derived from evil and the truth derived from good are opposites, they recognize the fact. But since people involved in evil feel and perceive only that evil is good (in fact, the evil pleases their senses, especially sight and hearing, and consequently pleases their thoughts and therefore their [deeper] perceptions), while they do indeed admit that evil and good are opposites, still once they are involved in something evil, its pleasure leads them to call evil good, and vice versa.

Let me take an example. If people have misused their freedom so as to think and do what is evil, they call that freedom; and its opposite, which is thinking what is good because it is intrinsically good, they call slavery. Yet this latter is truly free, while the former is servile. People who love acts of adultery call committing adultery free, and call the prohibition of adultery servile. They actually feel pleasure in raw sex and discomfort in chastity. People involved in a love of domineering because of self-love feel in that love a life pleasure that surpasses all other kinds of pleasure. So they call everything that belongs to that love "good," and label "evil" everything that goes against it. Yet the opposite is the case.

So even though everyone admits that evil and good are opposites, still people involved in evil things nourish an inverted concept of the opposition, and only people involved in good things nourish an accurate concept. No one can see what is good while involved in what is evil, but a person who is involved in something good can see what is evil. The evil is below, in a cave, so to speak, while the good is above, as if on a mountain.

272. Now since many people do not know what evil is like and that it is diametrically opposed to what is good, even though it is important to know

this, we need to present the matter, in the following sequence.

(i) *A natural mind involved in evil and false things is a form and reflection of hell.*

(ii) *A natural mind which is a form and reflection of hell descends by three levels.*

(iii) *The three levels of a natural mind which is a form and reflection of hell stand in opposition to the three levels of the spiritual mind, which is a form and reflection of heaven.*

(iv) *A natural mind which is a hell is in every respect directly opposed to a spiritual mind, which is a heaven.*

273. (i) *A natural mind involved in evil and false things is a form and reflection of hell.*

We cannot here describe what the natural mind is like in its own substantial form in a person, or what it is like in its own form, made up of substances from both worlds interwoven in the brain, where that mind, in its first principles, dwells. We will present a universal concept of that form below when we have to deal with the correspondence of mind and body.

Here we need only say something about its form in reference to its states and their changes, which are means to various kinds of perception, thought, intent, and purpose, and derived phenomena. For a natural mind that is involved in evil things and consequently in false ones is in these respects [perception, etc.] a form and reflection of hell. This form presupposes a substantial form as its subject. Actually, changes of state cannot occur without a substantial form as their subject, just as sight cannot occur without an eye, or hearing without an ear.

On this form or image by which a natural mind reflects hell: that form and reflection are of such nature that the ruling love and its cravings (which are the all-encompassing state of this mind) is in the position of the Devil in hell, while the false thoughts that arise from that ruling love are like the Devil's gang. This is exactly what the Devil and his gang mean in the Word.

The situation is similar. For in hell, a love of domineering derived from self-love is the ruling love. It is there called the Devil; and the false affections, together with the thoughts that arise from that love, are called its gang. The same holds true in each community of hell, with variations like the particular variations within a single genus.

A natural mind involved in evil and consequent false things is in a similar form. So natural people of this kind come after death into communities of hell that resemble themselves, and then act in unison with those communities in each and every respect. They have actually entered their own form—that is, the state of their own mind.

There is another love too, called Satan, subordinate to the former love called the Devil. This is a love of possessing others' property no matter what evil devices it requires. Various forms of devious malice and cunning are its gang. People in this latter hell are collectively called satans, while people in the former hell are collectively called devils. The ones who are not working under cover there do not reject their name. This is why the hells as a whole are called the Devil and Satan.

The reason two hells are marked off, broadly, according to these two loves, is that all the heavens are marked off into two kingdoms, heavenly and spiritual, according to two loves. The devilish hell corresponds inversely to the heavenly kingdom, while the satanic hell corresponds inversely to the spiritual kingdom.

The reader may see in the book *Heaven and Hell* (nn. 20-28) that the heavens are divided into two kingdoms, heavenly and spiritual.

The reason a natural mind of this sort is a hell in form, is that every spiritual form assembles itself in its largest and smallest occurrences. This is why every angel is a heaven in a smaller form, as has also been shown in the book *Heaven and Hell* (nn. 51-58). It follows from this also that each person or spirit who is a devil or a satan is a hell in a smaller form.

274. (ii) *A natural mind which is a form or reflection of hell descends by three levels.*

The reader may see above (nn. 222-229) that there are two kinds of level, called vertical and horizontal. This therefore includes the natural mind in its largest and smallest forms. Here we are dealing with vertical levels.

By virtue of its twin abilities called rationality and freedom, the natural mind exists in a state which enables it to climb by three levels and to descend by three levels. It climbs as a result of good and true things, and descends as a result of evil and false things. And when it climbs, the lower levels which lead toward hell are closed off; while when it descends, the higher levels which lead toward heaven are closed off. This is because they are involved in a reaction.

These three higher and lower levels are neither open nor closed in a newborn. Actually, at that point people are in ignorance of what is good and true and of what is evil and false. But as they involve themselves in such matters, the levels are opened or closed off on the one side or the other. When they are opened toward hell, the highest or most inward place is occupied by a ruling love which is a matter of purposing. The second or middle place is occupied by a thinking about what is false, which is a matter of discernment resulting from that love. The lowest place is occupies by the conclusion love reaches through thinking, or, which purposing reaches through discernment.

It is the same in this instance as with the vertical levels discussed above, which in proper sequence are goal [end], means [cause], and result [effect], or are like a first, an intermediate, and a final goal [end].

The downward progress of these levels is toward the body. As a result, they become cruder as they descend, and become material and carnal. If true elements from the Word have attended upon the formation of the second level, they are falsified as a result of the first level which is a love of what is evil, and they become servants and slaves. This enables us to determine the quality of the true elements of the church drawn from the Word in people who are involved in a love of what is evil, or whose natural mind is a hell in form. Specifically, since they are serving a devil as means, they are profaned. In fact, a love of what is evil, ruling in a natural mind which is a hell, is a devil, as stated above.

275. (iii) *The three levels of a natural mind which is a form and reflection of hell stand in opposition to the three levels of the spiritual mind, which is a form and reflection of heaven.*

We have already demonstrated the existence of three levels of the mind, called natural, spiritual, and heavenly, and have shown that the human mind composed of these levels looks toward heaven and bends around in that direction. This enables us to see that when a natural mind looks downward and bends around toward hell, it too is composed of three levels, with each of its levels standing opposite to a level of the mind which is a heaven.

I have been able to see the truth of this clearly in what I have seen in the spiritual world—in there being three heavens marked off by three vertical levels and three hells marked off by three vertical levels or by three levels of depth. Further, the hells stand opposite to the heavens in every detail, with the deepest hell opposite the highest heaven, the intermediate hell opposite the intermediate heaven, and the uppermost hell opposite the lowest heaven.

The same holds true for a natural mind which is in the form of a hell; actually, spiritual forms are alike in their largest and their smallest manifestations.

The reason the heavens and the hells are in this kind of opposition is that their loves are in this kind of opposition. Love for the Lord and a consequent love toward the neighbor make up the most inward level in the heavens, while love of self and the world make up the most inward level in the hells. The wisdom and intelligence that derive from these heavenly loves make up the intermediate level in the heavens, while the stupidity and madness (which look like intelligence and wisdom) that derive from these [hellish] loves make up the intermediate level in the hells. The consequences of these two [heavenly] levels, which either come to rest in the memory as information or take limited form in behavior, make up the lowest level in the heavens; while the consequences of the two [hellish] loves, which become either information or behavior, make up the most outward level in the hells.

The following experience will illustrate how good and true elements of heaven turn into evil and false things in the hells—turn into their own opposites, then.

I heard something divine and true flow down from heaven into hell and I heard it gradually change into something false as it went lower, so that in the lowest hell it had changed into its absolute opposite. I could see from this that the hells, level by level, are in opposition to the heavens in everything good and true, and that these become evil and false by flowing into forms which are turned the other way. For it is recognized that everything that flows in is perceived and felt according to the recipient forms and their states.

The following experience has also shown me that they are turned into something opposite. I was allowed to see the hells in their arrangement relative to the heavens, and the people there looked upside down—head down and feet up. I was however informed that they still seem to themselves to be standing up on their feet—we might compare this with our southern hemisphere.

We may conclude from what these experiences teach that the three levels of a natural mind which is a hell in form and reflection, are the opposites of the three levels of a natural [sic] mind which is a heaven in form and reflection.

276. (iv) *A natural mind which is a hell is in every aspect directly opposed to the spiritual mind, which is a heaven.*

When loves are in opposition, then all the elements of perception come into opposition. In fact, everything else flows from love—which makes up a person's very life—the way a stream flows from its spring. Anything not derived from this source sets itself apart in the natural mind from the things that are so derived.

What comes from one's dominant love is in the center; the rest is off to the sides. If these latter are true elements of the church from the Word they are set even farther off to the sides and eventually blotted out, at which point the person (or the natural mind) feels what is evil as good and sees what is false as true and vice versa. This is why such people believe that malice is wisdom, madness intelligence, cunning prudence, and black arts brilliance. At this point too they pay no attention to the divine and heavenly issues of the church and of worship, but lay tremendous stress on physical and worldly matters.

So they turn the state of their life upside down. That is, they tend to assign to the soles of the feet the things that belong to the head, and to trample them, while they assign to the head the things that belong to the soles of the feet. This is how people change from being alive to being dead. We call people living if their minds are a heaven, and dead if their minds are a hell.

EVERYTHING THAT BELONGS TO THE THREE LEVELS OF THE NATURAL MIND IS ENCLOSED IN DEEDS PERFORMED BY PHYSICAL ACTIVITY

277. The knowledge of levels set forth in this chapter enables us to disclose the following *arcanum*—that all the elements of people's minds (or their purposing and discernment) are within their acts or deeds, enclosed very much the way observable and invisible elements are enclosed within a seed or a fruit or an egg. The actual deeds or acts look like nothing more than their outward appearance would indicate; however, there are countless elements within them. There are in fact the cooperating forces of the motor fibers of the whole body, and all the mental elements that arouse and govern these forces. As presented above, there are three levels of these mental elements.

And since this includes all elements of mind, it includes all elements of purposing or of the affections of a person's love, which constitute the first level; it includes all elements of discernment, or all the thoughts of the person's perception, which make up the second level; and it includes all elements of memory, or all concepts of the thought closest to speech which are taken from memory, which are the basis of the third level.

It is the focusing of these in behavior that gives rise to deeds, which seen as to outward form do not reveal the prior elements which do nevertheless actually lie within them.

On the outmost as the complex, vessel, and foundation of earlier levels, see nn. 209-216 above; and on vertical levels finding their full existence in the outmost, see nn. 217-221.

278. The reason physical behavior looks, to the eye, as simple and straightforward as seeds or fruit or eggs in their outward form, or as nutmeats and almonds in a shell, while they still do enclose all the prior elements that give rise to them, is that every outmost has an outer covering which sets it off from prior things. Each level too is surrounded by a covering that sets it off from the next. This means that elements of the first level are not experienced by the second level, nor elements of the second level by the third.

For example, the love that belongs to purposing (which is the mind's first level) is experienced within the discernment's wisdom (which is the mind's second level) only through a kind of pleasure in thinking about a given topic. The first level (which as stated is the love that belongs to purposing) is experienced in the memory's information (which is the third level) only through a kind of gratification in knowing and talking.

It follows then that a deed, which is a physical act, does enclose all these things, even though it looks like a simple unit in outward form.

279. This is supported by the following. The angels who are with an individual perceive in detail the elements of mind within an action, spiritual angels perceiving the elements of discernment within it and heavenly angels perceiving the elements of purposing within it. This seems like a paradox, but it is true nevertheless. We must however realize that the mental elements that have to do with a projected or actual matter are in the center, with the others round about according to their relevance.

Angels say that an individual's quality can be perceived from a single deed, but that different deeds give different likenesses of a person's love depending on the way that love is focused into affections and then into thoughts.

In a word, every action or deed of a spiritual person is to angels like a delicious, nourishing, and beautiful fruit, which gives flavor, nourishment, and pleasure when it is picked and eaten. On angels' possession of this kind or perception of people's actions and deeds, see n. 220 above.

280. The same holds true of people's speech. From the sound of their speech, angels recognize people's love, from the articulation of the sound they recognize their wisdom, and from the meaning of the words they recognize their information. They also say that these three levels are present in each word because a word is like a closed unit with its own sound, articulation, and meaning. Angels of the third heaven have informed me that they perceive from the individual words of a speaker in their series the general state of that individual's spirit and some specific states.

In *The Doctrine of the New Jerusalem on Holy Scripture*, it has been amply shown that there is within the individual words of the Word something spiritual which belongs to divine wisdom and something heavenly which belongs to divine love, and that these are perceived by angels when the Word is read reverently by people on earth.

281. This leads to the conclusion that all evil elements and all the evil-derived false elements are present in the deeds of a person whose natural mind is descending by three levels into hell; and that all the good elements and their true elements are present in the deeds of a person whose mind is climbing into heaven; and that angels perceive both of these situations from a single statement or action by an individual.

This is why it says in the Word that people must be judged according to their deeds, and that we must give account of the meaning of our words.

CHAPTER IV

[THE METHOD OF CREATION]

THE LORD FROM ETERNITY, WHO IS JEHOVAH, CREATED THE UNIVERSE IN ITS ENTIRETY FROM HIMSELF AND NOT FROM NOTHING

282. It is known world-wide and acknowledged by every wise person on the basis of an inward perception, that there is one God who is the creator of the universe. It is known from the Word that God the creator of the universe is called *Jehovah*, from the verb "to be," because He alone Is. In *The Doctrine of the New Jerusalem about the Lord*, we have shown with many passages from the Word that the Lord from eternity is that Jehovah.

Jehovah is called the Lord from eternity because Jehovah put on a human nature to save people from hell. At that time he commanded his disciples to call him Lord. This is why Jehovah is called the Lord in the New Testament, as is evidenced by the following:

> You shall love Jehovah your God from your whole heart and your whole soul (Deut. 6:5).

and in the New Testament,

You shall love the Lord your God from your whole heart and your whole soul (Matt. 22:35).

The same occurs in other citations of the Old Testament in the Gospels.

283. Anyone whose thinking is based on clear reason will see that the universe was not created out of nothing, because he will see that nothing can be made out of nothing. "Nothing" really is nothing, and "making something out of nothing" is self-contradictory. Anything self-contradictory is contrary to the light of the truth, which comes from divine wisdom. And anything that does not come from divine wisdom does not come from divine omnipotence either.

Everyone whose thinking is based on clear reason will also see that everything was created from a substance that is intrinsic substance, this being the actual Reality [*Esse*] from which everything that exists can emerge. And since only the Lord is intrinsic substance and therefore intrinsic reality, we conclude that there is no other source for the emergence of [created] things.

Many people see this because reason enables them to see it. They have not dared to avow it, however, fearing that they might perhaps come to think that since the created universe is from God, it is God, or that nature is self-generated and that its inmost level is therefore what we call God.

For this reason, even though many people have seen that God (and His reality) is the only source of the emergence of everything, they have not dared to step beyond their first thoughts on the subject, lest they tangle their understanding in a so-called Gordian knot from which they will later be unable to untangle it.

The reason they could not extricate their understanding is that they are thinking about God and His creation of the universe on the basis of time and space. These are properties of nature, and no one can on the basis of nature perceive God and the creation of the universe. But everyone whose understanding enjoys a more inward light can perceive nature and its creation on the basis of God, since God is not within time and space.

On the divine not being within space, see nn. 7-10 above; On the divine filling all spaces of the universe without [being bound by] space, see nn. 69-72. And on the divine being within all time without [being bound by] time, see nn. 73-76.

We will see below that even though God did create the universe in its entirety out of Himself, still there is nothing whatever in the created universe that is God. We will also see other matters that will set this subject in their light.

284. In Chapter One of this book, we dealt with God—His being divine love and divine wisdom, His being life, and His being the substance-and-form which is the actual and only reality.

In Chapter Two, we dealt with the spiritual sun and its world, and the natural sun and its world, and with God's creation of the universe in its entirety by means of the two suns.

In Chapter Three we dealt with the levels which characterize each and every created thing.

Now in Chapter Four we must deal with God's creation of the universe.

The reason for dealing with all these topics is that angels have complained to the Lord about seeing nothing but darkness when they looked at this world, no knowledge among people about God, heaven, and nature's creation, knowledge on which their wisdom depends.

THE LORD FROM ETERNITY OR JEHOVAH COULD NOT HAVE CREATED THE UNIVERSE IN ITS ENTIRETY UNLESS HE WERE A PERSON

285. People who have a natural, physical concept of God have absolutely no way of understanding how God as a Person could have created the universe and everything that goes with it. In fact, they think to themselves, "How can God as a Person travel through the universe from place to place and create things? Or how can He utter a word from His place, and then whatever was spoken is created?"

This sort of thought comes to mind in describing God as Person for people who think about God-Man the same way they think about a person on earth, who think about God on the basis of nature and its properties, which are time and space.

However, people who do not think about God-Man on the basis of earthly people or on the basis of nature and its space and time, perceive clearly that the universe could not have been created unless God were a Person.

Transfer your thought to the angelic concept of God as being Person, banish the notion of space as completely as you can, and you will in your thinking come close to the truth. Even some scholars grasp the fact that angels are not within space because they grasp the spiritual as being apart from space. Actually, it is like thought—in spite of the fact that thought is within an individual, still it enables the person to be present somewhere else, anywhere, no matter how distant.

This is the kind of state characteristic of spirits and angels—who are people, even in body. They can be seen wherever their thoughts are, since spaces and distances in a spiritual world are "appearances" and behave in concert with the affection-based thought of spiritual people.

This enables us to conclude that God—who appears far above the spiritual world, as a sun, who can possess no appearance of space—must not be thought of in spatial terms. And then we can understand that

He created the universe not from nothing, but from Himself, that His human body cannot be conceived of as large or small or of any particular height, since these too are matters of space. We can therefore conclude that He is the same in first things and last, in greatest things and least, and even further that His human is the inmost level in every created thing, but is devoid of space.

On the constancy of the divine in things greatest and least, see nn. 77-82 above; and on the divine filling all space but being devoid of space, see nn. 69-72. And since the divine is not within space, it is not [extended along] a continuum either, the way the inmost level of nature is.

286. Discerning people can understand quite clearly that God could not have created the universe unless he were Person, because they cannot deny to themselves that there is love and wisdom in God, mercy and kindliness, the good and the true, since these things come from Him. Because they cannot deny this, they cannot deny that God is Person. Not one of these qualities actually can occur apart from a Person. For the human being is their subject, and to divorce them from their subject is to say that they do not exist.

Think of wisdom, and locate it outside any person—is it anything? Can you conceive of it as something airy or something fiery? No, except perhaps as within the air or flame; and if it is within them, it has to be wisdom in the kind of form a person has. It has to be in that complete form; nothing can be wanting if wisdom is to be within it.

In short, the form of wisdom is person; and since person is the form of wisdom, it is also the form of love, mercy, kindliness, the good, and the true because these act in unison with wisdom.

On the impossibility of love and wisdom occurring except in some form, see nn. 40-43 above.

287. We can establish the humanity of love and wisdom by the angels of heaven, who, to the extent that they are involved in love and therefore wisdom from the Lord, are people in full beauty. We can reach the same conclusion on the basis of what the Word says about Adam—that he was created in the image and likeness of God (Gen 1:26)—because he was created in the form of love and wisdom.

Everyone on earth is born into a human form physically. This is because their spirits—also called souls—are persons. And their spirits are persons because they have the ability to accept love and wisdom from the Lord. Further, to the extent that people's spirits or souls do accept, they become people after the death of the material bodies that surround them. And to the extent that they do not accept, they become monsters, with some human characteristics derived from the ability to accept.

288. Since God is a Person, the entire angelic heaven, taken in a single grasp, resolves into one person. This entity is divided into realms and sections that follow the members, organs, and viscera of a human being.

There are actually communities of heaven that make up a section including everything that belongs to the brain, and everything that belongs to the parts of the face, and everything that belongs to the body's inner organs. These sections are marked off from each other just the way they are in a person. Angels even know what section of the person they are in.

The whole heaven is in this model because God is a Person. And God is heaven, since the angels who make up heaven are accepting vessels of love and wisdom, and accepting vessels are models.

We have explained in *Arcana Coelestia* at the ends of several chapters, that heaven is in the form of everything human.

289. This enables us to see the idiocy of the concept people have who think of God as non-human and who think of divine attributes as not being in God as a Person. For separated from Personhood, these attributes are nothing but mental constructs.

On the essential humanity of God as the reason a person is a person depending on his acceptance of love and wisdom, see above (nn. 11-13). We are stressing the same point here for the sake of what follows, to make it possible to perceive that God created the universe because He is a person.

THE LORD FROM ETERNITY, OR JEHOVAH, BROUGHT FORTH FROM HIMSELF THE SUN OF THE SPIRITUAL WORLD, AND CREATED FROM IT THE UNIVERSE AND EVERYTHING IN IT

290. We discussed the spiritual world's sun in Chapter Two of this book, making the following points:

Divine love and divine wisdom are visible in the spiritual world as a sun (nn. 83-88).

Spiritual warmth and spiritual light radiate from that sun (nn. 89-92).

That sun is not God, but is an emanation from God-Man's divine love and divine wisdom: the same holds true from warmth and light from that sun (nn. 93-98).

The spiritual world's sun is at middle elevation, and seems to be as far from angels as the material world's sun is from us (nn. 103-107).

In the spiritual world, the east is where the Lord appears as the sun, and the other major regions depend on this (nn. 119-123, 124-128).

Angels are constantly turning their faces toward the Lord as the sun (nn. 129-134, 135-139).

The Lord created the universe and everything in it by means of that sun, which is the first emanation of divine love and divine wisdom (nn. 151-156).

The natural world's sun is nothing but fire, and the nature that has its origin in that sun is therefore lifeless. Further, the natural world's sun was created so that the work of creation could be wrapped up and finished (nn. 157-162).

Without this pair of suns, one alive and one lifeless, creation would not occur (nn. 163-166).

291. One of the points made in Chapter Two is that the [spiritual] sun is not the Lord, but is an emanation from His divine love and divine wisdom. It is called an emanation because that sun was brought forth from divine love and divine wisdom, which are intrinsic substance and form, and the divine emanates through it.

But human reason being what it is—not giving assent unless it sees a matter from its means [causa], that is, unless it grasps how (in this case, how the spiritual world's sun was brought forth, which is not the Lord but an emanation from Him)—we need to say something more about this.

I have talked with angels about this a good deal. They have stated that they grasp this clearly in their spiritual light, but that it is almost impossible for them to present it to a mortal in his natural light because there is such a difference between the two kinds of light and the resultant two kinds of thought.

They have however stated that it is like the sphere of affections and consequent thoughts that surrounds every angel, and is the means by which they establish their presence with people near and far. These surrounding spheres are not the actual angels, but come from each and every part of their bodies, from which substances are constantly flowing out like a river, with the outflow surrounding them. These attending substances of their bodies, constantly animated by means of the two wellsprings of his life's activity—heart and lungs—make the atmospheres respond to their activity, and thereby establish in other people a perception of something like the angels' presence. So there is not really some separate sphere of affections and consequent thought that goes out and keeps things going, even though we give it a name, since affections are simply states of the forms of the mind within.

They have also said that this kind of sphere surrounds every angel because it surrounds the Lord. The sphere around the Lord is from Him in this same way, and this sphere is their sun, or the sun of the spiritual world.

292. I have often been allowed to perceive that this kind of sphere does surround angels and spirits, as does a general sphere around many within a community. I have also been allowed to see it in different manifestations. Sometimes in heaven it looked like a subtle flame, in hell like a coarse fire; and sometimes in heaven it looked like a subtle and shining cloud, while in hell it looked like a coarse black cloud. Sometimes I have been allowed to perceive these spheres as various odors and scents. This has convinced me that everyone in heaven and everyone in hell is enveloped in a sphere made up of substances distilled and extracted from his body.

293. I have also perceived that the sphere does not flow only from angels and spirits, but flows from each and every visible thing in our world as well. It flows, for example, from trees and their fruits here, from gardens and their flowers, from herbs and grasses, even from soils and their smallest parts. I could therefore see that this is a universal characteristic of things both living and lifeless, each one being enclosed in something which is like what lies within it and which is continually being breathed from it.

People have recognized that the same holds true in the natural world because of the observations of many scholars that a wave of outflow is constantly flowing from people, from every animal, and from trees, fruit, gardens, flowers—even from metal and stone.

The natural world derives this from the spiritual world, and the spiritual world from the divine.

294. Since the constituent elements of the spiritual world's sun are from the Lord and are not the Lord, they are not intrinsic life but are stripped of intrinsic life. In the same way, the things that flow from an angel or a mortal and compose their surrounding spheres are not the angel or the mortal but are derived from them, stripped of their life. These can be part of the angel or person only by their agreement, since they have been extracted from their physical forms, which were forms of their life within them.

This is a mystery which angels with their spiritual concepts can see in thought and express in speech, though mortals with their natural concepts cannot, since it takes a thousand spiritual concepts to make one natural one, and a single natural concept cannot be resolved by mortals into any spiritual concept, let alone resolving it into all its spiritual concepts.

This is because they vary as to the vertical levels described in Chapter Three.

295. The following experience acquainted me with this kind of difference between angels' and mortals' thoughts.

They were told to think about something spiritually and then tell me what they were thinking. When they did this, and tried to tell me, they were unable to, and said that they could not express it. It was the same with their spiritual speech and with their spiritual writing. There was not a single word of spiritual language that was the same as a word of natural language, nor any element of spiritual writing that was the same as natural writing, including the letters, each of which would contain a complete meaning.

Remarkably enough, though, they said that they seemed to themselves to be thinking and talking and writing in the same way in their spiritual state as mortals in their natural state, when there is no resemblance.

I could see from this that the natural and the spiritual differ as to vertical level, and communicate with each other only through correspondences.

THERE ARE THREE THINGS IN THE LORD WHICH ARE THE LORD—DIVINE LOVE, DIVINE WISDOM, AND DIVINE USE. THESE THREE THINGS ARE PRESENTED IN SENSIBLE FORM OUTSIDE THE SPIRITUAL WORLD'S SUN—DIVINE LOVE BY MEANS OF WARMTH, DIVINE WISDOM BY MEANS OF LIGHT, AND DIVINE USE BY MEANS OF THEIR CONTAINING ATMOSPHERE.

296.   The reader may see above (nn. 89-92, 99-102, 146-150) that warmth and light emanate from the spiritual world's sun, the warmth emanating from the Lord's divine love and the light from His divine wisdom.

At this point, we need to state that the third emanation from that sun is atmosphere, the vessel of warmth and light, and that this emanates from the divine aspect of the Lord which is known as use.

297. Anyone who is thinking with some enlightenment can see that love has as a goal, and reaches toward, use, and brings forth use by means of wisdom.

Really, what is love unless there is something that is loved? That "something" is use. And since use is what is loved, and is brought forth by means of wisdom, it follows that use is the vessel of love and wisdom.

We have already explained (nn. 209-216, and elsewhere) that these three—love, wisdom, and use—

follow in a sequence determined by vertical levels, with the last level being the aggregate, vessel, and foundation of the antecedent levels. We can therefore now conclude that these three things—divine love, divine wisdom, and divine use, are in the Lord and are the Lord in essence.

298. We will be giving ample illustration later of the premise that the human being, both outwardly and inwardly viewed, is a form of all uses, and that all the uses in the created universe correspond to these uses. Here we need only mention it to make it known that the Lord as Person is the essential form of all uses, in which all the uses in the created universe find their source. So too the created universe viewed as to its uses is a model of Him.

By "uses" we mean things which are from God-Man—that is the Lord—in their proper pattern from creation. We do not mean things derived from the human ego [*proprium*]. This is actually a hell, and its derivatives are in conflict with the pattern.

299. Now whereas these three—love, wisdom, and use—are in the Lord and are the Lord, and whereas the Lord is everywhere and is in fact omnipresent, and whereas the Lord cannot make Himself present to any angel or mortal as He intrinsically is, or as He is within His sun, therefore He presents himself by means of the kind of thing that He can be in, presenting Himself as to love by means of warmth, as to wisdom by means of light, and as to use by means of an atmosphere.

The reason the Lord presents Himself as to use by means of an atmosphere is that the atmosphere is the vessel of warmth and light the way use is a vessel of love and wisdom.

In fact, the light and warmth that emanate from the divine sun cannot emanate in nothing—in a vacuum—but need some vessel as their substratum.

We call this vessel the atmosphere which surrounds the sun, takes it out in its embrace, and bears it to the heaven where angels are, thus establishing a presence of the Lord everywhere.

300. We have already explained (nn. 173-178, 179-183) that there are atmospheres in the spiritual world just as there are in the natural world; and we stated that the spiritual world's atmospheres are spiritual while the natural world's atmospheres are natural. Now because of the source of the spiritual atmosphere immediately surrounding the spiritual sun, we can conclude that every bit of it is essentially of the same quality as the sun within it.

Angels assert the truth of this, using their non-spatial spiritual concepts, by saying that there is only one substance, which is the source of everything, and that the spiritual world's sun is that substance. And since the divine is not within space and is the same in things greatest and least, this holds true for the sun which is God-Man's first emanation. Further, this only substance, the sun, establishes the varieties of all phenomena in the created universe according to sequential or horizontal levels and in keeping with distinct or vertical levels.

Angels have stated that there is no way to understand these matters without taking space out of one's concepts: if space is not removed, there is no way to prevent appearances from bringing in illusion. These illusions cannot enter as long as one is thinking that God is the essential reality which is the source of everything.

301. Beyond this, we can clearly see from non-spatial angelic concepts that nothing in the created universe is alive except the God-Man alone—the Lord, that is—and that nothing is active except by means of life from Him; also that nothing exists except by means of the sun which comes from Him. So it is the truth that in God we live and move and have our being.

THE ATMOSPHERES (WHICH IN EACH WORLD, SPIRITUAL AND NATURAL, ARE THREE) COME TO A CLOSE AT THEIR EXTREMITIES IN THE KINDS OF SUBSTANCES AND ELEMENTS THAT OCCUR ON EARTH

302. In Chapter Three (nn. 173-176), we set forth the existence in each world, spiritual and natural, of three atmospheres, distinct from each other according to vertical levels and shrinking progressively downward by horizontal levels. And since these atmospheres do shrink as they move downward, it follows that they become even more compact and inert, eventually, at their extremes, so compact and inert that they are no longer atmospheres but static substances—in a natural world the kind of fixed substances that occur on earth and are called elements.

This being the source of substances and elements, it follows *first* that there are three levels of the substances and elements, *second* that they are held together in interconnection by the surrounding atmospheres, and *third* that they are adapted in their forms to the production of all kinds of use.

303. As for the kinds of substances and elements that occur on earth being produced by the sun through its atmospheres, is there anyone who would disagree? —Anyone, that is, who does not think that there are ceaseless adjustments from beginning to end, that nothing can emerge except from something previous to it, ultimately then from a First—and the First is the spiritual world's sun, and that sun is God-Man or the Lord.

Now since the atmospheres are this "something previous" through which the sun makes itself present at the extremes and since these previous things do shrink in activity and in size all the way to the extremes, it follows that when their activity and size reach their lower limit, they become the kinds of substance and element that occur on earth. Because of the atmospheres they were born from, they retain in themselves an effort and impulse to bring forth uses.

If people do not set up a creation of the universe and everything in it by constant adjustments from a First, they cannot help building theories that are fragmentary and are broken away from their reasons. When light falls on these from a mind that explores things more deeply, they do not look like a house, but like a pile of rubble.

304. From this most general origin of everything in the created universe, all its particular components derive one feature—that they go from their first to their limits, which are relatively at rest, in order to come to a close and endure. So in the human body, the fibers move from their first forms all the way to becoming tendons; then fibers with little ducts move from their first forms all the way to becoming cartilages and bones, where they settle down and stay.

Since this kind of sequence from first to final forms occurs for fibers and ducts in a human being, there is a similar sequence for their states. Their states are varieties of sensation, thought, and affection. These also move along from their first forms, where they are in light, to their final forms, where they are in darkness. Or they move from their first forms where they are in warmth to their final forms where they are not in warmth. And since their sequence is of this nature, there is the same kind of sequence for love and everything about it and for wisdom and everything about it. In short, this kind of sequence applies to everything in the created universe.

This is just what we explained above (nn. 222-229)—that there are two kinds of level in the greatest and smallest forms of everything that has been created. The reason the two kinds of level occur even in the smallest forms of everything is that the spiritual sun is the only substance, the source of everything, in keeping with the spiritual concept of angels (n. 300).

IN THE SUBSTANCES AND ELEMENTS THAT CONSTITUTE THIS WORLD THERE IS NOTHING INTRINSICALLY DIVINE, BUT STILL THEY ARE FROM THE INTRINSIC DIVINE

305. We may conclude from the origin of earth discussed in the last section, that there is nothing intrinsically divine in its substances and elements, but that they are devoid of everything intrinsically divine. They are in fact, as we have said, the limits and boundaries of atmospheres, whose warmth has come to a close in chill, light in darkness, and activity in inertness.

Still, they have by their unbroken connection with the substance of the spiritual sun brought along what was from the divine there, which, as already mentioned (nn. 291-198) was the sphere surrounding the God-Man or Lord. From this sphere, through an unbroken connection with the sun, by means of the atmospheres, the substances and elements that constitute earth originated.

306. There is no other way to describe the origin of the world from a spiritual sun by means of atmospheres in words that come from natural concepts; but there are other ways in words that come from spiritual concepts, since these are non-spatial. And since they are non-spatial, they do not coincide with any words of a natural language.

You may see above (n. 295) that spiritual thought, speech and writing are so different from natural thought, speech and writing that they have nothing in common, and that the only way they communicate is through correspondence.

So it is adequate to understand the origin of the world naturally, in one way or another.

ALL USES, WHICH ARE THE GOALS OF CREATION, ARE IN FORMS, AND GET THEIR FORMS FROM THE KINDS OF SUBSTANCE AND ELEMENT THAT OCCUR ON EARTH

307. All the things we have discussed so far—the sun, atmospheres, and earths—are only means to goals. The goals of creation are the things brought forth by the Lord as a sun by means of the atmospheres and earths. These extend to the whole vegetable kingdom, the whole animal kingdom, and ultimately the human race and the angelic kingdom from it.

We call these "uses," because they are receptive of divine love and divine wisdom, and because they focus on God the creator, their source, and thereby unite him to his masterpiece so that they endure from him as they came into being, because they are united to him.

We say that they focus on God the creator, their source, and unite him to his masterpiece. But this is talking according to appearances, and means that God the creator makes them seem to focus and unite themselves on their own. In the following pages, we will be describing how they focus and thereby unite.

Some aspects of this have already been discussed in their proper places. For example, divine love and divine wisdom cannot help existing and manifesting themselves in other entities created from themselves (nn. 47-51): everything in the universe was created to be receptive of divine love and divine wisdom (nn. 55-60): the uses of all created things rise step by step to the human, and through the human to God the creator, their source (nn. 65-68).

308. Anyone will see clearly that the goals of creation are uses by reflecting that nothing can emerge from God the creator, nothing then can be created by him, except what is useful. To be useful, it is for others.

And what is useful to itself is also "for others." For usefulness to self is to be in a state that results in usefulness to others.

If we think this way, we can also reflect that what is genuinely useful cannot emerge from a human being, but in the human being from Him from whom only what is useful arises—from the Lord.

309. But since we are here dealing with the forms of what is useful, we shall discuss them in the following sequence:

(i) *There is in the earths an effort to bring forth uses in forms, or forms of uses.*

(ii) *There is in every form of use some reflection of the creation of the universe.*

(iii) *There is in every form of use some reflection of the human.*

(iv) *There is in every form of use some reflection of the infinite and the eternal.*

310. (i) *There is in the earths an effort to bring forth uses in forms, or forms of uses.*

The presence of this effort in the earths follows from their origin. The substances and elements the earths are made of are results and limitations of the atmospheres that emanate as uses from the spiritual sun as stated above (nn. 305-306). And since this is the source of the substances and elements the earths are made of, and their concentrations are held together by the pressure of the atmospheres, it follows that they possess in consequence a constant effort to produce forms of uses. They derive the very characteristic of productiveness from their origin, from being the limits of the atmospheres, with which they therefore accord.

We say that this effort and characteristic are "in the earths," but we mean that they belong to the substances and elements the earths are made of, whether these are within the earths or breathed from the earths in the atmospheres.

The abundance of things like this in the atmospheres is recognized. The presence of this kind of effort and characteristic in the substances and elements of the earths is obvious if we look at seeds. All kinds of seed are opened by warmth, right to their center. They are impregnated by the subtlest substances, which can only come from a spiritual source, and thus empowered to yoke themselves to use. This results in their ability to reproduce, and then, in combination with elements of natural origin, to construct forms of uses. Then they bring these forth, as if from the womb, so that they reach the light, and so sprout and grow. Thereafter, the effort is unceasing from the earth through the roots to the extremities, and from the extremities to first things where the use exists in its source.

This is how uses cross over into forms. And forms derived from use, which is like a soul, as they proceed from first to final and from final back to first things, derive the characteristic that each and every detail is of some use. We say that the use is like a soul because its form is like a body.

It also follows that there is a more inward effort, the effort to bring forth uses through sprouting, for the sake of the animal kingdom; for animals of every kind are nourished by plants. It also follows that there is a most inward effort—the effort to be useful to the human race.

These conclusions follow from three premises: (1) Plants are ultimate results, and within ultimate results are included all prior things in their pattern, in accord with what has been frequently presented above. (2) Both kinds of level are present in the greatest and smallest things, as presented in nn. 222-229 above. They are present also in the effort. (3) All uses are made by the Lord out of ultimate things, so within these ultimate things there exists the effort toward them.

311. All these efforts, however, are not alive. They are actually efforts proper to the lowest forces of life, which forces do nevertheless contain, because of the life they come from, an impulse to return by an indirect way to their source. In their last forms, the atmospheres become this kind of force, impelling earthly substances and elements into forms and holding them together from within and from without. There is not time for fuller exposition of these matters, since this is a major task.

312. The first work of the earths, when they had just been made and were in their rudimentary form, was the production of seeds. The first effort within the earths could not have been anything else.

313. (ii) *There is in every form of use some reflection of creation.*

There are three kinds of forms of uses: forms of use of the mineral kingdom, forms of use of the vegetable kingdom, and forms of use of the animal kingdom.

I cannot describe the forms of use of the mineral kingdom because they are not visible. The first forms are the smallest versions of the substances and elements that earths are made of. The second forms are concentrations of them, which occur with infinite variety. The third forms come from plant matter which has decayed into compost, and from dead animals. It comes also from this matter constantly giving off vapors and gases that combine with the earths and make their soil.

These three levels of use of the mineral kingdom reflect creation by producing (activated by the sun through the atmospheres and their warmth and light) uses in forms, which were the goals of creation. The image of creation in their characteristic efforts (see n. 310 above) is most obscure.

314. We can see a reflection of creation in the forms of use of the vegetable kingdom in their moving from

their first to their final forms and then back from final to first.

Their first forms are seeds; their final forms are stalks covered with bark. And by means of the bark, which is the outer shell [*ultimum*] of the stalk, they progress to seeds, which as stated are their first forms.

Stalks covered with bark reflect the plant covered with earths, from which the creation and shaping of all uses occurs. There is ample evidence that plant growth takes place through the leaves, bark, and layers, pushing out from the root-coverings that continue around the stems and branches into the beginnings of the fruit, and in like manner through the fruit into the seeds. The reflection of creation in these forms of use stands out in their gradual taking form from first to final stages, and from final back to first. It also stands out in the fact that every step has the goal of producing fruit and seed, which is useful.

We can see from this that the motion of the creation of the universe was from its first, the Lord clothed with the sun, to its final form, the earths, and from these, by way of uses, back to their first, the Lord. The goals of all creation, then, were uses.

315. We do need to realize that the warmth, light, and atmospheres of the natural world accomplish absolutely nothing toward this reflection of creation— only the warmth, light, and atmospheres of the spiritual world's sun. These bring the image with them, and clothe it with forms of use that belong to the vegetable kingdom.

The warmth, light, an atmospheres of the natural world simply open the seeds, maintain what they bring forth as they expand, and provide the elements that give them permanence. Nor do they accomplish this by any forces from their own sun, which forces are intrinsically quite negligible, but rather by forces from the spiritual sun, which are constantly impelling them to these activities. The natural forces, however, furnish absolutely nothing toward providing this reflection. The actual reflection of creation is spiritual. Still, so that it may be visible and may be stable and endure, it needs to be materialized—that is, filled out with elements of that world.

316. There is a similar reflection of creation in the forms of use of the animal kingdom. For example, from the seed sent into the womb, or the egg, a body is formed; and when this matures it produces new seeds.

This process is like the process that characterizes the forms of use of the vegetable kingdom. The seeds are the beginnings; the womb, or the egg, is like the earth. The prenatal state is like the state of a seed in the earth while it is forcing out its root; the state from birth to reproduction is like the state from the sprouting of the plant to its fruit-bearing state.

We can see from this parallelism that just as there is a likeness of creation in plant forms, there is one in animal forms as well—specifically, there is a process from first things to last, and from last things back to first.

A similar reflection of creation manifests itself in details within human beings. For there is a similar process of love through wisdom into uses, a similar process therefore of intent through discernment into action, and a similar process of charity through faith into works.

Intent and discernment, and charity and faith, are the first things, the sources. Actions and works are the last things. By way of pleasure in uses, there is a return from these last things to their first things, which as stated are intent and discernment or charity and faith.

It is obvious that the return occurs by way of pleasure in uses if we look at our conscious pleasure in actions and works. These are proper to each individual's love; they flow back to the first love, the source; and in this way there is a yoking together. The pleasures in actions and deeds are the pleasures we ascribe to use.

A similar process from first things to last and from last back to first stands out in the most purely organic forms of affections and thoughts within us. In our brains, there are star-like forms called the gray matter. Fibers leave this through the medullary substance and along the neck into the body. There they proceed to the extremities, and from the extremities return to their beginnings. The return of these fibers is accomplished by way of the blood vessels.

There is a similar process of all affections and thoughts, which are changes and variations of the states of these forms and substances. In fact, the fibers that leave these forms or substances are rather like the atmospheres derived from the spiritual sun, which are vessels of warmth and light. Bodily actions, further, are like the things brought forth from the earth by way of the atmospheres, whose pleasures in use return to the source they came from.

But it is hard to grasp with full discernment that these things have this kind of process, with a reflection of creation within, because the thousands on thousands of forces that are at work in an action seem like a single force, and because pleasures in use do not give rise to concepts in our thinking, but only influence us without our having any clear perception of them.

On these matters, you may refer to previous statements and explanations. For example, the uses of all created things rise by vertical steps to the human, and through the human to God the creator, their source (nn. 65-68). Further, the goal of creation takes form in the lowest things, and is the return of everything to the creator and the existence of a bond (nn. 167-172). But we will be able to see this in still clearer light in the next chapter, where we deal with the correspondence of intent and discernment with the heart and lungs.

317. (iii) *There is in every form of use some reflection of the human.*

This has already been demonstrated (nn. 61-64). We shall see in the following section that all uses from first to last and from last back to first bear a relationship to all elements of the human and have a correspondence with them, so that the human is therefore a universe in reflection, so to speak, and the universe, conversely, seen as to its uses, is a person in reflection.

318. (iv) *There is in every form of use some reflection of the infinite and the eternal.*

We can see a reflection of the infinite in these forms in their urge and ability to fill all the space in this world and in other worlds as well, to infinity. From a single seed comes a tree, shrub, or plant which fills its own amount of space. From each tree, shrub, or plant come seeds—several thousand, in some cases—which if sown and sprouted fill their own amounts of space. If all these new offspring were to arise over and over again from any one of these seeds, the whole globe would be filled in a matter of years. And if the reproduction still continued, many planets would be filled—so on to infinity. Multiply one seed by a thousand, and that thousand by ten, twenty, and a hundred thousand, and you will see.

There is a similar reflection of the eternal in these forms. Seeds are propagated year after year, and this propagation never ceases. It has not ceased from the creation of the world to the present day, and it never will.

These two facts are obvious indications, signs that bear witness to the fact that everything in the universe was created by an infinite and eternal God.

In addition to these reflections of the infinite and eternal, there is another reflection of the infinite and eternal in the variety of things. No substance, state, or thing can occur in the created universe that is the same as or identical to any other—not in the atmospheres, not in the earth, not in the forms that spring forth from them. So in any of the things that fill the universe, nothing can ever be brought forth which is the same as any other.

We see this obviously in the variety of people's faces everywhere. No two are identical in all the lands of the world, nor will there be to eternity. No two minds, then, whose imprints are faces, can be identical.

EVERYTHING IN THE UNIVERSE, LOOKED AT AS TO USES, REFLECTS AN IMAGE OF PERSON: THIS BEARS WITNESS TO THE FACT THAT GOD IS PERSON.

319. Early people called man a microcosm because the human reflects the macrocosm, which is the universe in its entirety. Nowadays, however, people do not know why the early people described man this way. In fact, all we can see in the human being of the universe or macrocosm is that we are nourished and live physically from its animal kingdom and its vegetable kingdom, and that we hear and breathe by means of its atmospheres. But these facts do not make us a microcosm the way the universe and all its contents is a macrocosm.

Rather, the early people derived their name "microcosm" or "little universe" for man from a knowledge of correspondences, which was characteristic of the earliest people, and from communication with heaven's angels. Heaven's angels actually know from what they see around them that everything in the universe, looked at as to uses, reflects an image of person.

320. We may state that the human is a microcosm or little universe because the created universe, looked at as to uses, is in the human image, but this cannot

penetrate anyone's thinking and move from there into knowledge as a result of a concept of that universe which is observable in the spiritual world. So there is no way the premise can be supported except by an angel who is in the spiritual world or by someone who has been granted presence in that world and a view of what is there. Since this has been granted to me, I can reveal this secret out of what I have seen there.

321. We need to realize that in outward appearance the spiritual world is just like the natural world. People see lands, mountains, hills, valleys, plains, lakes, rivers, and brooks, just the way they do in the natural world. So there are all the members of the mineral kingdom.

They also see parks, gardens, groves, and woods with all kinds of trees and shrubs bearing fruit and seeds; they see plants, flowers, herbs, and grasses. So there are all the members of the vegetable kingdom.

They see animals, flying creatures, and all kinds of fish; so there are all the members of the animal kingdom. The people there are angels and spirits.

We have prefaced this to let the reader know that the universe of the spiritual world is just like the universe of the natural world, the only difference being that things there are not fixed and static like things in the natural world because there is nothing natural there. Everything is spiritual.

322. We can demonstrate clearly that the spiritual world's universe reflects an image of person from the fact that everything we have just described (n. 321) is vividly visible and manifest around an angel and around angelic communities as though they had produced or created it. It stays around them and does not fade away.

We can show that this environment is as though they had produced or created it from the fact that when an angel leaves or a community moves, this environment is no longer visible. Further, when other angels arrive, the appearance of everything around them changes. The trees and fruits of the parks change, the blossoms and seeds of gardens change, the herbs and grasses of meadows change, and the kinds of animal and bird change.

The reason these things are present and change is that everything arises in accord with angels' affections and consequent thoughts. They are actually entities that correspond. And since they do correspond, they make one with what they correspond to, and are therefore its representative images.

The actual image is not visible when you focus on anything in its own form, but it is seen when you focus on the uses.

I have been allowed to see that when angels' eyes have been opened by the Lord and they see things from the correspondence of their uses, they recognize and see themselves within them.

323. Now, since angels' environments arise in accord with the angels' affections and thoughts, reflect a certain universe in being made up of earths, plants, and animals, and make thereby a representative image of the angel, we can see why the early people called man a microcosm.

324. The truth of this has been amply demonstrated in *Arcana Coelestia* and also in the book *Heaven and Hell*. There are also many supporting statements in the preceding pages of the present work, where we discussed correspondences.

We have also shown above that nothing occurs in the created universe that does not have a correspondence with some facet of the human—not just with our affections and consequent thoughts, but even with our physical organs and viscera. The correspondence is not with them as substances, but with them as uses.

This is why when the Word is dealing with the church and its members, trees like the olive, the vine, and the cedar are mentioned so often. So are gardens, groves, and forests, and animals, birds of the sky, and fish of the sea. They are mentioned there because they correspond, and by way of their correspondence make a one, as stated above.

So too, when things like this in the Word are being read by someone on earth, angels do not perceive them. In their stead they perceive the church or people of the church as to their state.

325. Since the whole universe does reflect an image of person, Adam is described as to wisdom and intelligence by the Garden of Eden, where there were trees of all kinds, and rivers, gems and gold, and the animals he gave names to—all of which mean the kinds of thing that were within him, and made what we call a person.

Quite similar things are said of Assyria in Ezekiel (31:3-9), meaning the church as to intelligence, and of Tyre (Ezek. 28:12, 13), meaning the church as to its insights into what is good and true.

326. This enables us to show that everything in the universe, if we look at its use, reflects an image of person, and that this bears witness to the fact that God is Person. For the kinds of thing described above do not happen around an angel-person out of the angel but out of the Lord through the angel. They actually arise from the inflow of divine love and divine wisdom into the angel, who is a recipient, and are brought forth in his field of vision the way the universe is created. So people there recognize that God is Person and that the created univere, if we look at its uses, is a reflection of Him.

EVERYTHING CREATED BY THE LORD IS A USE, AND IS A USE ACCORDING TO THE PATTERN, LEVEL, AND RESPECT IN WHICH IT RELATES TO THE HUMAN, AND THROUGH THE HUMAN TO THE LORD, ITS SOURCE.

327. We have already discussed the following points. Nothing but use can arise from God the creator (n. 308). The uses of all created things rise step by step from the lowest to the human, and through the human to God the creator, their source (nn. 65-68). The goal of creation takes form in lowest things, and that goal is that everything should return to God the creator, and that there should be a yoking together (nn. 167-172). Things are uses to the extent that they focus on their creator (n. 307). The divine cannot help existing and being present in others created from itself (nn. 47-51). Everything in the universe is receptive depending on its use, and this depends on its level (n. 58). If we look at uses, the universe is a reflection of God (n. 59). And there are more.

From these considerations, we can see this truth—that everything created by the Lord is a use, and is a use according to the pattern, level, and respect in which it relates to the human, and through the human to the Lord, its source.

Now we still need to say something specifically about uses.

328. "The human" to which uses relate does not mean simply the individual person, but also groups of people and smaller and larger communities—a nation, kingdom, or empire, for example—the largest community being that of the whole planet. Each of these is "the human."

It is the same in the heavens. In the Lord's sight, the whole angelic heaven is a single person. So is each community of heaven. This is why each angel is a person. You may see that this is so by referring to *Heaven and Hell* nn. 68-103. This explains what we mean by "the human" or "person" in the coming discussion.

329. We can determine what use is by considering the purpose of the creation of the universe. The purpose of the creation of the universe is the formation

of an angelic heaven. And since an angelic heaven is the goal, so too is the person or the human race, since this is where heaven comes from.

It follows then that all created things are intermediate goals, and that they are uses depending on the pattern, level, and respect in which they relate to the human, and through the human to the Lord.

330. Since the goal of creation is an angelic heaven from the human race, and is therefore the human race, all other created things are intermediate goals. Since they do relate to the human, they focus on these three aspects—our bodies, our rationality, and our spirituality, looking to our becoming yoked with the Lord.

People cannot be united to the Lord without being spiritual, nor be spiritual without being rational, nor be rational without being in a state of physical wholeness. It is like a house: the body is like the foundation, the rationality is like the house structure built on it, the spirituality like the furnishings of the house, and living in it is being united with the Lord.

This enables us to see the pattern, level, and respect in which uses, the intermediate goals of creation, relate to the human. Specifically, they relate to the maintenance of our bodies, the perfecting of our rationality, and to our receiving what is spiritual from the Lord.

331. *Things useful for the maintenance of our bodies* have to do with its nourishment, clothing, shelter, recreation and pleasure, protection, and preservation of state.

Created things useful for physical nourishment are all the members of the vegetable kingdom which can be eaten and drunk—for example, fruits, grapes, seeds, legumes, and herbs. Then there are all the edible members of the animal kingdom, like steers, cows, calves, deer, sheep, goats, kids, lambs, and the milk they give. Then there are many kinds of fowl and fish.

Created things useful for physical clothing are also many things from these two kingdoms, as are things useful for shelter. There are also many such things for recreation, pleasure, protection, and preservation of state. We will not enumerate them because they are familiar, and to list them would only fill up pages.

There are of course many things that do not yield anything useful to man. However, these "unnecessary" things do not destroy use, but enable useful things to survive. There is also the misuse of useful things. Misuse, however, does not destroy use; just as the falsification of something true does not destroy the truth except in the people who do it.

332. *Things useful for the perfection of rationality* are all those things that teach what we have just presented. They are called sciences and disciplines which have to do with nature, economics, civics, and morals. They are gleaned from parents and teachers, or from books, or from dealings with other people, or from oneself by reflection on such matters.

The higher the level of their use, the more they perfect rationality; and the more they are applied to life, the more enduring they are.

There is not room to list these uses, both because there are so many and because they relate to the common good in so many different ways.

333. *Things useful for receiving what is spiritual from the Lord* are all the things proper to religion and worship. This means things that teach an acknowledgment and understanding of God and an understanding and acknowledgment of what is good and true—things therefore that teach eternal life. These, like the disciplines [mentioned above], are gleaned from parents, teachers, sermons, and books, and especially by serious attention to life according to them. In Christendom, the means are teachings and sermons from the Word, and through the Word from the Lord.

We can describe these uses more extensively with the same categories applied to things useful to the body—nutrition, clothing, shelter, recreation and pleasure, and protection of state, for example. We simply apply these to the soul: nutrition to the good things of love, clothing to the elements of wisdom, shelter to heaven, recreation and pleasure to life's happiness and heavenly joy, shelter to [protection from] evils that besiege, and preservation of state to eternal life.

All of these are given us by the Lord to the extent that we realize that everything physical is also from the Lord, and that we are simply like appointed servants and stewards of our Lord's goods.

334. It becomes clear that these things have been given us for our productive use, as free gifts, if we look at the state of angels in the heavens. They too have bodies, rationality, and spirituality like earthly people. They are nourished gratis, for they are given food daily; they are clothed gratis because they are given clothing; they are sheltered gratis because they are given homes. They have no anxiety about any of these things, and to the extent that they are rational and spiritual together, they have pleasure, protection, and preservation of state.

The difference is that angels see that these things come from the Lord because these things are created in accord with the angels' state of love and wisdom (as explained in the preceding section, n. 322). People on earth do not see this because things recur in yearly cycles and do not depend on people's state of love and wisdom, but on their effort.

335. We may see that things are useful because they relate to the Lord through the human, but we still cannot say that they are uses from the human for the Lord. Rather, they are uses from the Lord for the human, because all uses are infinitely one in the Lord, and

none is in the human except from the Lord. In fact, a person cannot do what is good on his own, but from the Lord. What is good is what we call useful.

The essence of spiritual love is doing what is good for others not for our own sakes but for theirs. The essence of divine love is infinitely greater. This is like the love of parents for their children, in that they do them good out of love, not for their own sakes but for the children's.

People believe that because the Lord must be revered, worshipped, and praised, He loves reverence, worship, and praise for Himself. But He loves them for our sake, because this is how we come into a state for the divine to flow in perceptibly. For this is how a person removes that self-consciousness that blocks inflow and acceptance. Self-consciousness from self-love actually hardens and closes the heart.

This is taken away by the realization that on our own we can do nothing but evil and from the Lord nothing but good. This leads to a softening of the heart and a humility, from which flow reverence and worship.

It follows from all this that the purpose of the useful things the Lord provides from Himself through the human is that people may do good out of love. Since this is the Lord's love, this means receiving the joy of His love.

So let no one believe that the Lord is with people who only revere Him. Let them rather believe that He is with people who do His commandments—who do what is useful, therefore. He has His dwelling with the latter, not with the former (see also the discussion of these matters in nn. 47-49 above).

EVIL USES WERE NOT CREATED BY THE LORD, BUT AROSE TOGETHER WITH HELL

336. All the good things that come out in action are called uses, and all the evil things that come out in

action are called uses as well. But the latter are evil uses, while the former are good uses. Now since everything good comes from the Lord and everything evil comes from hell, it follows that only good uses come from the Lord, and that evil uses originate in hell.

The uses we are discussing specifically in this section mean everything we see on earth—all kinds of animal and all kinds of plant. Of these, the ones that are useful to humanity are from the Lord, and the ones that are harmful are from hell.

In similar fashion, "uses from the Lord" means everything that perfects our rational ability and enables us to receive something spiritual from the Lord. Conversely, "evil uses" means everything that destroys our rational ability and makes us incapable of becoming spiritual.

The reason we call things uses when they are harmful to us is that they are useful to evil people for doing evil, and also that they serve to absorb various kinds of ill will and therefore to heal. We use the term "use" in a double sense, like "love"—a good love or an evil love—and a love gives the name "use" to whatever is done by it.

337. We shall show that good uses are from the Lord and that evil uses are from hell, in the following order:

(1) *What earthly things we mean by "evil uses."*

(2) *All evil uses are in hell, and all good uses in heaven.*

(3) *There is a constant inflow from the spiritual world into the natural world.*

(4) *The inflow from hell is occupied with matters of evil use where things exist that are responsive.*

(5) *It is the lowest spiritual level, separated from what is above it, that does this.*

(6) *There are two forms into which this working by inflow occurs—the plant form and the animal form.*

(7) *Each form receives the ability to reproduce its own kind and the means of reproduction.*

338. (1) *What earthly things we mean by "evil uses."*

By "evil uses on earth," we mean everything harmful in each kingdom, animal and vegetable, and also everything harmful in the mineral kingdom. We cannot take the time to list all the harmful things in these kingdoms: that would be collecting names, and collecting names without pointing out the harm each kind does would not further the use which is the goal of this book.

As a matter of information, it will suffice to name a few at this point. In the animal kingdom, these include poisonous snakes, scorpions, crocodiles, lizards, owls, screech owls, mice, locusts, frogs, and spiders, also flies, drones, roaches, lice, and mites—in a word, animals that devour grasses, leaves, fruits, seeds, foods, and drinks, and that do harm to man and beast. In the vegetable kingdom, they include all destructive, irritant, and poisonous vegetation, and legumes and shrubs of the same character.

We can see from these few examples what "evil uses on earth" means. Actually, evil uses are all the things that oppose the good uses discussed in the section just above (n. 336).

339. (2) *All evil uses are in hell, and all good uses are in heaven.*

Before we can see that all the evil uses on earth come not from the Lord but from hell, we need first to say something about heaven and hell. Unless this is known, people might think the Lord responsible for evil uses as well as good ones, seeing them beginning together at creation or attributing them to nature and seeing their origin in nature's sun.

People cannot be rescued from these two errors without knowing that nothing takes form in the natural world which does not have a cause and source in the spiritual world, with anything good coming from the Lord and anything evil from the devil—that is, from hell. "The spiritual world" means heaven and hell.

In heaven, there are visible all the things that are good uses, discussed in the preceding section (n, 336). Conversely, in hell there are visible all the things that are evil uses, discussed and listed just above (n. 338)—all kinds of fierce animal, like snakes, scorpions, lizards, crocodiles, tigers, wolves, foxes, swine, horned owls, night-owls, screech owls, bats, mice, and rats, frogs, locusts, spiders, and many kinds of harmful insect.

There are also poisonous things—all kinds of hemlock, and aconite, in both plants and minerals. In brief, there is everything that is hurtful and deadly to humans. Things like this in the hells are visible in such forms quite vividly, exactly the way they are on earth and in the ground.

We refer to them as "visible" in hell. However they do not exist there the way they do on earth, being only correspondences of the cravings that spurt from the evil loves of the people there. These present themselves to others in forms like these.

Since these kinds of thing do exist in the hells, the hells are full of revolting fumes—of corpses, dung, urine, and decay, which the devilish spirits there enjoy the way foul-smelling animals do.

All this enables us to determine that similar phenomena in the natural world do not have their source in the Lord, were not created from the beginning, and did not spring from nature by way of its sun, but are rather from hell.

It is clear that they are not from nature by way of its sun, since what is spiritual flows into what is natural, and not vice versa. It is clear that they are not from the Lord because hell is not from Him; so neither is anything in hell that corresponds to the evils of its inhabitants.

340. (3) *There is a constant inflow from the spiritual world into the natural world.*

Anyone who does not know that there is a spiritual world, distinct from the natural world like the prior and the posterior or like a cause and its result, cannot know anything about inflow. This is why people who have written about the origin of plants and animals could only attribute it to nature. If they did believe God was the source, they thought that God at the beginning had endowed nature with the power of bringing them forth. In its own right, nature is in fact dead and contributes to the process of production no more than does a tool in the work of an artisan, which must be constantly propelled if it is to work.

It is the spiritual, with its source in the sun where the Lord is, emanating to the very boundaries of nature, that brings forth the forms of plants and animals, that sets up the extraordinary things we find within them, and that condenses them out of matter from the earth so that their forms are set and stable.

Recognizing, then, that there is a spiritual world, that the spiritual comes from the sun where the Lord is and which itself is from the Lord, and that this spiritual impels nature to activity the way something living impels something lifeless—recognizing this, we can see that there is no other source of the presence of plants and animals than through the spiritual world from the Lord, and that they are constantly becoming present through that world. We can therefore see that there is a constant inflow from the spiritual world into the natural. We shall present more support for this proposition in the next section.

The production on earth of harmful things through an inflow from hell happens under the same law of toleration by which evil things themselves flow from hell into people on earth. This law will be treated of in *Angelic Wisdom about Divine Providence.*

341. (4) *The inflow from hell is occupied with matters of evil use where things exist that are responsive.*

The things that respond to evil uses (that is, infectious plants and noxious animals) have to do with corpses, decay, excrement, and dung, foulness, and urine. So where we find these latter things, we find the kinds of plant and animal mentioned above. In tropical zones they are abundant—snakes, lizards, crocodiles, scorpions, mice, and the like.

Everyone knows that marshes, swamps, manure-heaps, and rotting humus teem with such creatures and that noxious flying things fill the air like clouds, while voracious grubs fill the ground and devour plants right to the roots. I once noticed in my garden that over a square yard all the dust was turned into minute flying things, for when I stirred it up with my walking-stick, they hovered like a cloud.

Experience alone enables us to see that carrion and decay agree with these vicious and useless animals, and are of the same nature. We can see this clearly from their underlying cause, which is that similar foul smells and fumes occur in the hells where little creatures like this appear. So these hells are given suitable names—some are called corpse-hells, some dung-hells, some urine-hells, and so on. But they are all roofed over so that their fumes will not leak out. For if they are opened only a little (as happens when demons are admitted), they stir up nausea and bring on headaches like a hangover. The ones that are also poisonous bring on fainting spells. Even the dust itself there has this characteristic, so its local name is "the damned dust." We can see from this that wherever there are such fumes, there are noxious creatures like this, because they correspond.

342. Now we need to ask whether creatures like this come from eggs carried in by the air or by rain or by seepage, or whether they come from these fluids and stenches themselves.

As for the possibility that the aforementioned kinds of vicious little creatures and insects are hatched from eggs brought in from elsewhere or hidden everywhere in the ground from creation, all experience dissents, since grubs turn up in tiny seeds, in nuts, in stones, even emerging from leaves. Then too, on small plants we find lice and grubs that are at home on them. We can also learn from the summer flies that appear all at once in great swarms in houses and fields and woods without springing from any egg-like matter. The insects that devour meadows and lawns, the destructive insects that fill the air in some tropical areas, and the ones we find in foul water, wine gone bad, and unhealthy air, are invisible as they swim and fly.

These observable phenomena support the people who claim that the actual smells and stenches and gases given off by the plants and soils and swamps also provide the first forms for this kind of creature.

The fact that they propagate themselves by eggs or by spawning once they have begun does not disprove their spontaneous beginnings, since every animal is given organs of generation and propagation (which we will discuss in n. 347 below) along with its other inner organs.

A supporting witness previously unrecognized is the observation that there are similar phenomena in the hells as well.

343. We can determine that the aforementioned hells have not only a communication but even a bond with similar phenomena on earth, from the fact that the hells are not remote from people but are around them—even within people who are evil—and are therefore touching our various lands.

Actually, as far as their affections, cravings, and consequent thoughts are concerned, and as to their derivative actions which are either good or evil uses, people are surrounded by angels of heaven or spirits of hell. And since the kinds of thing we find in our various lands also exist in the heavens and the hells, it follows that an inflow from the spiritual world is producing them directly when the earthly "climate" is favorable.

In fact, everything that can be seen in the spiritual world, both in heaven and in hell, is a correspondence of affections and cravings, since all such things come into being there in accord with these latter. So when affections and cravings, which themselves are of the spirit, encounter life or corresponding material on earth, we have present a spiritual factor which provides a soul and a material factor which provides a body. And intrinsic to everything spiritual is an impulse to clothe itself in a body.

The reason the hells surround human beings and are therefore touching our various lands is that the spiritual world is not within space, but occurs wherever there is a corresponding affection.

344. I once heard two presidents of the English [Royal] Society, Sir [Hans] Sloane and Sir [Martin] Folkes, talking to each other in the spiritual world about where seeds and eggs come from and about what comes from them on earth. The former attributed them to nature, claiming that from creation nature had been endowed with the ability and power to produce such things, aided by the warmth of the sun. The latter said that this power was a constant gift from God the creator within nature.

To settle the argument, Sir Hans was shown a beautiful bird. He was told to examine it and see whether it differed even slightly from a similar bird on earth. He held it in his hands for a while, examined it at some length, and said that there was no difference. All the while, he actually knew that the bird was nothing but the affection of a nearby angel, portrayed as a bird, and that it would vanish or cease to be when his affection ceased, as actually then happened.

Sir Hans was convinced by this experience that nature contributes nothing whatever to the production of plants and animals—it is only what flows in from the spiritual world into the natural.

He stated that if the bird had been filled out in its details with corresponding materials from earth, and thus given a fixed form, it would have been a lasting bird like birds on earth. He also said that it was the same with things from hell. He went on to say that if he had known what he now knew about the spiritual world, he would have attributed to nature no function but that of serving a spiritual element that came from God, by giving fixed form to things that are constantly flowing into nature.

345. (5) *It is the lowest level of the spiritual, separated from what is above it, that does this.*

In Chapter Three, we presented the following points. The spiritual flows down from its sun all the way to the lowest aspects of nature, and does so through three levels. These levels are called the celestial [or, "heavenly"], the spiritual, and the natural. These three levels are within people from creation and therefore from birth. They are opened as the life admits. If the celestial level is opened, which is the highest and most inward, the person becomes celestial. If the spiritual level is opened, which is intermediate, the person becomes spiritual. If only the natural level is opened, which is the lowest and most outward, the person becomes natural. If people become only natural, they love only physical and worldly things. To the extent that they love these, they do not love celestial and spiritual things and do not focus on God. To this extent, they become evil.

This enables us to determine that even though the more imperfect and harmful animals and plants begin from a direct inflow from hell, they are thereafter reproduced indirectly by means of seeds, eggs, or rooting. This means that the one hypothesis is not invalidated by the other.

346. (6) *There are two forms into which this working by inflow occurs—the plant form and the animal form.* It is recognized that only two universal forms are produced on earth, on the grounds of nature's two kingdoms, called the animal kingdom and the vegetable kingdom. It is also recognized that all the members of either kingdom have a great deal in common. The members of the animal kingdom, for example, have organs of sensation and organs of locomotion, as well as members and viscera activated by brains, hearts, and lungs. Members of the vegetable kingdom take root in the earth and produce stems, branches, leaves, flowers, fruit, and seeds.

As far as their productivity is concerned, both the animal kingdom and the vegetable kingdom in their [particular] forms have their source from an inflow and spiritual working out of heaven's sun, where the Lord is, and not from any inflow and working of nature out of its own sun except in giving them fixed form, as mentioned above.

All animals, large and small, have their source in something spiritual on that lowest level called "actual." Only man derives from all the levels—three in number, called celestial, spiritual, and natural.

Since each vertical or distinct level ebbs along a continuum from its perfect to its imperfect form, the way light wanes into darkness, so do animals, which means that there are perfect, less perfect, and imperfect animals.

The perfect animals are elephants, camels, horses, mules, cattle, sheep, goats, and the others that go in flocks and herds. The less perfect are the flying ones. The imperfect ones are fish and shellfish, which, being the lowest members of their level, are in the darkness, so to speak, while the former are in the light.

Still, since their life comes only from that lowest spiritual level called natural, they can only look toward the earth, focusing there on their food and, for the sake of propagation, on other members of their own species. For all of them, their soul is a natural affection, an appetite.

The same holds true for members of the vegetable kingdom. There are perfect, less perfect, and imperfect ones. The perfect ones are fruit trees; the less perfect are major vines and bushes; the imperfect are cereals. Plants, however, derive their spiritual aspect from being uses, while animals derived their spiritual aspect from being affections and appetites, as we have said.

347. (7) *Each form, while it is manifest, receives the means of reproduction.*
We have explained above (nn. 313-318) that there is an image of creation in everything the earth brings forth, whether it belongs to the vegetable kingdom or the animal kingdom, and also that there is an image of the human and even an image of the infinite and eternal. The presence of an image of the infinite and eternal comes out in the ability to reproduce to infinity and to eternity. This is why they all receive the means of reproduction, members of the animal kingdom by means of sperm and egg either in a womb or by spawning, and members of the vegetable kingdom by means of seeds in the earth.

This enables us to determine that even though the more imperfect and harmful animals and plants begin from a direct inflow from hell, they are thereafter reproduced indirectly by means of seeds, eggs, or rooting. This means that the one hypothesis is not invalidated by the other.

348. The following experience may serve to illustrate the fact that all uses, good and evil alike, come

from a spiritual source, that is, from the sun where the Lord is.

I heard that good and true things were being sent down through the heavens by the Lord to the hells, and that these very things, accepted level by level down to the bottom, were being turned into the evil and false things opposed to the good and true ones that were being sent down.

The reason this happened was that the receiving subjects turned everything that flowed in into the kinds of things that agreed with their own forms, exactly the way the pure white light of the sun is turned into hideous colors and into blackness in objects whose substances are more inwardly in forms that stifle and extinguish light. So too, swamps, manure, and carrion turn the sun's warmth into stenches.

This enables us to determine that even evil uses come from the spiritual sun, but that good uses are changed into evil ones in hell. We can therefore see that the Lord did not create and does not create anything but good uses, but that hell produces the evil ones.

VISIBLE FEATURES OF THE CREATED UNIVERSE WITNESS THAT NATURE HAS PRODUCED NOTHING AND PRODUCES NOTHING— THE DIVINE RATHER PROVIDES EVERYTHING FROM ITSELF, AND DOES THIS BY MEANS OF THE SPIRITUAL WORLD.

349. Many people in this world talk on the basis of the appearance that the sun, through its warmth and light, is producing what we see in plains, fields, gardens, and woods. They talk as though the sun were by its warmth pushing worms out of eggs and making the beasts of the earth and the birds of the air multiply, even making human beings live.

People who talk this way, wholly on the basis of the appearance, can do so as long as they do not attribute these powers to nature—as long as they are not really thinking about it. So people who speak of the sun as rising and setting, making days and years, being at one height or another, are likewise talking on the basis of an appearance. They can talk this way without attributing these powers to the sun. They are not actually thinking about the sun's stillness and the earth's motion.

But people who deliberately decide that the sun, by its warmth and light, is producing the things we see on earth, ultimately attribute everything to nature, even the creation of the universe. They become materialists, and finally atheists.

Later they may, of course, say that God created nature and endowed it with the power of producing this kind of thing. However, they say this because they are afraid of loss of reputation. When they speak of God the Creator, they still mean nature and the inmost of nature; and at this point they are wholly disregarding the divine things which the church teaches.

350. Still, we must forgive some people for giving nature credit for everything visible, and this for two reasons. *First*, they have had no knowledge of heaven's sun, where the Lord is, and of the inflow that comes from it. Nor have they had any knowledge of the spiritual world and its state, or of its presence with people on earth. So the only way they could think of the spiritual was as a purer form of the natural, meaning that angels are in the ether or on the stars. Then the devil must be man's evil—or if he does really exist, he is either in the air or in the depths. And then people's souls after death are either at the center of the earth or in some never-never land [*ubi seu pu*] until judgment day. Then there are other ideas of the same sort, suggested by fancy because of ignorance of the spiritual world and its sun.

The *second* reason for forgiving them is that they have had no way of knowing how the divine produces all these things on earth, where there are both good and evil things. They have been afraid to come to a decision because they did not want to attribute evil to God or adopt a material concept of God, making God and nature one and thus mixing them together.

These are the two reasons for forgiving people who have believed that nature produces everything visible by something instilled into it from creation.

However, people who have made themselves atheists by deciding in favor of nature are not to be forgiven, because they could have decided in favor of the divine. Ignorance does indeed excuse, but it does not annul what is false by conscious decision, since this kind of falsity fastens itself to what is evil, and therefore to hell. Consequently, people who decide in favor of nature to the point of severing the divine from it do not think of anything as sinful, since any sin is [sin because it is] opposed to the divine which they have severed and thereby cast aside. And people who in spirit do not think of anything as sinful, when they become spirits after death, dash hell-bound into the unspeakable practices that follow from their cravings, which have then been given free rein.

351. For people who do believe that the divine is at work in the details of nature, there are many things they see in nature that enable them to decide in favor of the divine, just as surely as people who decide in favor of nature and even more so. People who decide in favor of the divine pay attention to the marvels they observe in the growth of both plants and animals.

In the growth of plants, they observe that out of a tiny seed sown in the ground there emerges a root, then a stem by means of the root, and then in turn branches, leaves, blossoms, and fruit, right through to new seeds. It is exactly as though the seed knew the proper sequence or process for its own renewal.

Can any rational person think that the sun, which is nothing but fire, knows how to do this, or that it can endow its warmth and light to cause such results, and can even form the marvels plants contain and press toward a use? If a people's rational ability is raised upward, then when they see and ponder such phenomena, their only thought must be that they come from Him whose wisdom is infinite—that is, from God.

People who acknowledge a divine do both see this and think in this way. People who do not acknowledge a divine though, do not see and think like this because they do not want to. Further, in this way they lower their rational ability into their sensory [mind], which draws all its concepts from the light the physical senses are involved in; and they defend their illusions by saying, "Do you see the sun doing all this with its warmth and light? What is something you can't see? Is it anything?"

People who decide in favor of the divine pay attention to the marvels they observe in *the growth of animals*. Here I need mention only the example of eggs. Hidden within them are the chicks, in seed or in rudiments, together with everything needed to hatch them, and even every stage after hatching to becoming birds or flying creatures in the form of their parents. And if we pay attention to the actual nature of the form, we cannot, on deep reflection, help being stunned by the fact that the smallest and largest flying creatures alike—those too small to see as well as the visible ones—contain sensory organs for sight, smell, taste, and touch, and motor organs involving muscles, actually flying and walking, along with viscera surrounding a heart and lungs, controlled by brains.

The fact that even insignificant insects enjoy these organs has been recognized through anatomical research on them by a number of individuals, most notably Swammerdam in his *Biblia Naturae*.

People who give nature credit for everything do of course see things like this, but think simply that the phenomena are there and say that nature produces them. They say this because they have turned their minds away from thinking about the divine. And since they have turned away from thinking about the divine, when they see nature's marvels they cannot think rationally, let alone spiritually. They think in terms of sense-impressions and matter. So their thinking is confined to nature and depends on nature without rising above it, like that of the people in hell. The only difference between them and animals is in the strength of their rationality—that is, in the fact they they could understand and therefore think differently if they wanted to.

352. When people who have turned away from thinking about the divine see marvelous things in nature and become sense-centered as a result, they are not reflecting that [physical] eyesight is so crude that it sees a multitude of tiny insects as a single cloud. Yet each single insect is furnished with organs for sensation and motion—provided therefore with fibers and ducts, with minute hearts, lung-tubes, minute viscera, and brains. These are woven from the purest elements of nature, and the ways they are woven are responsive to a specific life, which activates the most minute parts individually.

If the eyesight is so crude that these countless creatures, each one comprising countless parts, look like a little cloud, and if sense-centered people think and draw conclusions on the basis of this sight, we can see how debased their minds are, and how benighted as to matters of the spirit.

353. Anyone who wants to can decide in favor of the divine on the basis of what can be seen in nature. People do make this decision if they think about God, on the basis of life. When they see the birds of the air, for

example, they can realize that each kind knows its own nourishment and where to find it. It knows its fellow-members by sound and sight, recognizing which are friends and which are enemies. Birds choose mates, couple sexually, build their nests ingeniously, lay their eggs, brood over them, know the incubation time, just when the chicks will hatch. They love them most tenderly, cherish them under their wings, search out food and nourish them. Yet they do all this on their own, and are able to do other similar things, begetting a family and perpetuating their kind.

Anyone who wants to think about a divine inflow through the spiritual world into the natural can see it in these phenomena. Anyone who wants to can say at heart, "Skills like this could not flow into them from the sun, through its light rays. The sun, which gives nature its beginning and essence, is actually nothing but fire, so its light rays are completely lifeless." This lets us conclude that things like this result from an inflow of divine wisdom into the lowest elements of nature.

354. Anyone can decide in favor of the divine on the basis of visible phenomena in nature by looking at worms. From the delight of their individual cravings, they strive and long for a changing of their earthly state into a kind of state that parallels the heavenly one. So they crawl into their nooks, put themselves into a womb, so to speak, in order to be reborn. There they turn into incipient and complete chrysalids, caterpillars, pupae, and finally butterflies. Then, with this transformation completed, endowed with lovely wings according to their species, they fly through the air as though it were their heaven. They play cheerfully there, they mate, they lay their eggs, and they provide themselves with descendants; and all the while they are nourishing themselves with a delightfully sweet food from flowers.

Can anyone who is deciding in favor of the divine on the basis of phenomena visible in nature fail to see some image of our own earthly state in them when they are worms, and an image of our heavenly state in them when they are butterflies?   In contrast, people who are deciding in favor of nature do see these processes, but because they have mentally denied the human heavenly state, they call them simply natural instincts.

355. Anyone can decide in favor of the divine on the basis of phenomena visible in nature by looking closely at what we know about bees. They know how to gather wax from plants and flowers, and how to suck out honey. They know how to build cells like miniature houses, how to arrange them in the form of a community with avenues for entering and leaving. From a distance they scent the flowers and plants from which they gather wax for their housing and nectar for their food, and once they are loaded full, they fly straight back to their hive. In this way, they provide themselves with food and housing for the coming winter, just as though they foresaw it and knew what they were doing.

They also appoint a regent for themselves, like a queen, who gives birth to their descendants. They build her a kind of throne room overhead and provide her with attendants. When egg-laying time arrives, she goes from cell to cell with her attendants and lays her eggs, which her retinue seals in to prevent any damage by exposure to the air. This is how their new generation is provided.

Later, when this generation has so come of age that it can do these same things, it is driven out of the home. Then the generation that has been driven out immediately collects itself into a swarm. Then in a troop, so as not to lose contact, it flies off to find a place to live.

Further, around autumn the useless drones are led out and their wings are shorn off to prevent their return and their use of food to which they contributed no labor; and there are other processes as well.

We can determine from this that they have, because of the use they serve to the human race, as a result of an inflow from the spiritual world, a form of government such as we can find among people on earth, and even among angels in the heavens.

Can anyone of sound reason fail to see that they do not get things like this from the natural world? What does the sun that nature comes from have in common with a government that resembles and parallels heavenly government?

Observing these and like phenomena among brute animals, the devotee of nature, the nature-worshipper, decides in favor of nature, while the devotee of God, the God-worshipper, sees the same things and decides in favor of the divine. For a spiritual person sees spiritual things within these phenomena and a natural person sees natural things in them— both see what resembles themselves.

As for me, things like this have been witnesses to the inflow of the spiritual into the natural, or of the spiritual world into the natural world, from the Lord's divine wisdom.

Reflect too, whether you could think analytically about any form of government, any civil law, any moral value, or any spiritual truth, if the divine did not flow in from wisdom through the spiritual world. As for me, I never could and I cannot now. I have been distinctively and sensibly aware of that inflow constantly for some nineteen years now, so I am speaking as a witness.

356. Can any natural thing have use as a goal, and arrange uses in patterns and forms? Only one who is wise can do this, and only God, whose wisdom is infinite, can organize and form the universe in this way.

Who or what else can foresee and provide all the things that serve people for food and clothing—food from the fruits of the earth and from animals, and clothing from the same sources? One of earth's miracles is that those insignificant creatures called silkworms dress us in silk and adorn us gloriously—women and men from queens and kings to maids and footmen. And those insignificant creatures called bees provide wax for the lights that add splendor to cathedrals and palaces.

These and many other phenomena are visible pledges that the Lord by Himself is controlling through the spiritual world everything that happens in nature.

357. I need to add that I have seen in the spiritual world people who have decided in favor of nature on the basis of visible phenomena, to the point of becoming atheists. In a spiritual light, their discernment seems opened downward but closed upward, because in thought they focused downward toward the earth, not upward toward heaven. There seemed to be a kind of film above their sensory level, which is the lowest level of discernment. In some of them it was flashing with a hellish fire, in some of them it was black as soot, and in some it was pale as a corpse.

Let each of us beware of decisions in favor of nature. Let each decide for the divine—there is no lack of means.

CHAPTER V

[THE GOAL OF CREATION]

THERE ARE WITHIN THE HUMAN BEING TWO RECIPIENT VESSELS AND DWELLINGS OF THE LORD, CREATED AND FORMED BY HIM, CALLED INTENTION AND DISCERNMENT. INTENTION SERVES HIS DIVINE LOVE, AND DISCERNMENT SERVES HIS DIVINE WISDOM.

358. We have discussed the divine love and divine wisdom of God the Creator, who is the Lord from eternity, and we have discussed the creation of the universe. Now we need to say something about the creation of humanity.

We read that humanity was created in the image of God, according to His likeness (Genesis 1:26). In this passage, "the image of God" means His divine wisdom, and "the likeness of God" means divine love. For wisdom is simply the image of love—love actually presents itself to be seen and recognized in wisdom. And since it is there seen and recognized, wisdom is its image.

Love, further, is the Reality [*Esse*] of life, and wisdom is the Presence [*Existere*] of life, from love. The "likeness-and-image" of God is clearly visible in angels. Love actually glows from within their faces and wisdom in their beauty; and beauty is the form of their love. This I have seen and recognized.

359. People cannot be images of God, according to His likeness, unless God is within them and is their life from the very center. God's presence within people, and His being their life from the very center, follows from what we have presented above (nn. 4-6)—that God alone is life and that angels and mortals are recipients of life from Him.

People have learned from the Word that God is within them and makes His abode there. And since this has been learned from the Word, preachers are in the habit of talking about preparing to receive Him, about His entering us and being in our hearts, and about our being His dwelling place. Devout people say the same sort of thing in prayer. It is applied even more explicitly to the Holy Spirit who they believe is within them when they are in holy zeal and are thinking, speaking, and preaching from that zeal.

We have explained in *The Doctrine of the Lord* (nn. 1-53) that the Holy Spirit is the Lord and not some God who is a self-contained person. In fact, the Lord says, "On that day you will realize...that you are in Me, and I in you (John 14:21)"; and there are similar statements in John 15:4, 5 and 17:23.

360. Now, since the Lord is divine love and divine wisdom, and these two are himself in essence, for Him to dwell in us and give us life it was necessary that He create and form within us recipient vessels and dwellings for Himself—one for love and the other for wisdom. These recipient vessels and dwellings in us are called intention and discernment. The recipient vessel and dwelling of love is called intention; the recipient vessel and dwelling of wisdom is called discernment.

We shall see in the following pages that these two belong to the Lord within us and that these two are the source of all our life.

361. Our possession of these two, intention and discernment, as distinct from each other as love and wisdom, is both known and unknown in the world. It is known to common sense and unknown to thought—even less known in the description that comes from thought.

From common sense, who does not realize that intention and discernment are two distinct things within us? In fact, everyone is sensing this who hears or says of someone else, "He means well, but he's not very discerning," or "He's very sharp, but he doesn't mean well," or "I like people who are perceptive and well-intentioned, but not people who are perceptive and malicious." But when the same people think about intention and discernment they do not make them two distinct entities, but muddle them together. This is because their thinking is shaped by their physical sight.

People like this lose track even more of the distinct duality of intention when they are writing. This is because at that point their thinking is shaped by their sensory level, which is the human self-image [proprium]. This is why some people can think and speak well but still cannot write well—a common situation with the female gender.

The situation is similar in many other areas. Who doesn't know, from common sense, that people who live well are saved and people who live badly are damned? Or that people who live well come to be with angels, and there see and hear and talk like people? Or that the people who have a conscience are the ones who do what is fair from a sense of fairness, what is right from a sense of rightness?

But if people drift away from common sense and subject these matters to thought, they no longer know what conscience is or that the soul can see and hear and talk like a person or what a good life is, beyond giving to the poor. However, if you write this sort of thing from thought, you confirm it with appearances and illusions, with words that have sound but no substance.

This is why many scholars who have done a great deal of thinking (and even more, scholars who have written on the subject) have crippled and beclouded and even destroyed their own common sense. And this is why simple folk see what is good and true more clearly than people who believe themselves wiser.

Common sense is the result of an inflow from heaven, and descends into thought all the way to sight. But thought severed from common sense descends into a kind of projection [*imaginationem*] that is born of [physical] sight and one's self-image.

I have experienced the truth of this. Tell people with common sense something true, and they will see it. Tell them that we have our being, live, and move from God and in God, and they will see it. Tell them that God dwells with human beings in love and wisdom, and they will see it. Tell them even that intention is the recipient vessel of love and discernment the recipient vessel of wisdom, and explain it a little, and they will see it. Tell them that God is love itself and wisdom itself, and they will see it. Ask them what conscience is, and they will tell you. But say the same things to scholars who have not been thinking from common sense, but rather from concepts garnered from the world through physical sight—they will not see. Then ponder who is wiser.

INTENTION AND DISCERNMENT, THE TWO RECIPIENT VESSELS OF LOVE AND WISDOM, ARE IN THE BRAINS—THROUGHOUT AND IN EACH PART—AND THEREBY THEY ARE IN THE BODY, THROUGHOUT AND IN EACH PART.

362. We need to explain this in the following sequence.

> (1) *Love and wisdom, and therefore intention and discernment, make up a person's very life.*

> (2) *A person's life occurs in its primary forms in the brains, and in derived forms in the body.*

> (3) *The quality of life overall and in each part depends on the quality of that life in its primary forms.*

> (4) *Through these primary forms, life comes from each part into the whole organism, and from the whole organism into each part.*

> (5) *A person's quality depends on the quality of his or her love and wisdom.*

363. (1) *Love and wisdom, and therefore intention and discernment, make up a person's very life.*

Hardly anyone knows what life is. When people think about it, it seems elusive, something that defies conceptualization.

It seems that way because people do not realize that God alone is life, and that His life is divine love and divine wisdom. So we can see that our own life is no different, and that there is life in us to the extent that we receive it.

It is acknowledged that warmth and light come from the sun, that all things in the universe are recipient of them, and that they flourish and brighten to the extent that they do receive. This is true also of that sun where the Lord is, whose radiant warmth is love and whose radiant light is wisdom, as we explained in Chapter 2. Life, then, comes from these two things that emanate from the Lord as the sun.

We can also determine that life is love and wisdom from the Lord from the fact that as love ebbs away from anyone, that person becomes sluggish, and that as wisdom ebbs away from anyone, that person becomes dull. If they ebb away completely, that individual is snuffed out.

There are many facets of love, variously labeled because they are derivatives. There are for example affections, cravings, appetites, and their forms of gratification and pleasure. There are also many facets of wisdom, such as perception, reflection, recall, thought, and concentration. Then there are many facets of love and wisdom together, like agreement, logical conclusion, and decision to act, among others. All of these do of course involve both love and wisdom, but they are assigned to the function that is dominant and closest to the surface.

The final derivatives of love and wisdom are the sensory processes of sight, hearing, smell, taste, and touch, together with their forms of gratification and charm.

It seems as though the eye sees; but discernment is seeing through the eye. This is why seeing is predicated of discernment. It seems as though the ear hears; but discernment is hearing through the ear. So hearing is predicated of that focus and listening that characterize discernment. It seems as though the nose smells and the tongue tastes; but discernment is both smelling and tasting through its ability to perceive. So smelling and tasting are predicated of perception. The list could be expanded.

The wellsprings of all these functions are love and wisdom. We can therefore conclude that these two make up a person's life.

364. Everybody sees that discernment is the recipient vessel of wisdom, but not many see that intention is the recipient vessel of love. This is because intention does not do anything by itself, but works through discernment. It is also because intention's love, as it moves across into discernment's wisdom, changes into affection first, and moves across in that form.

And affection is perceived only as a kind of pleasure in thinking or speaking or acting, to which we do not pay attention. Yet we can see that love is the source from the fact that people intend what they love and do not intend what they do not love.

365. (2) *A person's life occurs in its primary forms in the brains, and in derived forms in the body.*

"In primary forms" means "in first things," and "in derived forms" means "in things produced and formed from first things"; and by "life in its primary forms," we mean intention and discernment. These are the two things that are in the brains in their primary forms and in the body in their derived forms.

We conclude that the primary or first forms of life are in the brains on the following grounds.

(1) From actual feeling. When people concentrate their minds and think, they perceive themselves as thinking inside their brain. They draw in their eyesight, so to speak, furrow their brows, and perceive that a process of exploration is going on inside, especially behind and a little above the forehead.

(2) From human development in the womb. The brain or head comes first, and then gradually develops a body.

(3) The head is on top and the body below. It is orderly for higher things to act on lower ones, and not vice versa.

(4) Brain damage, whether in the womb, by injury, by disease, or by too much strain, results in shaky thinking, and sometimes the mind wanders.

(5) All the senses of the outer body—sight, hearing, smell, taste, and the all-inclusive sense called touch, and even speech—occur in the front part of the head called the face, communicate directly with the brains through

nerves, and get their sensitive and active life from the brains.

(6) This is why affections, which come from love, can be seen imaged somehow in the face; while thoughts, which come from wisdom, give a certain light to the eyes.

(7) Anatomy demonstrates that all the nerves come down through the neck into the body—none of them comes up through the body into the brains. Where we find the primary forms and beginnings of nerves, there are the primary forms and beginnings of life. Can anyone persist in denying that the beginning of life is at the beginning of the nerves?

(8) Ask anyone with common sense, "Where is your thinking, or where do you think?" The answer will be, "In my head." Or then ask people who would locate the seat of the soul in some gland or in the heart or somewhere else, "Where do we find affection and consequent thought in their first form? Isn't it in the brain?" They will either say no or claim ignorance. You may find the reason for this ignorance in n. 361 above.

366. (3) *The quality of life overall and in each part depends on the quality of that life in its primary forms.*

To understand this, we need to explain just where in the brains the primary forms are, and how they branch out.

Anatomy discloses just where in the brains these primary forms are. From anatomy, we learn that there are two brains, which are extended from the head into the spine. These brains consist of two substances, called "cortical substance" and "medullary substance." The cortical substance consists of countless things like tiny glands, and the medullary substance of countless things like fibers.

Now, since these tiny glands are the heads of the little fibers, they are also their primary forms. In fact, the fibers begin from them, reach out from there, and gradually gather into nerves; and bundled together or made into nerves, they reach down to the sensory organs in the face and the motor organs in the body, and form them. Check with any competent anatomist, and you will verify this.

This cortical or glandular substance makes up the surface of the brain, and the surface of the corpora striata from which the medulla oblongata comes, and it makes up the center of the cerebellum and of the medulla spinalis. The medullary or fibrous substance, on the other hand, begins throughout and continues outward. It is the source of the nerves, which are the source of everything in the body. Autopsies verify this.

People who know this, whether by knowing anatomy firsthand or by checking with people who know anatomy, can see that the primary forms of life are in no other location than where the fibers begin, and that the fibers cannot extend from themselves, but from these beginnings.

The primary forms or beginnings, which look like tiny glands, are practically innumerable. We could compare their abundance to the abundance of stars in the universe, and the abundance of derivative fibers to the abundance of rays that travel out from the stars and bring their warmth and light to their planets.

The abundance of these tiny glands could be compared to the abundance of angelic communities in the heavens, which are also beyond counting, and are arranged, I am told, in a similar design. And the abundance of little fibers reaching out could be compared to the true and good spiritual influences that flow down from those communities in a similar way, like rays.

This is why a human being is like a universe and like a heaven in its smallest form, as we have stated and explained so many times already.

This enables us to conclude that the quality of life in derived forms depends on its quality in its primary forms, or that the quality of life in its first forms in the brains determines its quality in dependent forms in the body.

367. (4)*Through these primary forms, life comes from each part into the whole organism, and from the whole organism into each part.*

This is because the whole organism, brain and body together, consists initially of nothing but the fibers that extend from their primary forms in the brains. This is the only source, as we can see from the explanations just above (n. 366). This means that the whole organism depends on each part. The reason life come through these primary forms from the whole organism into each part is that the whole organism provides each part its own proper share and need, thereby making it an integral part of the whole. In brief, the whole organism is formed [*existit*] from the parts, and the parts are maintained [*subsistunt*] by the whole. Many things in the body show us that there is this kind of mutual uniting, and a joining together as a result.

In fact, in the body as in a state, republic or kingdom, the larger whole is formed from individual people who are parts, and the parts or individuals are maintained by the larger whole. It is the same with anything that is characterized by form, especially in human beings.

368. (5) *A person's quality depends on the quality of his or her love and wisdom.*

This is because the quality of love and wisdom determines that of intention and discernment, intention being actually the recipient vessel of love and discernment the recipient vessel of wisdom, as we have explained above. These two functions make up the person and determine his or her quality.

Love is complex. It is so complex that its variant forms are beyond definition. This we can confirm by looking at the human race on earth and in the heavens. No one person or angel is so like another that there is no difference. It is love that makes the difference; each individual is in fact his or her own love.

People think that wisdom makes the difference, but wisdom comes from love. It is love's form. For love is the reality [Esse] of life, and wisdom is the presence [Existere] of life from that reality.

People in this world believe that discernment makes a person. But they believe this because discernment can be lifted into heaven's light (as explained above), and this makes people seem wise. But the very discernment that climbs up—that is, the discernment that does not belong to love—seems to belong to the person, as though the person were therefore like that discernment; but this is an appearance only. Actually, the discernment that climbs up belongs to a love of knowing and being wise but not to a love as well of applying to life the things one knows or is wise about. So in the world, it either eventually ebbs away or lingers outside the contents of the memory, at the edges, like a fallen leaf. So after death its connection is severed, and nothing of it is left except that part that is in harmony with the spirit's own love.

Since love constitutes a person's life—and therefore constitutes the actual person—all the communities of heaven and all the angels in those communities are arranged according to their affections, which are matters of love. No community, and no angel within a community, is given a place dependent on some discernment that is severed from its love. The same holds true for the hells and their communities, though their arrangement depends on loves that are opposite to heavenly loves.

These considerations enable us to conclude that the quality of love determines the quality of wisdom, and that this is the source of the quality of the person.

369. It is admitted that people's quality depends on the quality of their dominant love, but this is taken as referring only to their quality as to mind or personality [animum], not to their physical quality, and not therefore to their total quality. But an abundance of experience in the spiritual world has made me aware that people's whole quality—from head to toe, or from origins in the head to final effects [ultima] in the body—depends on the quality of their love.

In fact, all the people in that world are forms of their loves. Angels are forms of heavenly love, and devils are forms of hellish love. The latter are physically and facially deformed, while the former are physically and facially lovely. Further, when their love is attacked, their faces change, and if the attack is severe, they vanish. This is a unique feature of that world. It happens that way because their bodies are one with their minds.

We can see the reason in what has already been said. All the components of the body are derived—that is, woven out of fibers as a result of fundamental principles which are vessels recipient of love and wisdom. When the fundamental principles are of a given quality, their derivatives cannot have some other quality. So wherever the fundamental principles go, the derivatives follow. They cannot diverge.

This is why people who lift their minds to the Lord are wholly lifted to the Lord, and people who drop their minds into hell fall wholly into hell. So depending on the love, the whole person goes either to heaven or to hell.

One element of angelic wisdom is that a person's mind is the person because God is Person, and that the body is the mind's outside that senses and acts. They are therefore one and not two.

370. We need to note that the actual forms of a person's members and organs and viscera, seen as actually woven together, are made from fibers that start from beginnings in the brains. However, they are stabilized by typical earthly substances and materials, and by substances and materials derived from the earth in the air and ether, which happens by way of the blood. So if all parts of the body are to stay in their proper forms and thereby keep functioning properly, the person needs to be nourished by material food and constantly renewed.

INTENTION'S CORRESPONDENCE IS WITH THE HEART, AND DISCERNMENT'S WITH THE LUNGS

371. This needs to be presented in the following sequence.

(1) *All elements of the mind relate to intention and discernment, and all elements of the body to the heart and the lungs.*

(2) *There is a correspondence of intention and discernment with the heart and the lungs, and consequently a correspondence of all elements of the mind with all elements of the body.*

(3) *Intention corresponds to the heart.*

(4) *Discernment corresponds to the lungs.*

(5) *This correspondence enables us to discover many unknown facts about intention and discernment, and therefore about love and wisdom as well.*

(6) *The human mind is the human spirit: the spirit is the person: the body is an "outside" through which the mind or spirit senses and acts in the world of the body.*

(7) *The uniting of the human spirit with a body occurs by means of the correspondence of a*

person's intention and discernment with his or her heart and lungs, and severing occurs through non-correspondence.

372. (1) All elements of the mind relate to intention and discernment, and all elements of the body to the heart and lungs.

"Mind" means nothing but intention and discernment, which as aggregates are all the things that move a person and all things a person thinks. So they are all the things that belong to an individual's affection and thought. The things that move a person belong to intention, and the things a person thinks belong to discernment.

It is recognized that all the elements of human thought are matters of discernment, because people think as a result of discernment. But it is not equally recognized that all elements of human affection are elements of intention.

The reason this is not recognized is that when people are thinking, they do not pay attention to the affection but only to what they are thinking. It is like listening to someone talk and not paying attention to the sound but to the actual discourse; and the affection within thought is situated like the sound within speech. So people's affection can be recognized from the sound of their voice, and their thought from what they are saying.

The reason affection is a matter of intention is that all affection belongs to love, and the vessel recipient of love is intention.

Anyone who does not realize that affection is a matter of intention is mixing affection with discernment. Such people are claiming that they are one, when in fact they are not one, but rather act as one.

We can see this confusion in colloquial speech when someone says, "I think I'll do that," meaning "I intend to do it." Yet the fact that they are two things is also clear in colloquial speech when someone says, "I want to think that over." Within the thinking of discernment there is affection of intention, just as there is sound in speech, as we have stated.

It is recognized that all elements of the body relate to the heart and the lungs. But the correspondence of heart and lungs with intention and discernment is not recognized, so we need to discuss this next.

373. Since intention and discernment are vessels recipient of love and wisdom, they are two organic forms—that is, forms constructed out of the purest substances. They must be like this in order to be recipient vessels. The fact that their structure cannot be seen by the eye is no problem. It is beyond eyesight, even when that is amplified by a microscope.

The smallest insects—which have sensory and motor organs within them, since they sense and move and fly—are also beyond eyesight. Skilled observers, using microscopes, have discovered by dissection that they have brains, hearts, lung cavities, and digestive organs. If these little insects themselves are invisible to the naked eye (to say nothing of the minute organs they comprise) while we cannot deny that they are so constructed right down to their last details, then how can anyone claim that the two vessels recipient of love and wisdom, called intention and discernment, are not organic forms? How can the love and wisdom that are life from the Lord act into something which is not objective, into something which does not take substantial form? How else can thought be truly resident, and how can anyone talk from non-resident thought? Isn't the brain, where thought takes form, full, with every part of it structured? These organic forms are visible to the naked eye, discernible recipient vessels of elemental intention and discernment in the cortical substance, that look like very small glands (on this subject, see n. 366 above). Please do not base your thinking about these functions on the concept of a vacuum. A vacuum is nothing, and nothing happens in nothing, and nothing arises from nothing (on the concept of a vacuum, see n. 82 above).

374. (2) *There is a correspondence of intention and discernment with the heart and lungs, and consequently a correspondence of all elements of the mind with all elements of the body.*

This is something new, being unrecognized until now because people have not known what the spiritual is and how it differs from the natural, and therefore have not known what correspondence is. Correspondence is in fact a correspondence of spiritual phenomena with natural ones, and is the means of their being united.

We say that until now people have not known what the spiritual is, what its correspondence with the natural is, and therefore what correspondence is; and yet all this could have been known. Is anyone ignorant of the fact that affection and thought are spiritual? Is anyone ignorant of the fact that action and speech are natural, and that in consequence all facets of action and speech are natural? Is anyone ignorant of the fact that affection and thought, which are spiritual, enable people to act and speak? Is anyone then unable to know the nature of the correspondence of spiritual phenomena with natural ones? Doesn't thought enable the tongue to speak, doesn't affection in unison with thought enable the body to act?

These are two separable phenomena. I can think and not speak, and I can intend and not act. And we know that the body does not think, does not intend, but that thinking rather descends into speech and intention into action.

Doesn't affection radiate from the face, and display its own image there? Everyone recognizes this. Isn't affection spiritual by nature, and aren't the facial changes we call "expressions" natural? Is anyone incapable of drawing the conclusion, then, that correspondence exists, and that there is therefore a correspondence of all elements of the mind with all elements of the body? And since all elements of the mind relate to affection and thought (or, which is the same thing, to intention and discernment), and all elements of the body to the heart and the lungs, is anyone incapable of concluding that intention's correspondence is with the heart, and discernment's with the lungs?

The reason things like this have gone unrecognized is that people have become so "external" that they have been unwilling to admit anything except what is natural. This was their love's delight, and consequently the delight of their discernment. So raising thought above the natural to anything spiritual distinct from the natural was unpleasant for them. As a result, they have been unable to think of the spiritual, on the basis of their natural love and its delight, as anything but a rarefied natural, and they saw correspondence as something flowing in with no break whatever. In fact, completely natural people cannot conceive of anything separate from the natural—to them, this is nothing.

Another reason these matters have gone unseen and unrecognized until now is that people have taken all the elements of theology we call spiritual and put them away out of human sight. They have done this by means of the unreasoning principle, accepted throughout Christendom, that the spiritual theological matters which councils and some authorities have decided, are to be believed blindly—because, they say, they transcend comprehension. In consequence, they have come to think that the spiritual is like some bird that flies above the atmosphere in the ether, beyond the reach of eyesight. Yet in fact it is like a bird of paradise that flies so close to the eye that its lovely features brush the pupil, longing to be seen. Eyesight means the sight of discernment.

375. The correspondence of intention and discernment with heart and lungs cannot be established baldly [nude], that is, simply by reasoning; but it can be established by taking their effects into account.

It is the same as it is with the causes of things. We can see some of these by reasoning, but we see them clearly only through their effects. The causes are actually within the effects, and present themselves to view in them. The mind draws no conclusions about causes before taking this step.

We will be discussing the effects of the correspondence in question in the pages following. But first, so that no one slip back into preconceived, theorized concepts of the soul in connection with this concept, the material presented in the preceding section should be read through—nn. 363 and 364, for example, on love and wisdom (and therefore intention and discernment) making up a person's life; n. 365 on a person's life occurring in its primary forms in the brains and in derived forms in the body; n. 366 on the quality of life overall and in each particular depending on the quality of that life in its primary forms; n. 367 on life coming through those primary forms from each part into the whole and from the whole into each part; and n. 368 on the quality of people's life determining the quality of their wisdom and therefore the quality of their character.

376. In support of this, I may at this point cite a presentation of the correspondence of intention and discernment with heart and lungs 'which I saw in heaven with some angels.

By a marvelous flowing into intricate spirals, quite beyond words to describe, they kept forming an image of a heart and an image of lungs, including all their inner complexities; and they were following then the flow of heaven. For heaven impels itself into forms like these as a result of the inflow of love and wisdom from the Lord. So they were picturing the union of heart and lungs and at the same time their correspondence with the love of intention and the wisdom of discernment. They referred to this correspondence and union as "heavenly marriage," saying that it was the same through the whole body, even in its specific members, organs, and viscera. They said also that anywhere the heart and lungs are not working, each in turn, no impulse of life can occur from any intentional primary source, nor any sense of life from any cognitive primary source.

377. Whereas the subject of the next pages will be the correspondence of heart and lungs with intention and discernment, and this is the foundation of the correspondence of all the body's parts, namely the members, all of them, the sensory organs, and the body's viscera, and whereas the correspondence of natural with spiritual phenomena has been unrecognized until now, and has been fully presented in two works, one dealing with *Heaven and Hell* and the other, called *Arcana Coelestia*, dealing with the spiritual meaning of the Word in Genesis and Exodus, I should therefore like at this time to point out what has been written and explained in those two works on the topic of correspondence.

In the book *Heaven and Hell*:

> The correspondence of everything heavenly with everything human (nn. 87-102)
>
> The correspondence of everything heavenly with everything earthly (nn. 103-115)

In the work on the spiritual meaning of Genesis and Exodus, called *Arcana Coelestia*:

> The correspondence of the face and its expression with affections of the mind (nn. 1568, 2988, 2989, 3631, 4796, 4797, 4800, 5165, 5168, 5695, 9306).

The correspondence of the body, in reference to its behavior and actions, with matters of discernment and intention (nn. 2988, 3632, 4215).

The correspondence of the senses in general (nn. 4318-4330).

The correspondence of the eyes and their sight (nn. 4403-4420).

The correspondence of the nostrils and of smell (nn. 4624-4634).

The correspondence of the ears and of hearing (nn. 4652-4660).

The correspondence of the tongue and of taste (nn. 4791-4805).

The correspondence of the hands, arms, shoulders, and feet (nn. 4931-4953).

The correspondence of the loins and of the procreative organs (nn. 5050-5062).

The correspondence of the body's inner organs, specifically the stomach, the thymus gland, the chyle receptacles and ducts, and the mesentery (nn. 5171-5180, 5181).

The correspondence of the spleen (n. 9698).

The correspondence of the peritoneum, kidneys, and bladder (nn. 5377-5385).

The correspondence of the liver, and also of the hepatic, cystic, and pancreatic ducts (nn. 5183-5185).

The correspondence of the intestines (nn. 5392-5395, 5379).

The correspondence of the bones (nn. 5560-5564).

The correspondence of the skin (nn. 5552-5559).

Heaven's correspondence with the human being (nn. 911,1900, 1982, 2996-2998, 3264-3649, 3741-3745, 3884, 4051, 4279, 4403, 4524, 4525, 6013, 6057, 9279, 9632).

There is a correspondence of everything in the natural world and its three kingdoms with everything visible in the spiritual world (nn. 1632, 1831, 2758, 2990-2993, 2997-3003, 3213-3227, 3483, 3624-3649, 4044, 4053, 4116, 4366, 4939, 5116, 5377, 5428, 5477, 8211, 9280).

Everything visible in the heavens is a correspondence (nn. 1521, 1532, 1619-1625, 1807, 1808, 1971, 1974, 1677, 1980, 1981, 2299, 2601, 3213-3226, 3349, 3350, 3475-3485, 3748, 9481, 9570, 9576, 9577).

The correspondence between the Word's literal and spiritual meanings is the topic throughout the *Arcana*; and further material on this subject may be found in *The Doctrine of Sacred Scripture*, nn. 5-69.

378. (3) *Intention corresponds to the heart.*

This cannot be as clearly established by phenomena taken singly as by looking at intention in its effects, as stated above (n. 375). Looking at a single effect, we can establish the proposition by the fact that all affections, which are matters of love, bring about changes in the motions of the heart. We can perceive this from the pulse of the arteries, which synchronizes with the heart.

The heart's changes and motions in response to love's affections are beyond counting. All we can detect with the finger are that its beat may be slow or fast, high or low, weak or strong, regular or irregular, and so on. So it is different in happiness than in sorrow, in calm than in anger, in courage than in fear, in fevers than in chills, etc.

Since the motions of the heart (called systole and diastole) undergo various changes in response to the affections of particular loves, many early people and some contemporary ones have attributed affections to the heart and have also localized their residence there. This has led to such colloquialisms as great-hearted and faint-hearted, a happy heart and a sorrowful one, a soft heart and a hard one, a large heart and a petty one, a whole heart and a broken one, a heart of flesh and a heart of stone, a heart that is heavy or gentle or mild, putting our heart into our work, granting [people] one heart, granting a new heart, taking to heart, accepting in the heart, it doesn't touch my heart, hardening the heart, and a friend in heart. So we speak [using compounds of Latin *cor, cordis*, "heart," tr.] of concord, discord, and folly [*vecordia*], and many other things involving love and its affections. The Word speaks in the same way because the Word was written in correspondences.

It makes no difference whether you say love or intention, since the recipient vesel of love is intention, as stated above.

379. The presence of a vital warmth in people, and in every animal, is recognized, but its source is not. Anyone who talks about it does so on the basis of guesswork. For this reason, some people who have not known anything about the correspondence of natural things with spiritual things have attributed its origin to the warmth of the sun, others to the motion of particles, and others to life itself. But since these last have not known what life is, this has been simply a figure of speech.

But if we know that there is a correspondence of love and its affections with the heart and its derivative systems, we can know that love is the source of vital warmth. Love, in fact, emanates as warmth from the spiritual sun where the Lord is, and is also felt as warmth by angels. It is this spiritual warmth, which is essentially love, that flows by correspondence into the heart and its blood, giving it warmth and at the same time life.

It is recognized that people become warm, virtually aflame, in response to the level of their love, and that they grow numb and cold as it decreases. For this can be felt and seen—felt in warmth throughout the body, and seen in the blush of the face. Correspondingly, the stifling of love is felt in a bodily chill, and seen in facial pallor.

Since love is a person's life, the heart is the "first and final" of human life. And since love is a person's life, and soul leads its life in the body by means of the blood, blood is called "the soul" in the Word (Gen. 9:4, Lev. 17:14). Another meaning of "soul" will be discussed below.

380. Further, blood is red because of the correspondence of the heart and blood with love and its affections. There are actually all kinds of color in the spiritual world. Red and white are the basic ones, and the others derive their distinct hues from red and white and from their opposites, which are the color of sooty flame and black. In that world, red corresponds to love and white corresponds to wisdom.

The reason red corresponds to love is that it has its source there in the fire of the sun; and the reason white corresponds to wisdom is that it has its source there in the sun's light. Because of love's correspondence with the heart, then, blood can only be red, and point to its source.

This is why the light is flamy in the heavens where love to the Lord reigns, and angels there wear purplish clothes. In the heavens where wisdom reigns, the light is clear, and the angels there wear clothes of white linen.

381. The heavens may be divided into two kingdoms, one called "heavenly" and the other called "spiritual." In the heavenly kingdom, love to the Lord reigns; and in the spiritual kingdom, wisdom from that love reigns. The kingdom where love reigns is called the heart-system of heaven, and the kingdom where wisdom reigns is called the lung-system of heaven.

We need to be aware that the whole angelic heaven, in its entirety, reflects a single person, and in the Lord's sight looks like a single person. So its heart makes one kingdom and its lungs the other. There is in fact a cardiac and a pulmonary motion in a general way in the whole heaven, and in a specific way therefore in each angel. The general cardiac and pulmonary motion is from the Lord alone, since he is the only source of love and wisdom. In fact, these two motions exist in the sun where the Lord is and which comes from him, and thereby exists in the angelic heaven and in the universe.

To see the truth of this, draw back from space and think omnipresence, and you will find assurance. On the division of the heavens into two kingdoms, heavenly and spiritual, see *Heaven and Hell*, nn. 26-28. On the whole angelic heaven, in its entirety, reflecting a single person, see *ibid*., nn. 59-67.

382. (4) *Discernment corresponds to the lungs.*

This follows from what we have been saying about the correspondence of intention with the heart. There are in fact two reigning functions in the spiritual person or in the mind—intention and discernment. And there are two reigning entities in the natural person or in the body—the heart and the lungs. There is, as stated above, a correspondence of everything mental with everything physical. It therefore follows, given that intention corresponds to the heart, that discernment corresponds to the lungs.

Further, anyone may observe that discernment corresponds to the lungs by attending to our thinking and our speaking.

As to thinking, no one can think unless a "breathing spirit" accompanies and agrees with the process. So during silent thought, there is silent breathing; if the thought is deep, the breathing is deep. The person inhales and exhales, compresses and expands the lungs, in response to the thinking, which means in response to an inflow of affection from love—slowly, quickly, avidly, gently, cautiously. Further, if people repress this spirit, they cannot think except within their spirit, on the basis of its breathing, which is imperceptible.

As to speaking, not the slightest bit of a word can emerge from the mouth without the supporting force of the lungs. In fact, all the sound that is articulated into words arises from the lungs through the trachea and the epiglottis. So speech is intensified to shouting by the inflation of the [lungs as] bellows and the widening of their passageway, and as these contract, the volume lessens. If the passage is blocked, both speech and thought come to a halt.

383. Since discernment corresponds to the lungs, and thinking therefore to the lungs' breathing, "soul" and "spirit" are used in the Word to refer to discernment. For example,

> You are to love the Lord your God with all your heart and with all your soul (Matt. 22:37).
>
> God is to grant a new heart and a new spirit (Ez. 36:26, Ps. 51:10).

We have already explained that "heart" refers to love that belongs to intention. So "soul" and "spirit" are used to refer to the wisdom of discernment.

In *The Doctrine of the Lord*, it may be seen that "the spirit of God," also called "the Holy Spirit," is used to mean divine wisdom and therefore divine truth, the means to human enlightenment. Consequently,

> The Lord breathed on His disciples and said, "Receive the Holy Spirit" (John 20:22).

So too it is said that

> Jehovah God breathed the breath of life into Adam's nostrils, and he became a living soul (Gen. 2:7).

And a prophet was told to

> Prophesy to the spirit...and say to the wind...

"Come, O spirit, from the four winds, and breathe into these that are slain, that they may live" (Ez. 37:9).

There are similar statements elsewhere. This is why the Lord is called "the spirit of the nostrils" and also "the breath of life."

Since breathing occurs through the nostrils, the nostrils are used to refer to perception. A discerning person is described as "having a good nose," and an undiscerning person as "not getting the scent [*obesae naris*]." This is also why "spirit" and "wind" are the same word in Hebrew and in some other languages. In fact, the word "spirit" is derived from "filling with breath" [*animatione*]; so when someone dies we say that he or she "gives up the spirit [*emittat animam*]." This is also why people believe that the spirit is a wind or something airy, like a breath expelled from the lungs, and have a similar notion of the soul.

This enables us to determine that "loving God with all the heart and with all the soul" means loving him with all love and all discernment, and that "granting a new heart and a new spirit" means granting a new intention and a new discernment.

Since "spirit" refers to discernment, Bezaleel is described as "filled with the spirit of wisdom, discernment, and knowledge" (Ex. 31:3); Joshua as "filled with the spirit of wisdom" (Deut. 34:9); Nebuchadnezzar described Daniel as "having within him a surpassing spirit of knowledge, discernment, and wisdom" (Dan. 5:11, 12, 14); and we read in Isaiah, "They that wander in spirit shall know discernment" (Is. 29:24). There are similar statements in many other places.

384. Since all mental elements go back to intention and discernment and all physical elements to heart and lungs, there are two brains in the head, as mutually distinguishable as are intention and discernment.

The cerebellum is primarily for intention and the cerebrum primarily for discernment.

In similar fashion, the heart and lungs within the body are set apart from the other organs. They are set apart by the diaphragm, enclosed with their own membrane called the pleura, and make up that part of the body called the chest.

In the other parts of the body, which we refer to as members, organs, and viscera, the two are united because the parts are in pairs, like the arms and hands, the legs and feet, the eyes, the nostrils, and within the body the kidneys, ureters, and testes. And the viscera that are not in pairs are divided into right and left sides, especially the cerebrum itself, with its two hemispheres, the heart with its two ventricles, the lungs with their two lobes. Their right side goes back to the good that gives rise to what is true, and their left side to the true that come from what is good. Or in other words, the right side goes back to the good of love, from which the truth of wisdom comes, and the left side to the truth of wisdom from the good of love.

Further, since the union of the good and the true is mutual, and a virtual "one" is effected by that union, the paired members of a person act as a one and together in the processes of work and motion and sensing.

385. (5.) *This correspondence enables us to discover many unknown facts about intention and discernment, and therefore about love and wisdom as well.*

In this world, there is scarcely any awareness of what intention is and what love is, because people do not have the ability to love and to intend from love at will (ex se) the way they can discern and think, apparently at will. In much the same way, they cannot, on their own, make their heart move the way they can make their lungs move at will.

Now, since there is scarcely any awareness in this world of what intention and love are, while people are aware of what the heart and lungs are (these being visible to the eye, open to investigation, and having been investigated and described by anatomists, while intention and discernment are not visible to the eye and cannot be investigated), then once it is known that they correspond and act as one through their correspondence, many unknown facts about intention and discernment may be discovered that could not be discovered in any other way. These include facts about the union of intention with discernment, and the reciprocal union of discernment with intention, or about the union of love with wisdom, and the reciprocal union of wisdom with love. Then there are facts about the way love branches out into affections, about groups of harmonious affections, and about how they flow into perceptions and thoughts, and ultimately by correspondence into the actions and senses of the body.

These and many other unknown facts can be discovered and described on the basis of the union of heart and lungs, and of the inflow of the blood from the heart into the lungs and the return flow from the lungs into the heart, and the subsequent flow through the arteries into all of the body's members, organs, and viscera.

386. (6.) *A person's mind is that person's spirit; the spirit is the person: the body is an "outside" through which the mind or spirit senses and acts in the world of the body.*

As for this proposition—that a person's mind is that person's spirit, and that the spirit is the person—this can hardly be accepted with confidence by people who have thought that the spirit is a wind and the soul something ethereal, like a breath exhaled from the lungs. In fact, they say, "How can the spirit be a person when it is only a spirit? How can the soul be a person when it is only a soul?" They apply this to God as well, since he is called a spirit.

They have derived this concept of spirit and soul from the fact that in some languages "spirit" and "wind" are expressed by the same word. Then there is the fact that when someone dies, we say that he or she "gives up the ghost" or "the soul," and that life returns to people who have suffocated or fainted when the spirit or soul [*anima*] of the lungs returns. Since in these cases people do not observe anything but breath or air, they conclude on the basis of their eyes and their physical senses that people are not their spirits and souls after death.

From this physical evaluation of spirit and soul have sprung several theories, which in turn have given rise to the belief that the person does not become a person again until the day of the last judgment, waiting around somewhere or other in the meanwhile, as we have stated in *A Continuation Concerning the Last Judgment*, nn. 32-38.

Since a person's mind is that person's spirit, angels, being spirits as well, are called minds.

387. The reason a person's mind is that person's spirit, and the spirit is the person, is that "mind" is used to mean all the elements of a person's intention and discernment. These exist in their primary forms in the brains, and in derived forms in the body. So they constitute all the elements of the person, as far as their forms are concerned. This being the case, the mind (that is, intention and discernment) controls the body and everything it comprises, at will.

Doesn't the body do what the mind thinks and intends? Doesn't the mind impel the tongue and lips to speak, make the hands and fingers do what it pleases, make the feet walk where it wishes? Could the body be like this if the mind were not present in its derivative forms in the body? Is it consistent with reason to think that the body is obediently doing this because the mind wants it to? In this case, they would be two separate things, one above and the other beneath, one giving orders and the other heeding.

Since this is not consistent with any form of reason, it follows that a person's life occurs in its primary forms in the brains, and in derived forms in the body, as we have stated above (n. 365). Further, the quality of that life in its primary forms determines its quality overall and in each part (n. 366). And further still, through these primary forms life comes from each part into the whole organism and from the whole organism into each part.

In earlier sections, we have explained that all elements of the mind go back to intention and discernment, that intention and discernment are vessels recipient of love and wisdom from the Lord, and that these two capacities make up a person's life.

388. We can also see from what we have just presented that a person's mind is the essential person. In fact, the underlying form [*tela*, "warp"] of the human form, or the essential human form, comes in all detail from the primary forms extended from the brain through the nerves, as follows from other previous statements.

This is the form a person enters after death, the form which is then called a spirit or an angel, and which is perfectly human, but spiritual. The material form which is added and superimposed in this world is not the intrinsic human form, but is derived from it. It is added and superimposed so that the individual can do useful things in a natural world, and can also bring along a kind of stable container of spiritual things made from the purer substances of this world, thereby continuing and maintaining life.

It is a matter of angelic wisdom that the human mind—not only in general, but in every detail as well—is in a constant effort toward the human form, because God is Person.

389. If a person is to be a person, no part whatever can be wanting, either in the head or in the body, that occurs in the perfect person, since there is nothing in that person that does not participate in that form and make it. It is actually the form of love and wisdom, which seen in its own right is divine.

All the limited forms of love and wisdom are within it, which are infinite in the God-Man, but finite in His image, which is the person, angel, or spirit. If any part were wanting, some corresponding limited form would be wanting from the love and wisdom, a form through which the Lord could be with the person, from fundamentals, in extremes [*a primis in ultimis*], and could, out of His divine love by means of His divine wisdom, provide uses in the created world.

390. (7.) *The uniting of people's spirit with their body occurs by means of the correspondence of their intention and discernment with their heart and lungs, and severing occurs through non-correspondence.*

Since people have not been aware that a person's mind (meaning intention and discernment) is that person's spirit, and that the spirit is the person, and since they have not been aware that a person's spirit possesses heartbeat and breathing just as the body does, there has been no way to know that the spirit's heartbeat and breathing in a person flow into the body's heartbeat and breathing, and produce them.

Given the fact that our spirit does enjoy heartbeat and breathing just as the body does, it follows that there is a like correspondence of the heartbeat and breathing of a person's spirit with the heartbeat and breathing of that person's body. As stated, the mind is actually the spirit. So when the correspondence of these two motions fails, a separation occurs, which is death.

The separation or death occurs when the body, from whatever disease or accident, reaches a state in which it is unable to cooperate with its spirit: in this way the correspondence actually perishes, and with the correspondence the union perishes as well. This does not happen when only the breathing stops, but when the heartbeat stops as well. For as long as the heart is active, there is still love with its living warmth, protecting the life, as we can see in cases of fainting and suffocation, and also from the living state of the fetus in the womb.

In short, the life of a person's body depends on the correspondence of its heartbeat and breathing with the heartbeat and breathing of that person's spirit. When that correspondence stops, physical life stops: the person's spirit leaves and takes up its life in the spiritual world, a life so like its life in the natural world that it does not know it is deceased.

Most people are in the spiritual world two days after leaving the body. I have in fact talked with some people two days after their death.

391. There is only one source of solid support for the proposition that a spirit enjoys heartbeat and breathing just like an earthly person in a body—from spirits and angels themselves, when one is granted the ability to talk with them.

I have been granted this ability. So when I have asked them about this, they have told me that they are just as much "people" as are people in this world. They too enjoy bodies, albeit spiritual ones; they too feel their hearts beating in their chests, and the pulse of the arteries in their wrists, like people in the natural world. I have asked many angels and spirit about this, and they have all said the same thing.

As for the claim that the spirit of a person in a body is breathing, I have been granted knowledge by direct experience. Some angels were once given the ability to control my breathing, to lessen it at will, and finally to withdraw it to the point that only the breathing of my spirit was left, which I then sensibly perceived. The reader may see in the book *Heaven and Hell* (n. 449) that the same thing was done to me when I was allowed to know the state of people who are dying.

Then too, sometimes I have been brought into the breathing of my spirit alone, sensibly perceiving then that it was in harmony with the general breathing of heaven. Further, on many occasions I have been with angels, in a state like theirs, lifted up to them in heaven. At these times, I was in the spirit and out of my body, and I talked with them, using breathing the way it is used in this world.

These and other living illustrations have enabled me to see the following: that the human spirit is breathing not only within the body, but also after it leaves the body; that the spirit's breathing is so quiet that it is not perceived by the person; and that it flows into the observable breathing of the body, almost the way a cause flows into a consequence, or the way thinking flows into the lungs, and through the lungs into speech.

We can also see from this that an individual's union of spirit and body occurs by means of the correspondence of the two heart motions and the two lung motions.

392. The reason these two motions (of the heart and of the lungs) occur and continue is that the whole angelic heaven, overall and in detail, is involved in these twin motions. The reason the whole angelic heaven is thus involved is that the Lord imparts them from the sun where He is, and which is from Him. For that sun activates these two motions, from the Lord. And since everything in heaven and on earth depends on the Lord through that sun, in a particular chain because of their form, like a work linked together from beginning to end, and since the life of love and

wisdom comes from Him and all energy in the universe come from life, we can see that there is no other source.

It follows that the variation of these motions depends on the way love and wisdom are accepted.

393. We will be saying more about the correspondence of these motions in subsequent pages. We will discuss, for example, what this correspondence is like for people who breathe with heaven and what it is like for people who breathe with hell. We will also discuss what it is like for people who talk with heaven and think with hell—that is, what it is like for hypocrites, flatterers, phonies, and the like.

ON THE BASIS OF THE CORRESPONDENCE OF THE HEART WITH INTENTION AND DISCERNMENT WITH THE LUNGS [sic], IT IS POSSIBLE TO KNOW EVERYTHING KNOWABLE ABOUT INTENTION AND DISCERNMENT, OR ABOUT LOVE AND WISDOM, AND THEREFORE ABOUT THE HUMAN SOUL

394. In the learned world, a great many people have sweated over the inquiry into the soul. However, since they have not known anything about the spiritual world and the state of the soul after death, all they could do was construct theories—not theories about the nature of the soul, but theories about how it operates in the body. As to the nature of the soul, the only concept they could have was one of something very pure in the ether, and the only concept they could have of what encompasses the soul was of something like the ether.

They have not dared to publish more than a little of this however, fearing that they' would attribute something natural to the soul when they knew that it was spiritual.

Given this concept of the soul, and a recognition that the soul does operate in the body and produce everything that has to do with its sensing and moving, they as mentioned have sweated over an inquiry into the way the soul operates in the body, some claiming that it happens by means of an inflow and others that it happens by means of a harmony.

But since nothing has been discovered in this approach which offers the possibility of assent to a mind that wants to see whether something is true, I have been allowed to talk with angels and to be enlightened by their wisdom in this matter. What has emerged is this. The human soul, which lives after death, is the human spirit, and is a perfectly formed person. This soul has intention and discernment, whose soul is love and wisdom from the Lord. It is these two which make a person's life, which comes from the Lord alone. To the end that he may be accepted by people, the Lord makes it seem as though the life belonged to them.

However, to keep people from attributing life to themselves as their own possession, the Lord has also taught that everything of love called good and everything of wisdom called true comes from Him, and that no trace of it comes from us. And since these two are life, this means that all of life that is life comes from Him.

395. Since the soul, in respect to its essential reality, is love and wisdom, and these two are from the Lord within people, there are therefore two receivers within people, which are also the Lord's dwelling-places within us. One is for love, and the other is for wisdom. The one for love is called intention, and the other, for wisdom, is called discernment.

Now, whereas love and wisdom in the Lord are distinguishably one (see above, nn. 17-22), and whereas divine love belongs to His divine wisdom and divine wisdom belongs to His divine love (cf. nn. 34-39), and whereas they emanate in similar fashion from the

God-Man—that is, the Lord—so in human beings these two receivers and dwellings called intention and discernment have been so created by the Lord as to be distinguishably two, but nevertheless to make one in every activity and every sensation. In these functions, intention and discernment cannot be separated.

However, so that a person may become a receiver and dwelling-place, it has been worked out as necessary for that purpose that human discernment can be raised above an individual's self-conscious love into some measure of the light of wisdom, though the individual has no love for that light. In this way people see and are taught how they are to live in order to arrive at that love and thus enjoy blessedness forever.

Now, since the human race has misused the ability to raise discernment above self-conscious love, it has destroyed within itself the ability to be a receiver and dwelling-place of the Lord—that is, of love and wisdom from the Lord. It has done this by making intention the dwelling of love of self and the world, and discernment the dwelling of things that justify these loves.

This is the origin of the fact that these two dwelling-places, intention and discernment, have become dwelling-places of hellish love, and through justifications of these loves, dwelling-places of a hellish thinking which people in hell take for wisdom.

396. The reason love of self and love of the world are hellish loves, and that people have been able to move into them and thereby destroy intention and discernment within themselves, is that by creation love of self and love of the world are heavenly. They are in fact loves, proper to the natural person, serviceable to spiritual loves, the way foundations are serviceable to houses. For love of self and the world prompt people to value their bodies, to work to be fed, clothed, and housed, to pay heed to their homes, to look for jobs in

order to be useful, even to be respected according to the importance of the matters they are responsible for, for obedience' sake, and also to find enjoyment and recreation in this world's pleasures. All these things exist for a purpose, however, which must be a use. It is by means of them, in fact, that people are in a state to serve the Lord and to serve the neighbor. However, when there is no love of serving the Lord and serving the neighbor, only a love of serving self and the world, then that love changes from heavenly to hellish. For it so works that people plunge their minds and their consciousness [animum] into their self-images, which intrinsically are utterly evil.

397. Now to prevent people from being in heaven by their discernment and in hell by their intention and thereby having divided minds, after death all discernment above the level of the deliberate love is removed.

This is how intention and discernment ultimately act as one in everyone. People in heaven have intention that loves what is good and discernment that thinks what is true. People in hell, however, have intention that loves what is evil and discernment that thinks what is false.

People in this world do the same thing when they are thinking from their spirit, which happens in solitude, even though many of them act differently when they are physically aware, which happens when they are not alone. The reason they act differently is that they raise their discernment above their own level of intention or the love of their own spirit.

We have mentioned these things so that people might know that intention and discernment are distinguishably two, yet created to act as one, and that they are compelled to act as one at least after death, if not before.

398. Now since love and wisdom—and therefore intention and discernment—are what is known as the

soul, and since in the following pages we need to state how the soul acts into the body and makes everything in it work, and since this can be known from the responsiveness of the heart to intention and of the lungs to discernment, the principles that follow have been elicited by attention to that responsiveness.

(1) *Love or intention is human life itself.*

(2) *Love or intention is constantly striving toward the human form and toward all the elements of the human form.*

(3) *Apart from a marriage with wisdom or discernment, love or intention cannot do anything through its human form.*

(4) *Love or intention prepares a home or bridal chamber for its spouse-to-be, which is wisdom or discernment.*

(5) *Love or intention also makes preparations within its human form so that it will be able to act jointly with wisdom or discernment.*

(6) *Once the wedding has taken place, the first union occurs through an affection for knowing, giving rise to an affection for what is true.*

(7) *The second union occurs through an affection for discerning, giving rise to a perception of what is true.*

(8) *The third union occurs through an affection for seeing what is true, giving rise to thought.*

(9) *Through these three unions, love or intention is engaged in its own life of sensing and its own life of acting.*

(10) *Love or intention leads wisdom or discernment into all aspects of its home.*

(11) *Love or intention does nothing except in unison with the other.*

(12) *Love or intention unites itself to wisdom or discernment, and works things out so that wisdom or discernment is united in return.*

(13) *From the power given it by love or intention, wisdom or discernment can be raised up, accept things proper to light from heaven, and perceive them.*

(14) *Love or intention can be raised up in a similar fashion, and perceive things proper to warmth from heaven, if it loves its spouse to that degree.*

(15) *Otherwise, love or intention pulls wisdom or discernment back from being raised up, so that it may act in unison with it.*

(16) *Love or intention is purified by wisdom in discernment, if they are raised up together.*

(17) *Love or intention is polluted in and by discernment if they are not raised up together.*

(18) *Love purified by wisdom in discernment becomes spiritual and heavenly.*

(19) *Love polluted in and by discernment becomes nature-centered and sense-centered.*

(20) *But there still remain an ability to discern, called rationality, and an ability to act, called freedom.*

(21) *Spiritual and heavenly love is love toward the neighbor and love for the Lord; nature-centered and sense-centered love is love of the world and love of self.*

(22) *It is the same with charity and faith and their union as it is with intention and discernment and their union.*

399. *(1) Love or intention is human life itself.* This follows from the responsiveness of the heart to intention (discussed above, nn. 378-381), for as the heart acts in the body, so does intention in the mind. And just as all the elements of the body depend on the heart for their formation [*existentiam*] and for their motion, so do all elements of the mind depend on intention for their formation and their motion.

We say "on intention" meaning "on love," because intention is the receiver for love, and love is life itself (see above, nn. 1-3). And the love which is life itself comes from the Lord alone.

The reason we can look at the heart and its extension in the body through arteries and veins, and thereby know that love or intention is human life, is that responsive elements act in the same way, allowing for the fact that one is natural and the other spiritual.

We can see from anatomy how the heart acts in the body, for example that everything is alive, or is in obedience to life, where the heart is active through the tubes that extend from it, and that everything is lifeless where the heart through its tubes is not active.

Further, the heart is both the first and the last thing to be active in the body. We can determine that it is the first from embryos, and that it is the last from the dying. We can determine that it acts without the cooperation of the lungs from people who have been suffocated and from people who have fainted. This enables us to see that just as the subsidiary life of the body depends on the heart alone, so the mind's life depends on intention alone; and that intention remains alive when thinking ceases just as the heart does when breathing ceases—as we can also see from fetuses, the dying, those suffocated, and those who have fainted.

It follows from this that love or intention is human life itself.

400. (2) *Love or intention is constantly striving toward the human form, and toward all the elements of human form.* This we can see from the correspondence of the heart with intention, since it is recognized that all the parts of the body are formed in the womb and that they are formed by fibers from the brains and by blood vessels from the heart, with the tissues of all the

organs and viscera constructed of these two. We can see from this that everything human comes into being from the life of intention, which is love, everything coming from its beginnings out of the brain through fibers. We can also see that everything in the human body comes into being out of the heart through arteries and veins.

This makes it clear that life—which is love and consequently intention—is constantly striving toward the human form. And since a human form is made up of all the things that are in a person, it follows that love or intention is engaged in a constant effort and striving to form all those things. The reason this effort and striving is toward the human form is that God is Person, and His life is divine love and divine wisdom. This is the source of all life.

Anyone can see that unless life (which is the essential person) were active within that which is not intrinsically life, nothing within a person could have been formed as it is. For there are millions of things in a person that make a one and that work hand in glove toward an image of the life that is their source, to the end that the person may become the recipient and dwelling of that life.

This enables us to see that love, and intention because of love, and the heart because of intention, are constantly striving toward the human form.

401. (3) *Apart from a marriage with wisdom or discernment, love or intention cannot do anything through its human form.* This too we can see from the correspondence of the heart with intention.

The human fetus lives by its heart but not by its lungs. In fact, at that point the blood does not flow from the heart into the lungs, giving them the power to breathe. It flows rather through an opening into the left ventricle of the heart. For this reason, the fetus cannot then move any part of its body. It actually lies wrapped. Nor can it sense anything—the sensory organs are actually closed.

It is the same with love or intention, meaning that it still lives, but dimly—that is, without sensation or activity. However, as soon as the lungs are opened, which happens after birth, sensation and activity begin, and so do intending and thinking.

This enables us to determine that apart from a marriage with wisdom or discernment, love or intention cannot do anything through its human form.

402. (4) *Love or intention prepares a home or bridal chamber for its spouse-to-be, which is wisdom or discernment.* Throughout all creation and in its details there is a marriage of the good and the true. This is because the good is a matter of love and the true is a matter of wisdom, which two are in the Lord, and everything was created from Him.

How this marriage takes place in people can be seen mirrored in the union of the heart with the lungs. For the heart corresponds to love or the good, and the lungs to wisdom or the true (see above, nn. 378-381, 382-384).

We can see from this union how love or intention betroths wisdom or discernment to itself, and later leads it or begins a kind of marriage with it. It arranges the betrothal by preparing a home or bridal chamber for its partner. It leads by uniting its partner to itself by means of affections. And then it administers wisdom with its partner in their home.

We cannot fully describe the actual situation except in spiritual language, because love and wisdom (and consequently intention and discernment) are spiritual. Some of this can be rendered in natural language, but this will lead only to a dim perception, owing to ignorance of the nature of love and of wisdom, and ignorance of the nature of affections for the good and affections for wisdom, which are affections for the true.

However, we can still see what the betrothal and marriage of love with wisdom (or of intention with discernment) are like through the parallelism that stems from their correspondence with the heart and the lungs. The two situations are very much alike, so much so that there is absolutely no difference except that one is spiritual and the other natural.

We can conclude from the heart and lungs, then, that the heart first forms the lungs and afterwards unites itself with them. It forms the lungs in the fetus and unites itself with them after birth.

The heart does this in its home, called the chest, where they live together, separated from the rest of the body by a wall called the diaphragm and by an envelope called the pleura. It is the same with love and wisdom, or with intention and discernment.

403. (5) *Love or intention makes preparations within its human form so that it will be able to act jointly with wisdom or discernment.*

We talk about intention and discernment, but we need to know very well indeed that intention is the whole person. Intention is actually present with discernment in its primary forms in the brains and in its derived forms in the body; it is therefore in the whole body and in every part, as we have explained above (nn. 365-367). This demonstrates that in intrinsic form intention is the whole person, both generally and in all detail, and that discernment is its ally, as the lungs are the ally of the heart. Let people beware of nurturing a concept of intention as something separate from the human form—they are one and the same.

We can see from this not only how intention prepares a bridal chamber for discernment but also how it prepares everything in its house, which is the whole body, so that it will be able to act jointly with discernment. It makes things ready in such a way that each and every element of the body is united to discernment just as it is obedient to intention.

How each and every element of the body is prepared for a union with discernment like that with intention we can see only mirrored or imaged by an anatomical analysis of the body. This informs us how all things in the body are so connected that when the lungs breathe, each and every element in the whole body is impelled by the lungs' breathing, as it also is by the heartbeat.

We know from anatomy that the heart is united to the lungs by the auricles, and that these are extended into the inner reaches of the lungs. We also know that all the viscera of the whole body are connected to the chest cavity by ligaments, and so connected that when the lungs breathe, each and every part, overall and in detail, in some way receives an impulse from that breathing. In fact, when the lungs swell, the ribs enlarge the chest, the pleura is stretched, and the diaphragm is depressed. As these move, all the lower parts of the body, being connected by ligaments from them, receive some impulse from the respiratory motion. I forbear to mention many other things, lest readers who are not interested in anatomy will become confused about the subject because they are unfamiliar with the terminology of that science.

Just check with any practiced and competent anatomist as to whether everything in the whole body, from the chest all the way down, is not so connected that as the chest expands when the lungs breathe, each and every part is stimulated to move in time with the lungs.

This, then, enables us to see how the union of discernment is prepared by intention, involving the whole human form in all detail. Just search out the connections and examine them with an anatomist's eye; then, following the connections, observe how everything works together with the lungs as they breathe and with the heart; then for lungs think discernment and for heart think intention; and you will see.

404. (6) *Once the wedding has taken place, the first union occurs through an affection for knowing, giving rise to an affection for what is true.*

"The wedding" means the individual's first state after birth, from the state of ignorance all the way to the state of intelligence, and from this to the state of wisdom. The first state—one of utter ignorance—is not presently meant by the wedding, because in this state there is no discerning thought, only a vague affection which belongs to love or intentionality. This state is introductory to the wedding.

It is recognized that in the second state—that of one's youth—there is an affection for knowing. This is the means by which infants learn to talk, learn to read, and later gradually learn elements of discernment. We cannot doubt that the love of the intentionality is accomplishing this, for unless love or intentionality impelled it, it would not happen.

As for the proposition that every individual from birth on has an affection for knowing, which is the means of learning the things which discernment is gradually formed from, anyone who gives rational attention to experience will recognize this. We can also see that this is the source of the affection for what is true. For once someone has become intelligent because of an affection for knowing, that affection leads less toward knowing than toward reasoning, and toward defining the objects of love, whether these be domestic, civic, or moral matters. When this affection is raised all the way to spiritual concerns, it becomes an affection for spiritual truth.

We can see that its beginning, or introductory phase, was the affection for knowing, from the fact that the affection for what is true is a heightened affection for knowing. For being moved by things true is a result of wanting to know them, and on finding them, drinking them in with affectionate joy.

(7) *The second union occurs through an affection for discerning, giving rise to a perception of what is true.*

This anyone can see who is willing to let the light of rational insight shine on it. We can see from rational insight that the affection for what is true and the perception of what is true are twin abilities of discernment, which combine into one in some people, but not in others. They combine into one in people who want to perceive truths by discernment, and not in people who only want to know truths.

We can also see that people are involved in the perception of what is true in the measure that they are involved in the affection for discerning what is true. Given the affection for discerning what is true, its perception necessarily follows at the level of its affection. For no one of sound reason lacks perception of what is true, given the affection for discerning what is true.

We have explained above that everyone has the ability to discern what is true, the ability called rationality.

(8) *The third union occurs through an affection for seeing what is true, giving rise to thought.*

We are assuming that affection for knowing, affection for discerning, and affection for seeing are three different things (or that affection for what is true, perception of what is true, and thought, are three different things). This will be only dimly visible to people who cannot clearly perceive the workings of the mind, but it is clearly visible to people who can see them distinctly. The reason this is only dimly visible to people who do not clearly grasp the mind's workings is that they occur simultaneously in the thought of people involved in an affection for what is true and perception of what is true, and when they occur simultaneously, they cannot be distinguished.

People are in open thought when their spirit is thinking in the body, which happens primarily in the company of others. But when they are involved in an affection for discerning, and come by this route into a perception of what is true, then they are involved in the thinking of the spirit, which is meditation. This does descend into the thinking of the body, but silently. It is higher than this latter thought and examines the memory-based elements of thought as lower than itself, for it uses them either to draw conclusions or to confirm suppositions. The actual affection for what is true, however, goes unnoticed except as an impulse of intent springing from a kind of pleasure, which is given very little attention.

We can conclude on this basis that these three activities—affection for what is true, perception of what is true, and thinking—follow in sequence from love, and occur only within discernment. In fact, when love enters discernment (which happens when a union has been accomplished), it then first brings forth an affection for what is true, then an affection for discerning what it knows, and finally an affection for seeing in the thinking of the body what it discerns. Thinking is actually nothing but inner sight.

There is a kind of thinking that occurs first because it is a function of the natural mind, but thinking from a perception of the true which comes from an affection for the true, comes last. This thinking is wisdom's thinking, while the former is a thinking based on memory by means of the sight of the natural mind.

All the workings of love or intentionality outside discernment have to do with affections for what is good and not with affections for what is true.

405. By rational process, people can understand that these three activities follow in sequence from

love, which is proper to intentionality, in discernment; but it still cannot be seen clearly and thereby be confirmed as a matter of belief.

Now love (which is proper to intentionality) acts by correspondence in unison with the heart; while wisdom (which is proper to discernment) acts in unison with the lungs, as is explained above. For this reason, there is nowhere we can more clearly see and confirm the things just presented (n. 404) about affection for what is true, perception of what is true, and thinking, than in the lungs and their structure. So we need to describe these matters briefly.

After expelling the blood from its right ventricle, the heart sends it into the lungs, and after its passage through the lungs, it sends in into its left ventricle. The heart does this by means of the pulmonary arteries and veins.

There are the bronchial tubes of the lungs, which branch off and eventually terminate in vesicles, into which the lungs admit air and thereby breathe. Around the bronchial tubes and their branches are the arteries and veins called bronchial, which begin at the azygous veins or the vena cava and the aorta. These arteries and veins are distinct from the pulmonary arteries and veins. We can see from this that the blood flows into the lungs by two routes and out of the lungs by two routes. This is why the lungs can breathe in a rhythm different from that of the heart. It is acknowledged that the heart has one set of rhythms and the lungs another.

Now, since the correspondence of the heart and the lungs is, as shown, with intentionality and discernment, and since their union by correspondence is such that the one behaves like the other, we can see from the inflow of blood from the heart into the lungs how intentionality flows into discernment and does the things we have just said (n. 404) about affection for and perception of truth, and thinking. Correspondence has disclosed this to me, along with many other matters that cannot be described briefly.

Since love or intentionality corresponds to the heart, and wisdom or discernment to the lungs, it follows that the blood vessels from the heart to the lungs correspond to affections for what is true, and that the branches of the bronchial tubes correspond to perceptions and thoughts from these affections.

The person who explores all the fabrics of the lungs from their beginnings, and draws the parallel with intentionality's love and discernment's wisdom, can see in a sort of image what we have presented above (n. 404), and in this way support it so that it becomes a matter of belief. But since anatomical information about the heart and lungs is familiar to few, and since supporting something by the unfamiliar breeds obscurity, I shall refrain from showing the parallelism with more details.

406. (9) *Through these three unions, love or intention is engaged in its own life of sensing and its own life of acting.*

The reason love without discernment (or an affection of love without the thinking of the discernment) can neither sense nor act in the body, is that love without discernment is blind, so to speak, or affection without thinking is as though it were in deep darkness. Discernment is actually the light which enables love to see. Then too, discernment's wisdom comes from the light that emanates from the Lord as the sun.

So since intention's love sees nothing without discernment's light, the physical senses would be kept in blindness and dullness—not just sight and hearing, but the other senses as well. The reason this extends to the other senses is that every perception of what is true belongs to love in the discernment, as we have shown above, and all the physical senses derive their perceiving from the perceptions of their mind.

It is the same with every physical act. For an act done from love without discernment is like someone's act done at night—people then do not actually know what they are doing. So there would be no element of intelligence or wisdom in the act, which could not them be called a living act. An act derives its reality [*esse*] from love, and its quality [*quale*] from intelligence.

Further, all the power the good has is by means of the true. So the good acts in and thus through the true, and good being a matter of love, and the true a matter of discernment. We can determine from this that love or intention is engaged in its own life of sensing and its own life of acting through the three unions described above (n. 404).

407. We can establish the truth of this vividly by reference to the union of heart and lungs, because the correspondence between intentionality and heart, and between discernment and lungs, is such that the heart acts with the lungs on the natural level the way love acts with discernment on the spiritual level. So what we have just described can be seen as in an image presented to the eye.

We can determine that people are involved neither in a life of sensing nor in a life of acting as long as heart and lungs are not acting together, if we look at the state of an embryo or baby in the womb, and then at its state after birth. As long as a person is an embryo, or is in the womb, the lungs are closed. So he or she has neither sensation nor action. The sensory organs are closed, the hands, and feet as well, are restrained. But after birth, the lungs are opened, and as they are opened, the person senses and acts. The lungs are opened by means of blood impelled into them from the heart.

We can also see that a person is involved in neither a life of sensing nor a life of acting without the coworking of heart and lungs, if we look at people who have fainted. For them, the heart alone is working, not the lungs—breathing is actually taken away at such times. It is recognized that these people have neither sensation nor action.

It is the same with someone who is suffocated, whether by water or by something that blocks the larynx and closes the avenue for the lungs' breathing. It is recognized that at such times the subject seems to be dead, sensing nothing and doing nothing, and that the heart is still alive. A person actually returns to both lives—of sensing and acting—once the lungs' obstructions are removed.

In this interim, the blood is still circulating through the lungs through the pulmonary arteries and veins but not through the bronchial arteries and veins, and it is these latter which grant the person the ablility to breathe. It is the same with the inflow of love into discernment.

408. (10) *Love or intention leads wisdom or discernment into all aspects of its home.*

By "the home of love or intention" we mean the whole person as to all aspects of mind. Since these correspond to all the physical aspects (as explained above), "the home" also means the whole person as to physical aspects, called members, organs, and viscera.

On the basis of what has been presented above, we determine that the lungs are led into all these places in the same way that discernment is led into all aspects of mind. That is, love or intention prepares a home or bridal chamber for its spouse-to-be, which is wisdom or discernment (n. 402), and love or intention makes all preparations within its human form so that it will be able to act jointly with wisdom or discernment (n. 403), for example.

We can see from what has been said in these sections that absolutely everything in the whole body, through the ligaments that extent from the ribs, vertebrae, sternum, diaphragm, and peritoneum (which is suspended from the lungs), is so connected that as the lungs breathe, everything else is influenced and impelled into a similar alternating activity. We can determine by anatomy that the alternations of breathing do also enter the viscera themselves, all the way to their deepest recesses. For the ligaments just listed attach to the coverings of the viscera, and the coverings penetrate to their very center by means of extrusions, just as the arteries and veins do by means of their branchings.

So we can establish that the lungs' breathing, in complete conjunction with the heart, is in each and every detail of the body. So that the unison may be complete in all respects, the heart itself is included in the motion of the lungs. It actually lies within the lung cavity, is attached to them through the auricles, and rests above the diaphragm, which means that its arteries also take part in the pulmonary motion. And further, the ventricles are in a similar union by their attachment of the esophagus with the trachea.

We have cited these anatomical matters so that the reader may see the nature of the union of love or intention with wisdom or discernment, and the union of each in consort with all aspects of mind, for this is parallel [similis].

409. (11) *Love or intention does nothing except in unison with wisdom or discernment.*

With love having neither sensory life nor active life apart from wisdom, and with love leading discernment into all aspects of the mind (as explained in nn. 407 and 408 above), it follows that love or intention does nothing except in unison with discernment. What actually is "acting from love without discernment"? It can only be called irrational. Discernment, in fact, teaches what to do and how to do it. Love does not know this apart from wisdom. There is consequently a marriage between love and discernment, of such nature that even though they are two, they still act as one.

There is a similar marriage between the good and the true, since the good is a matter of love and the true is a matter of discernment. There is a marriage like this in the details of the universe, which have been created by the Lord. Their use goes back to the good, and the form of the use to the true. This marriage is the reason there is a left and a right in each and every particular part of the body, the right relating to the good which is the source of the true, and the left to the true from the good—therefore to a union.

This is why there are paired organs in the human being. There are two brains; there are two hemispheres of the cerebrum; there are two ventricles of the heart; there are two [lobes of the] lungs; there are two eyes, ears, nostrils, arms, hands, legs, feet, kidneys, testes, and so on. And where there are no pairs, there is a left and a right. This is because the good looks to the true in order to become effectively present, and the true looks to the good in order to exist. It is the same in the angelic heavens, and in their particular communities.

More on this may be seen above (n. 401), where we have shown that love or intention, without a marriage to wisdom or discernment, cannot do anything through its human form. We will discuss elsewhere the union of the evil and the false, which is opposite to the union of the good and the true.

410. (12) *Love or intention unites itself to wisdom or discernment, and works things out so that wisdom or discernment is united in return.*

We can see that love or intention unites itself to wisdom or discernment, from their correspondence with the heart and lungs.

Anatomical experience teaches that the heart may be in its life motion when the lungs are no longer in theirs. This is the teaching of experience in the case of people who are subject to fainting, and in people who suffocate, as well as for embryos in the womb and chicks in eggs.

Anatomical experience also teaches that when the heart acts alone, it forms lungs, and adapts them so that it can cause breathing in them, and that it also forms other viscera and organs so that it can exercise various uses in them. It forms the facial organs so that it can sense, the motor organs so that it can act, and the other organs in the body so that it can establish the uses that correspond to the affections of love.

The first conclusion we can draw from this is that just as the heart produces things like this for the various functions it is to perform in the body, so love produces similar things in its recipient vessel, which is called intention, for the various affections which make up its form. We have explained above that this form is the human form.

Now, since the first and most immediate affections of love are the affection for knowing, the affection for discerning, and the affection for seeing what one knows and discerns, it follows that love forms discernment for these functions and that it enters into them actively when it begins to sense and act, and when it begins to think. We can conclude that discernment contributes nothing to this process, from the parallel with the heart and the lungs discussed above.

We can see from this that love or intention unites itself to wisdom or discernment, and not wisdom or discernment to love or intention. This also enables us to conclude that the data which love gathers by its affection for knowing, the perception of the true it gets from its affection for discerning, and the thinking it gets from its affection for seeing what it knows and discerns—that these do not belong to discernment, but to love.

Thoughts, perceptions, and consequent data actually flow in from the spiritual world. They are not, however, received by discernment, but by love, according to its affections in discernment. It looks as though discernment received them, and not love or intention, but this is deceptive.

It also looks as though discernment united itself to love or intention, but this too is deceptive. Love or intention unites itself to discernment, and works things out so that this latter is united in return. The reason it is united in return is love's marriage with it. The union is therefore mutual, so to speak, from the life and consequent power of love.

The same holds true for the marriage of the good and the true, since the good is a matter of love and the true is a matter of wisdom. The good *does* everything, and accepts the true into its home, and unites itself to it to the extent that it is in harmony. The good can also let in true things that are not in harmony, but it does this from its affection for knowing, discerning, and thinking, as long as it has not limited itself to the uses which are its goals [*fines*] and are called its [specific forms of] good [*bona*].

There is absolutely no mutual union, or union of the true with the good. The fact that they are mutually united stems from the life of the good. This is why every mortal, and every spirit and angel, is regarded by the lord according to his or her love or good, and no one according to discernment or truth separated from love or good. In fact, people's life is their love, as shown above, and their life depends on the way they have highlighted particular affections by means of things true, that is, the way they have perfected affections from wisdom. For affections of love are highlighted and perfected through things true, therefore through wisdom, and then love acts in unison with it—works out of it, so to speak. However, it is acting through it on its own, as though it were acting through its own form, which derives nothing whatever from discernment, but everything from some focusing of love, which is called an affection.

411. Love calls everything that favors it "its good possessions"; and everything conducive, as means, to its good ends, it calls "its true possessions." Further, since these latter are means, they are loved and come to belong to its affection, thereby becoming affections in form. So "the true" is nothing other than the form of affection which is a matter of love.

The human form is simply the form of all of love's affections. Beauty is its intelligence, which it gains through truths, which it receives through inner and outer sight or hearing.

These are the elements which love arranges in the form of its affections—forms which occur in great variety, but which all derive a similarity from their general form, which is the human one. All these forms are beautiful and dear to the love, but others are ugly and unlovable to it.

We can conclude from this too that love unites itself to discernment, and not the reverse, and that even mutual union stems from love. This is what it means to say that love or intention works things out so that wisdom or discernment is united in return.

412. These statements can be seen in image, so to speak, and thereby supported by reference to the correspondence of the heart with love and of the lungs with discernment, discussed above. For given that the heart corresponds to love, then its limited forms, which are arteries and veins, correspond to affections, with the ones in the lungs corresponding to affections for what is true. Too, since there are other vessels in the lungs as well, which are called air passages,

through which breathing takes place, these vessels therefore correspond to perceptions.

It must be throughly known that the arteries and veins in the lungs are not affections, and that the processes of breathing are not perceptions and thoughts—they are rather correspondent entities, since they act responsively or synchronously. The heart and lungs likewise are not love and discernment; they are correspondent entities. And since they are correspondent entities, the one can be seen in the other.

Knowing the whole structure of the lungs from the study of anatomy, one can see clearly, by comparing this structure with discernment, that discernment does nothing on its own. It neither perceives nor thinks on its own, but depends wholly on affections that belong to love, called, in the discernment, affection for knowing, discerning, and seeing (these have been dealt with above). All the states of the lungs depend on the blood from the heart and from the vena cava and the aorta; and the breathing processes that take place in the bronchial tubes occur in keeping with their state. For once the blood flow stops, breathing stops.

We could unveil a great many more things by comparing the structure of the lungs with discernment. But since few people are familiar with the science of anatomy, and since explaining or supporting something by means of the unknown puts the matter into obscurity, I am not at liberty to say more about these matters.

From my familiarity with the structure of the lungs, I am fully convinced that love, through its affections, unites itself to discernment, and that discernment does not unite itself to any affection of love, but is rather united in return by love, to the end that love may have a sensory life and an active life.

We must above all know that the human being has a double breathing—one breathing of the spirit and the other of the body. The breathing of the spirit depends on fibers from the brain, and the breathing of the body on blood vessels from the heart, and on the vena cava and the aorta. Particularly, it is evident that thought produces breathing, and it is also evident that affection of love produces thought. For thought apart from affection is just like breathing apart from a heart—it cannot occur. So we can see that affection, which is a matter of love, unites itself to thought, which is a matter of discernment, as stated above, the way the heart does in the lungs.

413. (13) *From the power given it by love or intention, wisdom or discernment can be raised up, accept things proper to light from heaven, and perceive them.*

We have shown above, in many places, that people can grasp secrets of wisdom when they hear them. This human ability is what we call rationality, which everyone has from creation. It is by this ability—which is the ability to understand things more deeply and to make decisions about what is just and fair, what is good and true—that people can be distinguished from animals. It is also what we mean by saying that discernment can be raised up, can accept things which are matters of light from heaven, and can grasp them.

The truth of this can also be seen in image, so to speak, in the lungs, since the lungs correspond to discernment.

In the lungs, this can be seen in its small-cell substance, which consists of the extensions of the bronchia all the way to the smallest sacs, the receptors of air in the processes of breathing. These are what thought acts in unison with, by correspondence.

The nature of this sac-like substance is such that it can expand and contract in two states, one together with the heart, and the other almost separated from the heart. In a state of union with the heart, the expansion and contraction take place through the pulmonary arteries and veins, which come exclusively from the heart. In the state of virtual separation from the heart, they take place through the bronchial arteries and veins, which come from the vena cava and aorta. These latter vessels are outside the heart.

This is true of the lungs because discernment can be raised above love proper, which corresponds to the heart, and receive light from heaven. Still, when discernment is raised above love proper, it does not retreat from it, but draws from it what we call an affection for knowing and discerning for the sake of some element of prestige, glory, or profit in this world. This element clings to each love like a coating, so that the love glows dimly on its surface; but in wise people, love is translucent.

We have cited these facts about the lungs to support the proposition that discernment can be raised up, and can accept and perceive matters proper to heaven's light; it is in fact a full correspondence. Correspondence enables us to see the lungs from [the standpoint of] discernment, and discernment from [the standpoint of] the lungs, and so from both together to see the confirmation.

414. (14) *Love or intention can be raised up in a similar fashion, and accept things proper to warmth from heaven, if it loves its spouse to that degree.*

In the preceding section, and in a number of earlier passages, we have demonstrated discernment's ability to be raised into heaven's light and to draw wisdom from it. We have also demonstrated that love or intention can likewise be raised, if it loves matters of heaven's light, or matters of wisdom. Love or intention, however, cannot be raised by having any element of prestige, glory, or profit as its goal, only by a love of use—not for its own sake, that is, but for the sake of the neighbor. And since this love is given only from heaven by the Lord, and is given by the Lord when people flee evils as sins, it is by this means that love or intention can be raised, and apart from this means it is impossible.

Love or intention, though, is raised into heaven's warmth, while discernment is raised into heaven's light. Further, if they are both raised a marriage is accomplished there for them which is called "the heavenly marriage" because it is a marriage of heavenly love and wisdom. This is why we say that love too is raised if it loves wisdom, its spouse, to that degree.

Love for the neighbor, from the Lord, is the love of wisdom, or the genuine love of human discernment.

It is like light and warmth in this world. Light does occur without warmth, and it also occurs together with warmth. It occurs without warmth in winter, and with warmth in summer; and when there is warmth with the light, everything blossoms.

In the human being, the light that corresponds to winter light is wisdom without its love, and the light in people that corresponds to summer light is wisdom together with its love.

415. In the union of the lungs with the heart, we can look at a kind of image of this union and disunion of wisdom and love. Because of the blood it sends out, the heart can be united to the clustered sacs of the bronchial system, and it can also be united because of the blood that does not come from itself but from the vena cava and the aorta. By this latter means, the body's breathing can be separated from the spirit's breathing; but when the blood moves only from the heart, then the two kinds of breathing cannot be separated.

Now, since thoughts act in unison with breathing, by correspondence, we can also see from the twofold respiratory state of the lungs that an individual can think one way (and speak and act one way from thought) when in the company of others, and think differently (and speak and act from thought different-ly) when not in company, that is, when there is no fear of any loss of reputation.

In the latter case, one can think and speak against God, the neighbor, the spiritual concerns of the church, and moral and civil principles. One can also act against them by stealing, getting revenge, blas-pheming, and committing adultery. But in company, with the fear of loss of reputation, the same individual can speak, preach, and act exactly like a spiritual, moral, and civic person.

This enables us to conclude that love or intention can, like discernment, be raised, and receive things proper to heaven's warmth, if only it loves wisdom to that degree, and that if it does not love wisdom, it can be apparently separated.

416. (15) *Otherwise, love or intention pulls wisdom or discernment back from being raised up, so that it may act in unison with it.*

There is natural love, and there is spiritual love. A person who is involved in natural love and spiritual at the same time is a rational person. However, one who is involved only in natural love can think rational-ly, just like a spiritual person, but still is not a rational person. Such people actually do raise their discern-ment all the way to heaven's light—to wisdom, there-fore—but nevertheless the matters of wisdom or of heaven's light are not matters of their love. It is indeed love that effects this, but from an affection for prestige, glory, and profit.

So when they perceive that they are not getting any-thing that suits them from this raising up (which hap-pens when they are thinking internally, on the basis of their natural love), then they do not love matters of heaven's light or wisdom. They therefore then pull their discernment back from its height, so that it will act in unison with them.

For example, when discernment is involved in wisdom by being raised, then love sees what justice, sincerity, chastity, and even genuine love are. A natural love can see this by its ability to discern and explore things in heaven's light; it can even talk about and preach about and describe them as virtues at once moral and spiritual.

But when discernment is not in its uplifted state, then if the love is merely natural, it does not see these virtues. It sees rather injustice instead of justice, deceit instead of sincerity, wantonness instead of chastity, and so on. If it then thinks about the things it discussed before, while its discernment was in its uplifted state, it can mock them, and think that they are useful only for ensnaring people's minds.

This enables us to conclude how to understand the proposition that love, unless it loves its spouse wisdom to that degree, pulls it back from its height so that it acts in unison with it. On love's ability to be raised if it does love wisdom to that degree, see above (n. 414).

417. Now since love corresponds to the heart and discernment to the lungs, what we have just said can be supported by their correspondence—that is, how discernment can be raised beyond its proper love all the way into wisdom, and how discernment is pulled back from that height by the love, if the love is merely natural.

People have two kinds of breathing, one of the body and one of the spirit. These two kinds of breathing can be separated, and they can also be united. In people who are merely natural, especially in hypocrites, they are separated; but they are rarely separated in spiritual and sincere people. So merely natural people or hypocrites whose discernment has been raised up, and who thereby have many elements of wisdom dwelling in their memory, can in public talk wisely on the basis of thought from memory. But the same people not in public think not from memory but from love. They breathe in the same way as well, since thinking and breathing act correspondentially. We have already explained that the nature of the construction of the lungs enables them to breathe from the blood from the heart and from blood from outside the heart.

418. It is commonly thought that wisdom makes a person. So when we hear people speak or teach wisely, we may think they are what they seem—in fact, they themselves believe this at the time. This is because when they are speaking and teaching in public, they are thinking from memory, and if they are merely natural, this is from the surface of their love, which is an affection for prestige, glory, and profit. When the same people are alone, though, they think from the deeper love of their own spirit, and then they do not think wisely, but insanely.

We can conclude from this that no one should be judged on the basis of wise speech, but rather on the basis of life—that is, on the basis not of wise speech separated from life, but of wise speech united to life. "Life" means love: we have explained above that love is life.

419. (16) *Love or intention is purified in discernment, if they are raised up together.*

From birth, people love nothing but self and the world, since this is all they seem to see, and therefore their minds dwell on nothing else. This love is natural-physical, and can be called material. Further, this love has become impure because heavenly love has been separated from it in the parents.

This love cannot be separated from its impurity unless people have the ability to raise discernment into heaven's light and see how they must live so that their love can be raised together with discernment into wisdom.

Through discernment, love (that is, the person) sees what evils are corrupting and polluting the love. It also sees that if it flees those evils as sins and turns away from them, it loves the things that are opposed to those evils, which are all heavenly. Then too, it sees the means through which it can flee those evils as sins and turn away from them. The love (that is, the person) sees this by using the ability to raise its discernment into heaven's light, which yields wisdom.

Then, to the extent that love puts heaven in the first place and the world in the second, and at the same time puts the Lord in the first place and self in the second, love is ridded of its uncleanness and purified. That is, it is to that extent raised into heaven's warmth and united to the light of heaven that discernment is in, and a marriage occurs which is called the marriage of the good and the true—that is, of love and wisdom.

Everyone can grasp intellectually that to the extent that people flee and turn away from theft and cheating, they love honesty, fairness, and justice. So to the extent that people flee and turn away from revenge and hatred, they love the neighbor; and to the extent that they flee and turn away from adultery, they love chastity, and so on. In fact, hardly anyone knows what there is of heaven and the Lord in honesty, fairness, justice, love for the neighbor, and other affections of heavenly love, before the things that oppose them have been removed.

When these opposing elements have been removed, then the individual is involved in these virtues, and recognizes and sees them from [being involved in] them. Until then, there is a kind of veil in the way. It does let some of heaven's light through to the love, but since the love does not love its spouse, wisdom, all that much, it does not accept it. In fact, it resists and rejects it vigorously when it comes back from its height. But still, it is mellowed by the fact that the wisdom of discernment can be useful to it as a means to prestige, glory, and profit. It is however putting self and the world in the first place, and the Lord and heaven in the second. Whatever is put in second place is loved to the extent that it serves it, while if it does not, it is renounced and discarded—after death, if not before.

This establishes the truth that love or intention is purified in discernment if they are raised up together.

420. The same process is reflected in the lungs, whose arteries and veins correspond to affections which belong to love, and whose breathing cycles correspond to perceptions and thoughts which belong to discernment, as stated above. An abundance of experience demonstrates that the heart's blood purifies itself from unassimilated elements in the lungs, and also enriches itself with suitable elements from the air that is drawn in.

We observe *that the blood purifies itself from unassimilated elements in the lungs* not simply from the blood flowing in, which is venous and therefore loaded down with chyle gathered from ingested solids and liquids, but also from the exhalations—they are moist, and have an odor which other people smell. We also note that a lessened amount of blood flows back into the left ventricle of the heart.

We observe *that the blood enriches itself with suitable elements from the air that is drawn in* from the vast supply of odors and gases constantly given off from shrubs, flowers, and trees, from the vast supply of various minerals and liquids from soils and rivers and swamps, and from what is given off by people and animals, all of which saturate the air. We cannot deny that these flow into the lungs when air is drawn in, and since this is undeniable, so is the fact that the blood draws suitable elements in from this source. The elements that are suitable are the ones that correspond to its love.

This is why there are, in the sacs or smallest parts of the lungs, vast numbers of small veins with minute mouths that take in these kinds of element. It is also obvious that the blood flowing back into the left ventricle of the heart is arterial, and looks bright. These facts show that the blood is purifying itself from alien materials and enriching itself with congenial ones.

As to the proposition that the blood purifies and enriches itself in the lungs in a way that corresponds to the affections of the spirit, this has not yet been recognized, but it is widely recognized in the spiritual world. In fact, angels who are in the heavens take special delight in the odors that correspond to their love of wisdom, while spirits in hell take special delight in odors that correspond to love opposed to wisdom. These latter odors are stenches, while the former odors are fragrances.

It follows that people in this world saturate their blood with similar elements, according to the correspondence with the affections of their love. What a person's spirit loves, his or her blood correspondingly is hungry for, and draws in by means of breathing.

It follows from this correspondence that people are purified as to love if they love wisdom, and that they are polluted if they do not love it. Further, all human purification takes place through matters of truth that belong to wisdom, and all human pollution takes place through matters of falsity opposed to wisdom's truths.

421. (17) *Love or intention is polluted in and by discernment if they are not raised up together*, because if love is not raised up, it remains impure (as stated above, nn. 419, 420). As long as it remains impure, it loves impure things, such as various forms of vengefulness, hatred, cheating, blasphemy, and adultery. At this point, these are actually its affections, which are called cravings, and it rejects things that have to do with charity, justice, candor, truth, and chastity.

We have stated that love is polluted in and by discernment. It is polluted *in discernment* when the love is moved by these impure things. It is polluted by *discernment* when love makes elements of wisdom become its slaves, and even more when it perverts, falsifies, and adulterates them.

On the corresponding state of the heart or its blood in the lungs, we need say no more than has already been said (n. 420), only that a defilement of the blood occurs instead of a purification, and instead of the blood being nourished by fragrances, there is a nourishing by decaying substances, exactly the way it happens in heaven and in hell.

422. (18) *Love purified by wisdom in discernment becomes spiritual and heavenly.*

People are born nature-centered, but as their discernment is raised into heaven's light, and their love is raised with it into heaven's warmth, they become spiritual and heavenly. They then become like a garden of Eden which is in the light of spring and in the warmth of spring at the same time. Discernment does not become spiritual and heavenly, but love does, and when love does, it also makes discernment, its spouse, spiritual and heavenly.

Love becomes spiritual and heavenly by a life according to the truths of wisdom which discernment teaches and displays. Love draws these in through its discernment, and not independently. For love cannot raise itself up unless it knows things that are true, and it cannot know them except by means of a discernment that has been raised up and enlightened. Then love is raised up to the extent that it loves the truths by doing them. For discerning and intending are two different things—that is, talking and doing are two different things.

There are people who understand and discuss truths of wisdom, but still do not intend and do them. So when love does the truths of light that it understands and discusses, then it is raised up. Reason alone enables us to see the truth of this. What would you call people who understand and discuss truths of wisdom, when they contradict them in life—that is, when they intend and act contrary to them?

The reason love purified by wisdom becomes spiritual and heavenly is that people have three levels of life, called natural, spiritual, and heavenly, dealt with in Chapter Three of the present work. Further, people can be raised from one level to another; but they are not raised by wisdom alone, only by a life in accord with wisdom, since a person's life is his or her love. So people love wisdom to the extent that they live by it; and they live by wisdom to the extent that they purify themselves from the unclean things that are sins. To the extent that they do this, they love wisdom.

423. Correspondence with the heart and lungs does not enable us to see very well that love purified by wisdom in discernment becomes spiritual and heavenly, because no one can see the quality of the blood through which the lungs are kept in their state of breathing. Blood can be teeming with impurities and still be indistinguishable from pure blood. Then too, the breathing of a merely natural person seems like the breathing of a spiritual person. However, this is precisely distinguishable in heaven, where everyone breathes in accord with his or her marriage of love and wisdom. So just as angels are recognized by this marriage, they are recognized by their breathing. This is why anyone who is not in this marriage, on arrival in heaven, feels chest pains, and struggles to draw breath, like someone in the throes of death. So they throw themselves down from heaven headlong, and find no rest until they are in the company of people whose breathing is like their own. Then, by correspondence, they are involved in like affection and therefore in like thought.

This enables us to conclude that for a spiritual person it is the purer blood—which some call the soul-spirit [*spiritus animalis*]—which is purified, and that it is purified to the extent that the individual is involved in a marriage of love and wisdom.

It is this purer blood that is most intimately responsive to that marriage, and since it flows into the physical blood, it follows that this latter too is purified by means of it. The opposite is true of people in whom love has been polluted in discernment.

But as we have stated, no one can investigate this by any experimentation with blood. We must rather look to affections of love, since these correspond to the blood.

424. (19) *Love polluted in and by discernment becomes nature-, sense-, and body-centered.*

Natural love separated from spiritual love is opposed to spiritual love. The reason is that natural love is love of self and love of the world, and spiritual love is love of the Lord and love of the neighbor. Further, love of self and the world looks downward and outward, while love of the Lord looks upward and inward. So when natural love is separated from spiritual love, it cannot be raised up from the person's self-image [*proprio*] but remains submerged in it and, to the extent that it loves it, mired in it. If at this time discernment does rise up, and sees by heaven's light the sorts of thing proper to wisdom, then natural love drags it back and united it to itself in its self-image, where it either rejects the matters of wisdom, falsifies them, or arranges them around itself so that it can enhance its reputation by talking about them.

In the same way that natural love can climb up step by step and become spiritual and heavenly, it can also climb down step by step and become sensory and physical. It does climb down to the extent that it loves dominance without any love of use as source, only out of self-love. This is the love called "the devil."

People involved in this love can talk and behave like people involved in spiritual love, but when they do, it is either on the basis of memory or on the basis of discernment raised independently into heaven's light. The things they say and do, however, are rather like fruits that look lovely on the surface, but are full of decay inside. Or they are like nuts whose shells look sound, but which have been wholly eaten by worms inside.

In the spiritual world, they call these the illusions through which the harlots called sirens put on beauty and deck themselves with attractive clothes, though once the illusions are dispelled, they look like specters. They are also like devils who make themselves angels of light. For when that physical love pulls its discernment down from its height (which happens when it is in privacy) and thinks on the basis of its own love, then it thinks against God and in favor of nature, against heaven and in favor of the world, against the true and good elements of the church and in favor of the evil and false elements of hell—that is, against wisdom.

This enables us to determine the quality of the people called "physical people." They are not actually physical as far as their discernment is concerned, but they are physical as far as their love is concerned. That is, they are not physical as to discernment when they are talking in public, but they are when they talk to themselves in the spirit. And since this is what they are like in spirit, after death they become in both respects—both love and discernment—the spirits who are called "physical spirits." People who in the world were in the highest love of dominance out of a love of self, and also in an elevation of intellect above others, look physically like Egyptian mummies, and are mentally crude and inane.

Who in the world nowadays knows that this love is like this intrinsically? However, there is a love of dominance out of a love of use—a love of use not for the sake of self, however, but for the sake of the common good. But it is hard for people to tell the two apart, even though the difference between them is like the difference between heaven and hell. The difference between these two loves of dominance may be seen in the book *Heaven and Hell* (nn. 551-565).

425. (20) *But there still remains an ability to discern, called rationality, and an ability to act, called freedom.* We have discussed these two abilities, which are proper to human beings, above (nn. 264-267).

People have these two abilities so that they can become spiritual from being natural, which is being regenerated. For as stated above, it is a person's love which becomes spiritual and is regenerated, and it cannot become spiritual, or be regenerated, unless it knows by means of its discernment what is evil and what is good, and thereby what is true and what is false. When it knows this, it can choose one or the other; and if it chooses the good, then it can be taught by its discernment about the means for attaining to the good.

Knowing and discerning these means is the result of *rationality*; intending and doing them is the result of *freedom*. Freedom is also intending to know, discern, and think them.

People who believe, because of their church doctrine, that spiritual or theological matters surpass understanding and are therefore to be believed without being understood, are unable to know anything about these abilities called rationality and freedom. They cannot help denying the ability called rationality. And people who from their church doctrine believe that no one can do good independently and that therefore good done intentionally is not a means to salvation, cannot help denying on religious grounds the existence of each of these abilities which people possess.

A further consequence is that after death, people who have confirmed themselves in these opinions are deprived of both these abilities, in accord with their belief. Instead of being able to be in heavenly freedom, they are in hellish freedom; and instead of being able to be in heavenly wisdom from rationality, they are in hellish insanity. Further, remarkably, they recognize the occurrence of each ability in doing evil things and thinking false things, unaware that the freedom to do evil things is slavery, and the rationality to think false things is irrationality.

It should however be clearly realized that both these abilities—freedom and rationality—belong not to the person but to the Lord with the person, and that they cannot be claimed by the person as possessions. Further, they cannot be given to the person as possessions, but belong constantly to the Lord with the person. Still, they are never taken away. The reason is that without them, people cannot be saved; for without them they cannot be regenerated, as stated above. This is why we are taught by the church that we cannot think what is true on our own or do what is good on our own.

But since people perceive only that they think what is true on their own and do what is good on their own, we can see clearly that they ought to believe that they think what is true in apparent independence [*sicut a se*] and do what is good in apparent independence. For if they do not, then either they do not think what is true or do what is good, thereby having no religion, or they think what is true and do what is good and then attribute what is divine to themselves.

426. (21) *Spiritual and heavenly love is love toward the neighbor and love for the Lord; nature- and sense-centered love is love of the world and love of self.* By "love toward the neighbor" we mean a love of uses, and by "love for the Lord" we mean a love of performing uses, as explained above.

The reason these loves are spiritual and heavenly is that loving uses and doing them from a love of them is distinct from a love of one's self-image. For people who love uses spiritually are not focusing on themselves, but on others outside themselves, whose welfare moves them.

Opposed to these loves are the loves of self and the world, since these do not focus on uses for the sake of others, but for the sake of self. People who do this are inverting the divine design, putting themselves in the Lord's place and the world in heaven's place. This is why they are looking away from the Lord and from heaven, and looking away from these is looking toward hell. But there is more on these loves above (n. 424).

However, people do not feel and perceive a love of performing uses for the sake of uses as clearly as they feel and perceive a love of performing uses for self's sake. So too they are unaware, when they are performing uses, whether they are acting for the sake of uses or for the sake of self. May they realize, then, that they are performing uses for uses' sake to the extent that they avoid evils. For to the extent that they do avoid evils, they are not performing the uses on their own, but from the Lord. The evil and the good are in fact opposed to each other, so to the extent that people are not involved in the evil, they are involved in the good.

No one can be involved in evil and in good at the same time, because no one can serve two masters at the same time.

The reason for mentioning this is to let it be known that even though people do not sensibly perceive whether the uses they are performing are for the sake of the uses or for the sake of self (that is, whether they are spiritual or merely natural), they can still tell by noting whether they think of evils as sins or not. If they think they are sins, and therefore do not do them, then the uses they do are spiritual. And once they are avoiding sins out of a repugnance for them, then they begin to perceive sensibly a love of uses for the sake of uses, out of a spiritual delight in them.

427. (22) *It is the same with charity and faith and their union as it is with intention and discernment and their union.*

There are two loves by which the heavens are distinguished—heavenly love and spiritual love. Heavenly love is love for the Lord, and spiritual love is love toward the neighbor. These loves are distinguished by this: heavenly love is a love of what is good, while spiritual love is a love of what is true.

The marriage of heavenly love is with wisdom, while the marriage of spiritual love is with intelligence. The part of wisdom is to do what is good on the basis of what is good, while the part of intelligence is to do what is good on the basis of what is true. So heavenly love does what is good, while spiritual love does what is true.

The difference between these two loves can be described only as follows. People who are involved in heavenly love have wisdom engraved on their lives, not on their memories. This is because they do not talk about divine truths, but do them. But people who are involved in spiritual love have wisdom engraved on their memories. So they do talk about divine truths, and do them on the basis of principles in their memories.

Since people who are involved in heavenly love have wisdom engraved on their lives, the moment they hear anything they perceive whether it is true or not. And when they are asked whether it is true, they reply simply that it is or that it is not. They are the people meant by the Lord's words, "Your speech must be "Yes, yes; no, no" (Matthew 5:37). Since they are like this, they do not want to hear anything about faith. They say, "What is faith? Isn't it wisdom? And what is charity? Isn't it action?" And when they are told that faith is believing what you do not understand, they turn away and say, "He's raving." These are the people who are in the third heaven, and who are the wisest of all.

People got that way in the world if they applied directly to their lives the divine things they heard, turning away from evils as hellish, and revering the Lord alone. Because they are in innocence, they look like little children to others. And because there is no trace of pride in their speech, they also seem simple. However, when they hear someone talking, they know all his or her love from the tones of voice, and all his or her intelligence from the words.

These are the people who are in the marriage of love and wisdom from the Lord, and who have to do with the region of heaven's heart discussed above.

428. In contrast, people who are involved in spiritual love, which is love toward the neighbor, do not have wisdom engraved on their lives; instead, they have intelligence. For wisdom is doing good from an affection for what is good, while intelligence is doing good from an affection for what is true, as stated above.

These people do not know what faith is, either. If someone mentions faith, they understand "truth," and if someone mentions charity, they understand "doing the truth." If someone talks about the necessity of believing, they call this a meaningless phrase and say, "Who doesn't believe what is true?" They say this because they are seeing what is true in the light of their heaven. So they call believing the unseen either naivete or folly. These are the people who make up the pulmonary region of heaven, discussed above.

429. But people who are involved in a natural-spiritual love have neither wisdom nor intelligence engraved on their lives. Instead, they have a kind of

faith from the Word, to the extent that the Word is united to charity. Since they do not know what charity is or know whether faith is truth, they cannot mingle with people in the heavens who are involved in wisdom and intelligence; they can mingle rather with people who are involved only in information. Still, the ones who have avoided evils as sins are in the farthest heaven, and are in a light there like that of a moonlit night.

But as for people who have not settled into a belief in the unknown, and who have at the same time been involved in some affection for what is true, once they have been taught by angels (depending on their openness to truths and their life according to them), they are raised into communities of people who are involved in spiritual love and thereby in intelligence. They become spiritual, while the rest remain natural-spiritual.

However, people who have lived in a faith separated from charity are taken away and dispatched to wastelands because they are not involved in anything good. They are therefore not in any marriage of the good and the true, the marriage everyone in the heavens is involved in.

430. Everything we have said in this section about love and wisdom can also be said about charity and faith, if we simply take charity to mean spiritual love and faith to mean truth as the means to intelligence. It is the same if we say intentionality and discernment or love and intelligence, since intentionality is the recipient vessel of love and discernment the recipient vessel of intelligence.

431. I may add the following matter of interest. In heaven, all the people who perform uses from an affection for uses derive from the fellowship they belong to a greater wisdom and a greater happiness than other people have. For them, performing uses in heaven is behaving honestly, rightly, fairly, and reliably in the task

assigned to them. This they call charity, and the reverent acts of formal worship they call signs of charity. The rest they call obligations and privileges, saying that when anyone does his or her job honestly, rightly, fairly, and reliably, the larger whole takes solid and lasting form in that good work. They also say that this is "being in the Lord," because everything that flows in from the Lord is a use, and flows from the parts in [sic] the whole, and from the whole to the parts. "The parts" there are the angels, and "the whole" is their community.

THE NATURE OF THE BEGINNING OF THE HUMAN BEING FROM CONCEPTION

432. No one can know the nature of the beginning of primal form of the human being in the womb after conception, because it cannot be seen. Further, it is made up of spiritual substance, which does not fit into sight by the light of nature. Whereas then some people in this world are inclined to turn their minds to the exploration of the primal human form (the seed from the father, which is the agent of conception) and whereas many of them have slipped into the error of believing that the person is complete from the very first, which is rudimentary, and is completed [simply] by growing larger, the nature of this rudimentary or first form has been disclosed to me.

It was disclosed to me by angels to whom it was revealed by the Lord. Because they made this a matter of their wisdom, and because the delight of their wisdom is to share what they know with others, they were given leave to present the beginning human form to my eyes in image in heaven's light. It was like this.

I saw a kind of minute image of a brain with a very faint outline of a face on the front, without anything extending from it. The upper, convex part of this rudimentary form was a complex of adjoining little globes or spheres, and each little sphere was a complex of still smaller ones, and each of these likewise a complex of the very smallest ones. So there was a trine of levels. In front, on the flattened part, something was outlined that looked like a face. The protruding part was enclosed by a very thin membrane or lining, which was transparent.

The convex part, which was an image of a brain to the smallest detail, was divided into two prominences, so to speak, just as the brain on a larger scale is divided into two hemispheres. I was told that the right prominence was the recipient vessel of love and the left prominence the recipient vessel of wisdom, and that by marvelous interconnections they were virtual consorts or intimate companions.

Then I was also shown, in a heavenly light that dawned, that the inner structure of this minute brain was in the design and form of heaven, both as to its arrangement and as to its pattern of flow. I was also shown that its outer structure was set in opposition to that design and that form.

After I had seen and been shown these things, the angels said that the two inner levels, which were in the design and form of heaven, were recipient vessels of love and wisdom from the Lord, and that the outer level, which was set in opposition to heaven's design and form, was the recipient vessel of hellish love and madness. This is because people are born into all kinds of evil as a result of hereditary defect, and these evils dwell in the outmost reaches. This defect is not removed unless the higher levels are opened, the levels which, as stated, are recipient vessels of love and wisdom from the Lord.

Further, since love-and-wisdom is the actual person, and love-and-wisdom in its essence is in fact the Lord, and this rudimentary human being is a recipient vessel, it follows that there is therefore in this rudimentary form a constant striving toward the human form, which is done step by step.